A Guide to
Stockpicking

A Guide to Stockpicking

GILLIAN O'CONNOR

CENTURY
BUSINESS

This edition first published by Century Ltd
Random House, 20 Vauxhall Bridge Road, London SW1V 2SA

Random House Australia (Pty) Limited
16 Dalmore Drive, Scoresby
Victoria 3179 Australia

Random House New Zealand Limited
18 Poland Road, Glenfield
Auckland 10, New Zealand

Random House South Africa (Pty) Limited
PO Box 2263, Rosebank 2121, South Africa

Random House UK Limited Reg. No. 954009

Papers used by Random House UK Limited are natural, recyclable products made from wood grown in sustainable forests. The manufacturing processes conform to the environmental regulations of the country of origin.

ISBN 0 7126 6086 0

Typeset by Deltatype Limited, Birkenhead, Merseyside
Printed and bound in Great Britain by Mackays of Chatham plc, Chatham, Kent

Companies, institutions and other organizations wishing to make bulk purchases of any business books published by Random House should contact their local bookseller or Random House direct:
Special Sales Director
Random House, 20 Vauxhall Bridge Road, London SW1V 2SA
Tel 0171 973 9000 Fax 0171 828 6681

Contents

Acknowledgements

Many people have given generously of their time, knowledge and experience in helping me produce this book. I am extremely grateful for all their help and encouragement.

In particular I would like to thank Michael Hughes and his team at BZW, and Geoffrey Holmes and Alan Sugden. All are living proof of the maxim – if you want a job doing well, ask a busy man. Michael read most of the manuscript himself, valiantly seconded by Ian Burgess on the accounting chapters, and came up with several predictably acute and interesting comments and suggestions. His criticisms were invariably constructive and so courteously expressed that I almost believed I was the one doing him a favour. Not so.

I had already leaned heavily on Geoffrey and Alan's own accountancy classic in writing my accounting chapters. But with extreme kindness they took time out from revising it to provide line by line comments on my chapters.

Other experts provided detailed comments on particular chapters. David Damant of Credit Suisse Asset Management read both the accountancy and the chart chapters. David Charters and Richard Marshall at Investment Research of Cambridge read the chart chapter and provided invaluable sample charts. Andrew Fowler of UBS made several useful criticisms of my Sainsbury case study. Peter Jeffreys of Fund Research Limited was similarly helpful and forthright over my comments on unit and investment trusts. Peter Temple checked and improved the Appendix on investment software. And David Wells of Binder Hamlyn and Andrew Radice, who also specialises in advising individuals on tax, both vetted the Appendix on Tax-efficient Investment.

Thanks also to the friends and colleagues who took on the job of reading large chunks of the book at various stages. Bernard Gray, Shekhar Das, Philip Coggan and John Train all spent precious weekends doing so, and all produced helpful and constructive suggestions.

Good illustrations are vital to any publication. So my sincere thanks go to Joe Russ, Graham Lever and Keith Fray of the *Financial Times* for their painstaking work in producing illustrations which are both pleasing and accurate.

Two other debts demand acknowledgement. First, my thanks to inspired stockpickers such as Benjamin Graham, Warren Buffett and Peter Lynch. I have leaned heavily on their published maxims in many places. But, even more important, if they did not exist, I would have had nothing to write about. My second debt is to all my colleagues and former colleagues at the *Financial Times* and the *Investors Chronicle*. Again, if those publications did not exist, this book would not exist either.

The contribution made by these people was great; the mistakes remain mine.

G.O'C.
June 1996.

List of Illustrations

Preface

When I had finished the *Investors Chronicle Beginners' Guide to Investment* one thing worried me. I had tried to give readers a background to how investment works and some kind of framework within which to make decisions, but I was not sure I had taken investors all the way. I still had an uncomfortable image in my mind of a reader, armed with all of this information, opening the back page of the *Financial Times* and seeing 2,000 stock prices swimming before his eyes. 'OK,' he says in a heavy tone, 'I understand all that, but which shares do I buy?'

Eventually I decided it was simply impractical to include everything about investment in a single book. *Beginners' Guide* was already very long, and if all of the details of how to pick stocks had been added, readers would have needed a wheelbarrow to carry the book around. So the *Guide* stayed as it was, focused on giving readers the fundamentals they needed about markets and investment. But there remained a further job to be done.

Happily, my colleague Gillian O'Connor has now picked up that challenge. In *A Guide to Stockpicking* she gives investors the tools they need to weed through the hundreds of stocks in the newspaper. Because successful investment is an art, not a science, there can be no definitive answers to picking a winning portfolio or to good market timing. Yet there are plenty of tools which investors can use to spot shares which they should avoid like the plague, and to pick out the gems which will shine.

Gillian sets out these tools in a way which picks the reader up from where *Beginners' Guide* left off and takes them a long way towards becoming an investment analyst. Then, in a very readable way, she explains the techniques of some of the great investors. Her aim is to give readers an *a la carte* selection of investment methods, so that everyone

can find something which suits their palate and their
personality.

In the *Guide to Stockpicking* I think Gillian has succeeded
in giving the reader a powerful and valuable investment aid,
and I warmly commend it to anyone who enjoys the fun of
the stockmarket ride.

Bernard Gray
August 1996.

Introduction

Successful professional investors are passionate about picking shares. It may be their job, but like all the best jobs it is also their hobby. They are 'amateurs' in the original sense of the word. Ordinary people who want to succeed as stockmarket investors need to be amateurs in both senses. If you don't find picking shares a wonderfully enjoyable challenge, don't pick shares. Buy an index-tracking unit trust, which will mimic the stockmarket's performance, and spend your leisure doing something you do enjoy.

For, like most hobbies, investment is demanding. Novices often regard it as a gamble – like a flutter on the horses or the lottery. Successful investors work very hard at making money. Mike Milken, the former American junk bond king, used to ride the subway to work at crack of dawn wearing a miner's helmet to read prospectuses by, because he hated to waste time. Jim Rogers, an emerging markets pioneer, saw two marriages break up because his wives could not understand his passion for hard work.

But it is perfectly possible for a private investor to become a successful stockpicker. Indeed, in many ways it is easier to operate as an amateur than as a professional. Most professional investors have several masters. They have to satisfy both the fund management group they work for, and its clients, many of whom have unrealistic and conflicting demands and expectations.

The private investor is answerable only to himself. He can work out his own strengths and weaknesses and play to his strengths. He can set his own targets and monitor his own progress. He can spot and profit from opportunities not open to the manager of a large fund. And if he doesn't like a share or doesn't understand the business, he can simply walk away and look for one he does like and understand.

There are over 2,000 shares traded on the London stockmarket. A private investor normally picks between 10 and

30 shares for his portfolio – roughly one per cent of the market. So he can afford to be choosey.

But too wide a choice can be a problem. Open the share price pages of the *Financial Times*, and an army of names and statistics fight for your attention. How do you know which ones to choose? This book is dedicated to answering that question.

It assumes that the reader already has a basic understanding of stockmarket mechanics, and has decided what his broad investment objectives are. These subjects were addressed in the *Beginners' Guide to Investment*, to which this book is the sequel. This book is designed to help the reader who is ready to commit some money to shares and trusts, but does not know where to start.

You need a financial plan . . .

First, though, it's worth recapping on some basic financial planning rules. Unlike a professional investment manager, a private investor needs to choose a stockmarket strategy which will fit into his broader financial plan. Most people will only consider stockmarket investment after they have already bought a house, made appropriate pension and insurance arrangements and put some cash aside for crises.

But within that general framework shares can still be used to perform several different jobs. Younger people will probably be using them to produce long term capital growth. Older ones may think of them primarily as a source of additional income. Each reader will have his own particular needs.

And these needs will affect both what your investment objective is and what kind of shares you buy to achieve it. If, for example, you are young and single, you can sensibly take a long term view, and – if you are comfortable with the idea – take greater risks than someone twice your age.

If you are nearing retirement you will probably be far more cautious. This will usually mean both that the proportion of your wealth invested in shares is lower, and that the shares you choose will be less risky and less rewarding. You may even decide to put the majority of your money into something predictable, such as index linked gilts, and keep a few shares for fun. Alternatively, whatever age you are, you may prefer to put most of your money into professionally managed funds, such as unit and investment trusts, and invest only a small amount yourself.

Deciding what role your share portfolio will play in your life is up to you. But it is crucial that you are very clear about what its function is before you start choosing shares.

. . . and you need an investment strategy

You also need a coherent investment strategy. Not all successful investors use the same approach when choosing shares. But they all have some method: a disciplined selection and monitoring process, criteria, a game plan.

They know why they are buying this company or share rather than that one and they know what they expect it to do for them. They use filters and yardsticks to help them select shares in the first place. And when they are checking on their portfolio afterwards, they usually have benchmarks against which to measure the performance of a company and its shares, so that any decision to hold or sell is more than a whim.

Some people like to map out an overall view of what they think is going to happen in financial markets over the next few years, and then deploy their assets accordingly, like a general deploying his troops. First they pick the stockmarkets they like, then they decide to put a relatively large proportion of their total money in industries they expect to do well, and only then do they start looking at individual companies. Thereafter they will move their troops from one part of the battlefield to another (from one country to another and one industry to another), depending on how the campaign develops.

Other investors concentrate on companies: they are stockpickers through and through. At heart they are romantics. They scour the world looking for a soulmate: the perfect share. Perpetually on the alert, they turn every corner hoping that this time they will walk straight into a wonderful little company, preferably a virgin unsullied by other investors' attention. But they conduct this hunt in various ways.

Some literally walk round the local shopping centre, hoping their experiences as a consumer will point them towards the perfect share. Those more mathematically inclined spend hours scouring through balance sheets, looking for signs that a particular company is being unfairly neglected by other investors. Others find fascination and profits in using share price charts, which study investor behaviour patterns in order to predict future price movements.

The time scale over which people invest also differs. Many of the most successful investors, such as Warren Buffett, who has built up a multi-billion dollar company through wise stockmarket investment, believe in long term relationships with the companies they invest in. Others, such as Peter Lynch, who ran a very successful American unit trust, reckon that the length of the relationship depends on the share and there is nothing wrong with a holiday fling. Speculators, such as George Soros, have their eyes on the exit even before they say 'hello'.

Private investors tend to be romantic stockpickers rather than generals. This is partly because they seldom have a large enough portfolio to make the military approach feasible, partly because they find picking companies more interesting. But stockpicking should never be regarded as the easy option. Successful stockpickers need to be just as disciplined as the generals.

Although men such as Buffett and Lynch have evolved a distinctive style, they already had a thorough understanding of traditional fund management methods before they branched off on their own. Most professional investors experiment until they find a technique which works for them. And private investors need to do the same thing. But beware of trusting too much of your money to your stockpicking skills while you are still learning the ropes. Your education could prove expensive.

How this book can help

Investment is an art, not a science. And just as different

styles of painting require different brushes, so different investment techniques require different investment tools. This book first discusses how the main investment tools work and how to use them. Then it looks at how investors with different styles use these tools. Finally it explains how you can put the theory into practice in your own stockmarket investments. No book can make your mistakes for you or turn you into an experienced investor overnight. But it may help you learn faster.

All investors believe in buying shares when they are likely to go up, rather than down. But they disagree about the extent to which you can fine tune your timing. Chapter 1 explains how professionals use fundamental analysis, their assessment of what's happening in the outside world, to make stockmarket forecasts. Such forecasts are based on things like the outlook for the economy, company profits and interest rates. The main rival to fundamental analysis is charting, formally known as technical analysis. Chapter 2 discusses some of its theories and practices.

Many ordinary people believe that analysis is all very well, but that most successful investment is in practice based on insider knowledge. Chapter 3 examines some popular ways of timing your purchases and sales, following indicators such as company directors' dealings in the shares of companies whose boardrooms they grace.

Academic studies suggest that even if stockmarket movements can be rationalised in the long term, they are often unpredictable over the short term. If so, many short term stockmarket movements may be based as much on emotion as on fundamental developments in the real world. Chapter 4 considers the part psychology plays in investment.

Then it is down to the nitty gritty of company analysis in Chapters 5 to 7. These focus on company accounts, a mine of useful information for stockpickers, but one which you need the right equipment to exploit. They explain how to use accounts to understand what is going on in the business and how to see through the camouflage some companies use to make their figures look better than they are.

But shares in a good business are not necessarily cheap – indeed, they are very seldom cheap. So professional investors and analysts also use a number of different filters and yardsticks to decide which shares look worth buying. Chapter 7 goes through the main investment yardsticks, explaining what each one tells you.

Assembling an investment toolkit is one thing; using it to build a portfolio is another. Chapters 8 and 9 provide several role models for new investors: they discuss the strategies of half a dozen of the most influential modern investors. Men such as Warren Buffett, Peter Lynch and George Soros are extremely clear about the process they use to achieve success. And in most cases their chosen techniques can be copied by an intelligent private investor.

Unfortunately few people have the chance to chat about investment with masters such as Buffett on an everyday basis. So the next couple of chapters look at the investment comment you are most likely to hear about or read: the reports produced by stockmarket analysts and newspapers. What are they trying to do and how can you make use of it?

The book's aim throughout is to help the reader to turn theory into practice. But the final section, Chapters 12 to 14, concentrates on the practicalities. It applies the different tools and techniques discussed earlier to a specific case study, Sainsbury. It discusses ways of managing your portfolio. And it considers the alternative to stockpicking: investing through unit and investment trusts. Appendices list useful sources of information, set out how computer software can help the private investor, and explain how to take advantage of government tax concessions.

If this menu sounds a bit daunting, don't worry. The book aims to give you a taste of a number of different investment approaches. But then it is up to you to decide which to follow up. No professional investor uses all the tools and techniques outlined here. Indeed, attempting to do so would probably be counterproductive. The important thing is to choose a system that works for you, one you are comfortable with.

People invest in shares to make money. But that's not the only reason. They also do it because they enjoy it. Like most arts, the more you understand about stockpicking, the more enjoyment you are likely to get out of it. This book aims to increase your knowledge of stockpicking, your wealth and your enjoyment.

Introduction

IN A NUTSHELL

1. Private investors can be successful stockpickers. They even have some advantages over the professional: they have only themselves to answer to; and they only need to choose a few shares out of the 2,000 on the London stockmarket. But too big a choice can be a problem. This book is designed to help you choose.

2. First you need to work out how your shares fit into your overall financial plan. Are you looking for capital growth or income and over what time scale?

3. Then you need to work out a coherent investment strategy. There are lots of different ways of approaching equity investment, and lots of different ways of picking individual shares. But all successful investors have a disciplined process for doing so. Private investors need one too.

4. This book tries to shorten the new investor's learning process. It discusses how to time purchases and sales to best advantage. It explains how the main investment tools work and how to use them. It looks at the winning strategies of some of the world's best known investors. And it suggests how you can adapt these tools and techniques to your own stockmarket investments.

Section One:
Investment Timing

Chapter 1
Market Analysis

Investors often talk about the stockmarket as if it was a dangerous wild animal or a mob on the rampage. A bull market, when share prices thunder onwards and upwards, provides marvellous opportunities to make profits. But never trust a bull: it can turn round and gore you in a trice. That's what commentators call a correction.

A bear market, when share prices fall, is thoroughly nasty from beginning to end. And if you think the bear has raged its way out, and venture back into the market, you may well get trapped by a sucker's rally. The message is that anyone who tries to make money out of the stockmarket does so at his peril.

The major turning points are always obvious with hindsight. At the time the signals are usually less clear. But a body of folklore has built up, which investors use to try and identify the peaks and troughs. Markets usually overdo the enthusiasm at the top and overdo the gloom at the bottom.

General euphoria can provide a warning that a bull market is near the top. Typical signs are headlines about the bull market in even the popular newspapers; penny share mania among people who do not usually buy shares; shares on unusually low dividend yields and high price earnings ratios; wise men explaining why 'this time is different'; a bevy of new issues and bids made with shares rather than cash. Low interest rates often make alternatives, such as cash deposits, look unappealing.

Anyone studying the detail of what is happening can often see the rot beginning. Share prices fail to respond to good news, but move down on bad news. Investors seem to be putting the worst possible interpretation on any event. The shares which have led the bull market up start to fade, and the only reason that the market as a whole keeps rising is that optimists are giving some hitherto neglected shares a whirl. That's the kind of market in which to take defensive action: by

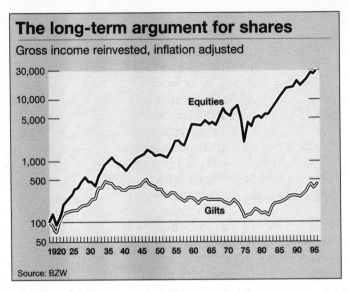

The long-term argument for shares

Gross income reinvested, inflation adjusted

Source: BZW

Fig 1.1 Over the long term shares have produced significantly higher returns than gilts, mainly because inflation reduces the real value of gilts. Reinvested income makes the major contribution to returns.

all means keep your solid long term growth companies; but jettison anything fashionable and vulnerable.

At the end of a long or serious bear market, both sentiment and signs are almost a mirror image of those at the top of a bull market. Ordinary people take it as read that the stockmarket is finished for good; novice investors who have clung on like grim death all the way down finally sell; interest rates are high and newspapers pretend that investing in cash deposits is exciting; shares look cheap but pundits explain why they are not worth buying; there's nary a new issue or unit trust launch to be seen.

The more detailed signs that a recovery could be imminent are that share prices appear already to have discounted Armageddon; so when bad news comes they do not fall further. This is the time to start cautiously looking for bargains. Keep hanging on to your long term investments, but think about moving some more of your money back into the market.

If this all sounds remarkably unscientific to you, you are right. The trouble is no one has yet invented a reliable way of predicting stockmarket movements. That is one reason why stockmarket investment is intrinsically dangerous. Shares have performed substantially better than most rival investments such as gilts over the long term (Fig. 1.1), but in the short term they can damage your wealth. Anyone thinking of putting money into the stockmarket at all hopes that his returns will at least equal the long term average. Anyone going to the trouble of picking his own shares usually hopes to beat the market. But how realistic are these hopes?

The City is full of highly paid investment analysts trying to help professional investors beat the averages. Most market research is based on fundamental analysis: the analysts look at 'real' factors, such as company earnings and dividend prospects and inflation and interest rate expectations, in order to make their forecasts. The traditional alternative is technical analysis, or charting, which bases its conclusions on the analyst's interpretations of price charts. (See Chapter 2.) Quantitative analysis, a more recent arrival from the US, uses sophisticated computer models to improve portfolio selection and trading techniques.

But beating the market is easier said than done, since all investors are playing the same game. Analysts and investors both devote a lot of time and computing power to working out what is likely to happen both to company profits and to the economy; they make judgements about probable social and political developments; they assess whether shares look attractive compared with alternative investments; and they look for sectors which seem relatively good value. Investors then buy or sell shares in anticipation of what they expect to happen to fundamentals. So today's prices already reflect investors' expectations. That is what people mean when they say that the market discounts the future.

What investors and analysts are always looking for is a mismatch: reasons for thinking that the expectations built into current price levels are inaccurate or incomplete. If the investor's reasoning is correct, prices should eventually move to a more appropriate level, and he will make money.

But glaring anomalies are rare. And even when the market does seem to have got it wrong, it does not necessarily correct its mistake just because you have spotted it. Periods of overvaluation and undervaluation can last a long time.

Private investors who invest money on the assumption that an overvalued market is bound to fall in the very near future can learn the hard way that it doesn't work like that.

Different investors have different attitudes to market timing. Some of the most successful, such as Warren Buffett, pay very little attention to the market's gyrations; they concentrate on stockpicking, and welcome a fall in the market because it provides more opportunities to buy good shares cheaply.

Buffett's own mentor, Benjamin Graham, compared the market to a manic-depressive partner. Sometimes he overvalued your shares ludicrously, sometimes he grossly undervalued them. But he was always willing to buy you out at his own price. Graham argued that you should never be influenced by 'Mr Market's' view. But you should sometimes take advantage of his folly to sell high and buy low.

How efficient is the market?

Most professional investors are being paid to beat the market. But some academic theories suggest that even if they succeed it is due to luck, not skill. The two most often cited are the Random Walk and the Efficient Market Hypothesis (EMH). The first suggests that share price changes are random and unpredictable. The second says that all relevant information is quickly assimilated by investors and reflected in share prices. Both can be used to argue that anyone trying to beat the market consistently is on a hiding to nothing.

However, most investors and academics now agree that, although markets are broadly efficient, they are not totally efficient. Pockets of inefficiency do exist and provide the intelligent investor with his opportunities. So trying to beat the market can be worthwhile. But only a handful of investors will consistently succeed.

Professional analysts have also been fighting back by making a distinction between long term and short term forecasts. They argue that, even if short term share price movements are essentially irrational and unpredictable, the same is not true of stockmarket movements over longer

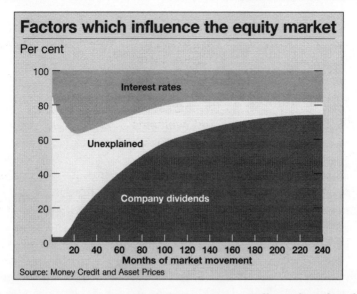

Factors which influence the equity market

Fig 1.2 The market's short term behaviour is essentially random, though interest rates have some influence on it. But over longer periods of time company profitability becomes increasingly influential.

periods of time. The longer the period analysed, the more rational stockmarket behaviour becomes.

The chart above (Fig 1.2.) shows the result of a study which traced the relationship between movements in the equity market and two possible influences: company profitability, as reflected in dividend growth, and interest rate movements. It shows that in the short term the stockmarket's behaviour is indeed almost entirely random. The most important influence on it is interest rates, but even they are pretty marginal. There is virtually no link with company profitability.

But the longer the period of time for which market behaviour is analysed, the more susceptible it becomes to rational explanation. For the first four years interest rates remain the most important identifiable influence. But at that point corporate profitability reasserts itself and becomes steadily more dominant. And when it comes to periods as long as a decade the market tracks company profitability very closely.

Since different factors affect short and long term market

behaviour, analysts use different tools for making short and long term forecasts. It may seem superficially surprising that they bother much with short term forecasts, since the market is so unpredictable in the short run. And short term forecasts tend to be much less reliable than longer term ones. But professional investors want short term forecasts, so analysts supply them.

Long term market forecasts

Any investor should have a long term strategy: a game plan, which he reviews periodically. The better the initial plan, the less it should need changing. The main investment choices for individuals are deposits, conventional and index-linked gilts, UK and overseas shares and property (usually your own house). The general shape of an individual investor's total portfolio will depend on his personal financial situation.(See Chapter 13.) But deciding whether shares look cheap or expensive on a long term view can influence the actual division of resources at any given time.

Do you, for example, use an inheritance to pay off a mortgage or do you put it into the equity market? It will only make sense to choose shares if you expect the return on them to exceed the cost of servicing your mortgage. This is the kind of situation where long term forecasts for the equity market can help your financial planning. They are not an everyday tool.

Over the long term share prices follow growth in company dividends closely. Dividends do not rise steadily. They have periods of strong growth, and periods where they stagnate or fall, roughly in line with the business cycle. But real dividend growth (adjusted for inflation) has averaged around 1 per cent to 2 per cent a year. And, unless there is a particular reason for expecting unusually good or bad growth, most long term forecasts for the equity market assume that future dividend growth for the next decade or so will be similar to the underlying trend.

But the actual return investors get from shares will depend on whether the market is cheap or expensive at the time they invest. Analysts have several different ways of judging this, including a couple familiar to most private investors, dividend yields and price earnings ratios. As a rule of thumb, the higher the dividend yield when you buy, the higher the real long term return you can expect.

Say, for example, the yield on the FT-SE-A All Share index is 4 per cent when you buy. Add on the 1 to 2 per cent average growth in dividends, and the total real long term return (income plus capital growth) is likely to be around 5 to 6 per cent. If, however, the initial dividend yield when you buy is 6 per cent, the likely real long term return would rise to 7 to 8 per cent. Shares will probably prove a better long term buy when the initial yield is 6 per cent, even though the background may well look relatively gloomy.

This kind of calculation is part of the process pension funds go through when deciding how to split their money between different types of investment. They compare the probable returns on shares with those on overseas shares, gilts, cash, property and so on. Private investors can do the same.*

Say you want to compare what you are likely to make from shares with what you know you will get from index-linked gilts. Shares are regarded as an inflation hedge, but index-linked gilts are the real thing: both capital and income are guaranteed to rise in line with inflation.

The *Financial Times* publishes the yields on index-linked gilts every day. Say it shows a yield of 3.5 per cent on index-linkers which will be repaid in 10 years time. Since that is an inflation-proofed yield, it is fair to compare it with the estimated real return on shares: 5 to 6 per cent if the current dividend yield is 4 per cent. So you stand to get 1.5 to 2.5 percentage points more from shares.

Does that make shares the better bet? Not necessarily. The return on shares is a guesstimate; the yield on index-linkers is guaranteed, provided you hold them until they are repaid. Given the additional risks of shares it would be silly even to consider them unless you expected them to produce higher

* Two complications for private investors are tax and costs. The calculations here pay no attention to either. Their effects will depend on your individual circumstances, but can substantially alter the balance of advantage. Appendix C discusses tax efficient investment.

returns. The jargon name for the difference is the equity risk premium.

Is a premium of 1.5 to 2.5 percentage points enough to make the extra risk you incur by buying shares acceptable? Unfortunately even professional investors cannot decide what the risk premium 'ought' to be. As a private investor you may well stick with the gilts if you are the cautious type. If you are young and optimistic you may feel the extra returns likely from shares justify the extra risk.

Private investors should not place too much emphasis on these sums. They are back of the envelope calculations based on forecasts which may well be wrong. But they can be useful as a rough guide to help you weigh one type of investment up against another. And doing them forces you to work out what you expect your investments to do for you before you buy. This gives you a yardstick against which to measure both their subsequent performance and your forecasting ability.

Remember though that the comparisons are only used for relatively long term forecasts, ten years or so. Over shorter periods share prices may fail to track dividend growth, and dividend growth may deviate substantially from its long term average. So a forecast of short term equity returns based on long term trends could be wildly out. Short term forecasters use different tools.

Short term market forecasts

The market's short term behaviour is essentially unpredictable, but professional investors who should know better, such as unit trust managers, often advertise their short term performance triumphs. No wonder cynics compare the market with a casino, with lucky punters trying to sell their system to the innocent and ignorant.

Fund managers blame the customers for demanding short term performance. Analysts blame the fund managers for demanding short term forecasts. No one personally admits to having short term performance targets, but everyone agrees there's a lot of it around. And most market forecasts have a time horizon as short as 12 to 18 months.

Stockmarket strategists, who usually have a background in economics, argue that they could be more useful if they were encouraged to forecast at least three years and preferably five years ahead. For over a five year period company profitability and interest rates, things economists are trained to forecast, are the main drivers of stockmarket performance. With a shorter time frame the strategists are trying to predict an essentially random process.

But if fund managers want forecasts with a time horizon as short as 12 to 18 months, strategists have to comply. Economic factors remain central to their forecasting process. But most strategists also toss other considerations into the pot from time to time: the relative attractions of other investments, the pull of other markets, the political situation, institutional liquidity, domestic investor confidence, tidal waves of foreign money, demographic trends, global warming.

The shorter the time horizon, the more these extraneous factors can matter. For they may affect what investors actually do. And if short term market movements are essentially unpredictable, guessing what everybody else is likely to do is as good a recipe for success as any other. Keynes compared this type of investment with someone judging a beauty competition by trying to work out which competitor the other judges were likely to prefer.

Unfortunately, even if you stick to the 'rational' economic factors, there is no simple way to put the jigsaw together. Sometimes a factor has more than one effect. For example, if companies borrow to finance capital spending, this may be good for future company profits, but bad for share prices in the short term, because their borrowing sucks money out of the stockmarket.

What's more the effect of a given factor often depends on the context. The market generally approves of tax cutting when the economy is in recession, but is suspicious of it at other times.

But it is not just the context that determines the market's responses: the market itself is enduringly fickle. It minds about different things at different times. To the outsider it often appears to have tunnel vision: at any given time it concentrates on one factor to the exclusion of others. This can present useful buying opportunities, but only if you can see a reason why its focus will change. There is no point in being the only one in step.

It is dangerous to assume that because the market often acts like a manic depressive mob, it can safely be ignored. As one stockmarket analyst sadly commented: 'Forecasting can be dangerous, even if the predictions are correct. This is because profits are made out of being one step ahead of the market. Being two steps ahead as a result of correct forecasts can lead to losses. One can be too clever for one's own good.'*

Economic growth and business cycles

Economic growth – or the lack of it – is at the heart of equity investment. For that is what produces the higher company profits and dividends investors are looking for. But there are two types of growth. At different periods different countries experience sustained economic growth: Britain did during the industrial revolution, and the emerging economies, notably those in Southeast Asia, are enjoying it now.

Investors are often willing to pay more for company profits from economies experiencing this type of 'secular' growth. And investors with a large portfolio are often advised to have some of their money in the economies which are currently in the fast lane. This can mean buying shares in the relevant overseas companies, or unit trusts which do so. But it can also mean looking for UK shares of companies which operate in the fast-track countries. Such shares may be relatively unmoved by the ups and downs of the UK economy.

But the UK market as a whole is influenced by Britain's business cycle. All modern economies appear to be tied to an economic big dipper, which moves from recession to recovery and back again. Company profits as a whole rise and fall roughly in line with the cycle, but not all companies are affected equally. Investors attempt to anticipate the various stages of the cycle. This is one reason why the market often

* Gordon Pepper in *Money, Credit and Asset Prices.*

does well when the economy is depressed. But investors often get it wrong, because every cycle is different.

One City economist produced this potted analysis of a 'typical' business cycle:*

Typical business cycle

I. Recovery. Stimulatory economic policies; confidence picks up; inflation is still falling.

Market reaction. Short term interest rates fall; bond yields bottom; share prices and commodity prices rise.

II. Early upswing. Increasing confidence; healthy economic growth; inflation remains low.

Market reaction. Short term interest rates bottom; bonds are stable; share and commodity prices are strong.

III. Late upswing. Boom mentality; inflation gradually picks up; government economic policy becomes restrictive.

Market reaction. Short term interest rates rise; bond yields rise; share prices top out but commodity prices are still rising strongly.

IV. Economy slows or enters recession. Confidence suddenly drops; inventory correction begins (ie companies start running down their stocks); inflation continues to accelerate.

Market reaction. Short term interest rates peak; bond yields top out; share prices fall and so do commodity prices.

V. Recession. Production is falling; inflation peaks; confidence is weak.

Market reaction. Short term interest rates drop; bond yields drop; share prices start rising but commodity prices stay weak.

---

* See the *Pocket Guide to Economics for the Global Investor* by John Calverley.

Investors have two ways of profiting from business cycles. If they invest during the recession but before share prices have started to pick up, they can sometimes make very good profits. Alternatively they can leap from one group of shares to another as the cycle progresses, aiming always to hold the ones set to do comparatively well.

But investing when the market is in the pits is not for wimps. In 1989–90, when British short term interest rates were 15 per cent and inflation was just starting to fall from about 10 per cent, the UK joined the European Exchange Rate Mechanism and cut interest rates. The economy was deep in recession, despite assurances to the contrary from the then chancellor, John Major. But with inflation already falling it was pretty clear at that point that interest rates were likely to be starting a long term decline. (Fig 1.3.) That was the moment to buy shares and benefit from the coming recovery. But it took a lot of courage.

Investors hopping from one sector to another as the cycle

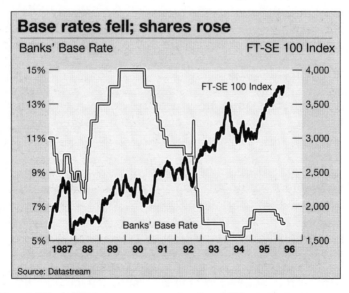

Fig 1.3 When UK interest rates started to fall in 1990 investors were deeply reluctant to move their money out of high interest deposit accounts. Investors who had the courage to buy shares then prospered mightily.

progresses are following a well-trodden path. It is common knowledge that companies producing necessities, such as food tend to plod on regardless of the business cycle, while shares of firms in areas such as engineering, car components or big-ticket consumer goods are cyclical: the companies are badly hit in recession, but do unusually well when it is going at full throttle. This is partly because of the things they produce, but also because of their operating structure. They often have high fixed overheads or high borrowings, or both.

Since everybody knows the pattern, shares in such companies tend to move up long before the recovery materialises. So investors can only make money by investing before the crowd. This can be an expensive mistake, since the recovery sometimes fails to materialise, or the green shoots wither prematurely. For example, building and construction shares started to pick up in the early 1990s, as interest rates fell, but the shares subsequently relapsed as it became obvious that demand was not picking up.

Even if the recovery does materialise, you may discover you have bought shares in one of the weaker companies whose collapse benefits the others, but leaves you losing money. And if you succeed in buying the right shares at the right time, you need to be ruthless about selling as soon as the share price starts flagging. Even investors who like cyclical shares agree that they should never be valued as highly as those of companies which can grow consistently over the long term.

Effects of inflation

An economic tradition going back to the eighteenth century argues that low inflation – about 3 per cent – is good for profits and so should be good for shares. The thinking is that if employers can raise prices without workers noticing, wage increases will lag behind price increases, and so profits will rise.

But in the post-war period reality has departed from this script. During the big upsurges of inflation in the 1970s and early 1980s, the forces driving prices up came from the cost side – big increases in oil prices and wages. Companies did eventually manage to increase their own prices, but initially their profits were squeezed. And when governments tried to curb inflation by tight monetary policies – which meant high interest rates and a strong pound – profits were squeezed a second time.

The experience of the seventies and eighties also showed that medium or high inflation is bad for company profits in the long run, because it creates uncertainty. Once inflation rises above very low levels it becomes unstable and its future course is hard to predict. Company managers take investment decisions on the basis of assumptions about the future. And if these become very uncertain, they often 'go on strike': stop investing at all.

But if high inflation is bad for equities, it is fatal for conventional gilts. That is why equities have acquired the reputation for being an inflation hedge. The table below shows average investment returns during periods of low, medium and high inflation.

Investment returns and inflation

Inflation range %	Equities %	Gilts %	Cash %	Avge.inflation %
1.9–4.6	17.9	10.3	8.0	3.2
4.6–7.8	15.0	7.0	9.5	6.0
7.8–24.9	11.1	10.1	12.2	13.8

Source: PDFM Ltd

If you knock off the average inflation from the nominal returns on equities, they were highest when inflation was low, and actually negative when inflation was high.

You can profit from inflation if you can anticipate changes in the inflation rate when the market does not. This is easiest for gilts. When inflation rises to politically unacceptable levels, the government usually tries to bring it down through a very tight monetary policy; ie it raises interest rates to very high levels. Gilt prices fall and their yields rise. But often the market remains sceptical. This is an opportunity. If you judge correctly that the policy will work – that inflation and hence interest rates will fall faster than the market reckons – you can do well by buying gilts.

Anticipating changes in inflation correctly can also dictate good investment tactics for the equity market. When inflation rises there tends to be a flight out of money into solid objects such as property. If you can anticipate a rise in inflation before the market, you might do well by investing in property shares. For many people a more obvious strategy would be to move money out of shares and buy a larger house. But then you must be equally ready to trade your large house in for a smaller model when the inflationary bubble is pricked.

Effects of interest rates

Interest rates affect investors in several ways. They are an important ingredient of business cycles, and affect consumer demand, business confidence and company profitability. But they also have a direct impact on stockmarkets. In the short term they have a more important influence on the equity market than corporate profits.

Short term interest rates are the main instrument of government monetary policy. And monetary policy is the main instrument the government uses in trying to control the economy. In the 1990s the government's objective has been to control inflation while keeping the economy moving ahead. It is not an easy balancing act.

The government's emphasis on keeping inflation down explains the puzzle of why investors often respond favourably to signs of an economic slowdown and are worried by excessive economic growth. They believe slower growth will save the government from having to damp the economy down by increasing interest rates. It also helps explain why shares and gilts so often move together nowadays. Inflation has always been the key issue for bond markets. The bond market's preoccupations now matter to equities as well.

If interest rates rise, companies and individuals who borrow will have to pay more in interest and so will have less money to buy goods or to invest. Equally savers may be more inclined to leave their money in the bank rather than spend it. Raising interest rates thus tends to damp down the economy. Small companies, which are often dependent on bank borrowing, tend to be worse hit than larger ones.

The interest rate lever can also be used in reverse. If the economy is sluggish because interest rates are high, the government will often cut rates. It is trying to encourage individuals to spend rather than save, and companies to borrow for new capital investment.

But interest rates also have a far more direct impact on the markets. For they affect the relative attractiveness of shares, compared with cash deposits or gilts. Short term interest rates are what matter in the comparison with cash deposits; gilt yields are the key in equity/gilt comparisons.

Cuts in interest rates are generally good for gilt prices. Yields move down with, or more often in anticipation of, cuts in base rates. As gilt prices rise, gilts become more expensive relative to equities. So investors buy shares and share prices also rise. Another reason for the market's sensitivity to interest rates is simply that falling rates increase the amount of money investors put into the stockmarket.

As interest rates fall, it becomes less attractive for investors to hold cash deposits, and, if they do not wish to spend their money, they have to find another investment home for it. Shares are an obvious alternative, particularly as they are likely to be rising in anticipation of higher company profits. So as rates fall, the weight of money shifting from deposits to shares tends to boost equity prices. Similarly, when interest rates start to rise, there is a tendency for investors to switch money from the stockmarket to interest-bearing deposits.

There is often a considerable time lag between the peak or trough in interest rates and investors' reaction to it. For example, when UK interest rates started to fall in 1990 private investors were deeply reluctant to move their money out of high interest deposit accounts. With short term rates at 15 per cent, it was difficult to imagine that they could fall to only 5.25 per cent over the next four years. But they did. And the FT-SE 100 index, which stood at about 2,300 in 1990 rose to a peak of just over 3,500 in early 1994.

Effects of tax changes

For about three decades after the War the prevailing economic orthodoxy – Keynesianism – put fiscal policy at the centre of economic policy. Its job was to iron out fluctuations in the economic cycle: when the economy got too hot, the government would raise taxes to dampen demand; when the economy was going into a downturn, it would cut taxes to stimulate demand. Insufficient demand was thought to cause unemployment, excessive demand inflation.

Since the mid-seventies, this sort of demand management has fallen out of favour, partly because the nature of unemployment has changed – it stays high even when demand is strong – and partly because governments have become more concerned about inflation than unemployment.

Nowadays the main effect of the government's fiscal policy on the equity market is through the gilt market. The gilt market is directly concerned with the government's overall balance between taxation and spending because it has to finance most of the difference. When the difference is large, the supply of gilts increases and, other things being equal, gilt prices fall – and their yields rise. This tends to depress equities too. The opposite effect comes into play when government borrowing shrinks.

Changes in taxation also affect equities directly. If the government raises taxes, the amount people have left to spend out of their total pay – their disposable income – will fall, or rise by less than it would otherwise have done. This is likely to have a depressing effect on consumer spending, which accounts for more than half of all spending in the economy. Even a small change in personal taxes affects the whole economy, but sectors which depend wholly on consumer spending, such as retailing, are likely to be more affected than others.

Companies pay tax as well as individuals and if the government changes the corporation tax rules, the returns for investors will be affected in a relatively straightforward way. The government also sometimes tinkers with the rules governing capital allowances for new investment and depreciation of assets, which can have a substantial effect on company profits. Tax changes which affect specific industries, such as the duties on cigarettes, alcohol and petrol may have a knock-on impact on share prices, but only if the changes were unexpected.

In practice the market often anticipates what the government is likely to do. And by the time the Whitehall machine has lumbered into action, the policy change is already all in the price. Investors hoping to profit from changes in interest rates or tax need to read what the pundits are saying the government will do, and act as soon as it becomes reasonably clear what is likely to happen.

Effects of currency changes

If sterling falls, as it did after Black Wednesday in September 1992, companies which export can drop the prices they charge in foreign currencies in order to take a bigger share of the international market. Alternatively, and this is what they usually do, they can leave their foreign currency prices unchanged and turn their foreign currency receipts into a larger number of pounds than before the fall in sterling. This increases their sterling profit margins and so boosts corporate profits.

Companies with a high proportion of their business in exports, normally the larger FT-SE 100 companies, can thus glow quietly as they see their profits and stock prices rise following a fall in sterling. Smaller companies with markets in the UK also benefit indirectly. For foreign companies exporting to the UK (and UK importers) will either have to raise their prices or cut their profit margins in order to remain competitive. Domestic producers face no such dilemma, which makes it easier for UK companies to take a bigger share of the UK market following a fall in sterling.

Conversely, a rise in sterling can cause a problem for exporters and put pressure on companies operating in the domestic market. But sterling does not often present British industry with this problem.

A major currency change can have a significant impact on the stockmarket over quite a long period of time. Investors who bought UK shares after Black Wednesday, even after the market's initial knee-jerk reaction, made good profits.

Effects of elections

Although markets may start talking about imminent elections a year or more before they happen, some studies suggest that share prices as a whole only really respond when the election is about three to five months away. Specific sectors, such as the privatised utilities, may react earlier because they are seen as particularly likely to be affected.

What share prices do before the election depends, unsurprisingly, on which party is expected to win. But it is not at all clear that past patterns will hold in future elections. For investors' expectations may alter along with changes in the parties' own agendas. Or they may reckon that agendas and acts are different things.

A paper by broker Robert Fleming analysed the effects of elections between 1966 and 1992. Its conclusions were:

- When a Labour victory is expected, the market is unlikely to rise sharply, and may well fall.
- When a Tory victory is expected the market is likely to rise.
- When Labour wins there is no consistent outcome.
- When the Tories win the market rises if the result is unexpected. But if it had already been anticipated the election marks the high for the next few months.
- The financial sector tends to do badly in the run-up to the election, whichever party is expected to win.
- After a Tory win, composite insurance, merchant banks and property companies have normally recovered best.

Stockmarket historian David Schwartz points out that UK stockmarket swings in the run-up to the election have grown more pronounced in recent years. This could be because of the increasing prevalence of opinion pollsters. He has calculated that in the five month run-up to the election the biggest swings have occurred when the incumbent government is unusually popular or unpopular.

The UK market often benefits indirectly from US elections. Schwartz notes that markets on both sides of the Atlantic normally do well in the year before an American presidential election. He suggests that this is because the date of the next US election is fixed. The incumbent government has every opportunity to try to get the economy in good order before polling day. Wall Street responds to the improving economic prospects. And London tends to track Wall Street. (See Fig 1.6 page 25.)

Shares versus gilts

Equities are not the only game in town. Inside the UK the main competition to shares comes from gilts. The usual yardstick is the gilt-equity yield ratio, published every day in the *Financial Times* on the stockmarket report page.

(It is the yield on gilts divided by the yield on shares.) In recent decades this number has normally hovered somewhere between 2 and 2.5 with occasional forays up to 3 or lurches down to 1.5. (See Fig 1.4.) In other words gilts usually yield between two and two and a half times as much as shares.

Within the range 2 to 2.5, the ratio tells investors comparatively little, though it does provide warnings that either gilts or equities are moving towards the cheap or expensive ends of

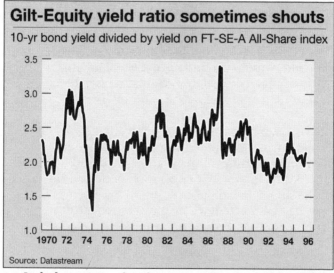

Fig 1.4 In the last 25 years the gilt-equity yield ratio has normally ranged between 2 and 2.5. When it gets well outside that range, it's time to review your strategy.

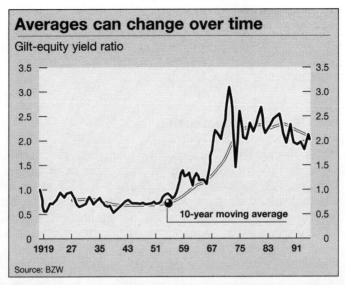

Averages can change over time

Gilt-equity yield ratio

10-year moving average

1919 27 35 43 51 59 67 75 83 91

Source: BZW

Fig 1.5 The cult of the equity is now so well established that many people forget that it is comparatively recent. In the early years of this century equities usually yielded more than gilts because they were riskier.

their ranges. Very occasionally, though, the ratio gives a screaming signal to investors. By the end of 1974, for example, when investor gloom was so pervasive that NatWest had to put out a tape message denying rumours that it was in trouble, a ratio of 1.5 was the prelude to a long bull market.

In 1987 the ratio moved above 3. The message was either that shares were very expensive or that gilts were cheap. But the stockmarket powered blithely ahead for most of the year, as interest rates were cut in the run-up to a general election, and equity markets boomed worldwide.

When the stockmarket crash came in October, Wall Street fell 508 points in a day, but bond prices boomed, as investors finally cottoned on to the fact that the two types of investment had got wildly out of line. That wily entrepreneur Sir James Goldsmith was credited with uncanny intuition for having sold at the market peak in the summer of 1987. But the simple signal from the gilt-equity yield ratio was there for any level-headed investor to read.

But like all yardsticks, the gilt-equity yield ratio needs to be used intelligently. Earlier this century, before inflation took off, equities used to yield more than gilts. BZW's Equity Gilt Study shows that the long term average for the ratio is only 1.4 and for the period 1919 to 1959, the range was 0.5 to 1.1. (See Fig. 1.5 on the previous page.) Investment yardsticks are carved in water, not stone.

The international dimension

Britain's stockmarkets are less insular than many of its inhabitants. So British investors must also consider how international investment flows may affect the UK stockmarket. If institutional investors think that Wall Street offers better prospects for profits, they will divert money there from the UK. How closely stockmarkets in different countries track together will in the long term depend on the performance of their individual economies and local investment conditions. In the short term relationships are sometimes less rational.

Traditionally, the UK has taken its lead from New York, and at times the correlation between the two markets has been extremely close. Indeed, the links remain far closer than those with continental European markets, despite the fact that they are now Britain's largest economic trading partners.

But the extent of the linkage is not constant. Periodically market commentators celebrate the arrival of decoupling. In 1994–95, for example, the correlation between London and New York weakened. Wall Street streaked ahead, while London made more modest gains. (See Fig 1.6 opposite.)

Whatever the relative performances of these markets in the longer term, professional investors' rigid adherence to conventional yardsticks cost them (or more precisely the beneficiaries of the funds) money in the short term. Relationships are not immutable, and those who identify changes early profit from their acumen.

To say that international markets have links is not at all the same as saying that they operate under the same conventions. You cannot, for example, assume that, if the outlook for economic growth and interest rates are similar in two countries, the markets will have similar price earnings ratios and are likely to produce similar investment returns. Accounting conventions, taxation, and valuation norms and methods all differ from one market to another.

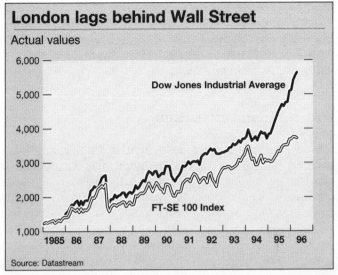

London lags behind Wall Street

Actual values

Dow Jones Industrial Average

FT-SE 100 Index

6,000 — 5,000 — 4,000 — 3,000 — 2,000 — 1,000

1985 86 87 88 89 90 91 92 93 94 95 96

Source: Datastream

Fig 1.6 Traditionally the London stockmarket has mirrored Wall Street very closely. But in 1994–95 the correlation weakened as Wall Street streaked ahead. A one-off readjustment or the long awaited 'decoupling'?

Local investment fashions mean that a stock which looks fully valued in its own country can sometimes appeal to foreigners and vice versa. In a few industries, such as drugs, investors do analyse industries globally. But making any but the most general comparisons between markets is dangerous.

First pick your strategy

The novice investor may by now be getting a touch restive. The behaviour of the stockmarket as a whole can only sensibly be predicted in the long term. Yet many fund managers are judged by their short term performance. Most share prices are broadly where they 'ought' to be, given the current state of knowledge. Yet most fund managers spend their days buying and selling shares in an expensive and abortive attempt to beat the market. Can he really do better than the pros?

Fortunately the private investor is not under the same pressures as the professional fund manager. He can choose his own time frame. But he needs to choose one which suits his overall strategy. Otherwise he risks being tossed to and fro by the crowd.

The dedicated stockpicker. It is perfectly possible for the private investor to decide simply to ignore the market, and stick to picking stocks. Providing he is investing over a sufficiently long term, and provided he can stomach some bad years, he ought to be all right in the end. But if he wants to get the best value from his stockpicking, he needs to keep at least half an eye on the market's vagaries.

The fundamental investor. If you are investing for the medium to long term, say three to five years, one of the most profitable strategies is to identify key turning points. Buying when interest rates had peaked in 1990 is a good example. With hindsight it is always easy to see how a small number of well-timed decisions could have produced an outstanding investment performance. Identifying those turning points at the time is a bit trickier.

The market timer. Some investors are not content with spotting major turning points; they want to ride every wave in every market from the trough to the peak. Thus they move from shares to bonds and back again at different stages of the economic cycle. They hop from one type of share to another at different stages of the cycle. And, if they have an international outlook, they may also leap from one world market to another: Europe one year, the US the next, Japan or Emerging Markets the next.

Their investment choices may be based on economic fundamentals, but they also need to make sure that they have spotted an incipient trend before other investors. And since everybody is playing the same game, this can often mean buying so early that there is a real danger of the trend failing to materialise. They buy and sell far more frequently than the fundamental investor, and tend to have more than a hint of the trader in their make-up.

The trader. A trader may sometimes do the same thing at the same time as a fundamentalist. But he works on a much shorter time frame, and he is interested in fundamentals only if he thinks investors have got them wrong and will soon appreciate their mistake. Some traders operate on a time scale of a few weeks or less. Peter Lynch is a trader in some contexts; George Soros in all. (See Chapter 9 pages 228–32.)

The trend follower. The trend follower is a humble version of the market timer. He waits for major market movements and hopes to jump aboard soon after they start and, and jump off again soon after they stop. This strategy can be applied to the whole market, groups of shares or individual stocks.

Many trend followers are chartists. The chartist argues that the sensible way to treat a mob is to join it, and keep your eyes skinned for signs that its mood is changing. But when the mood of the stockmarket mob changes as rapidly as it did in 1987, fellow travellers do not have time to jump clear.

Know yourself

The point to note is that the different strategies require different skills and demand different disciplines. See how you measure up.

Stockpicking. If you like picking stocks but find the market baffling, ignore it, and invest for the long term. But that can mean gritting your teeth and riding out some sickening short term upsets.

Investing on fundamentals. If you find the broader business picture interesting, and have a rational and independent turn of mind, try your hand at fundamental analysis, and invest for at least the medium term. But you may find yourself buying when everybody else is gloomy and selling when everybody else is optimistic. That demands mental stamina.

Market timing. If you enjoy the thought of pitting your wits against the market, market timing could be your forte. But beating the professionals without access to the same information sources is a very tall order. Buying and selling is expensive, particularly for the private investor. So even if you get your timing right, your gains may be frittered away in higher dealing costs. You need to have a lot of spare time to study the market, and be extremely disciplined about working out what your price objectives are over what period of time. Only go ahead if the game is worth the candle.

The trader. The same caveats apply only more so, particularly if you attempt to trade on a regular basis. If, however, you fancy yourself as a crowd psychologist and have the patience to trade only when you think the market is in a manic or depressed mood, you could make money. But remember that market valuations can remain stretched for long periods before they snap back. You are bound to get it wrong sometimes, and lose money. That hurts.

The trend follower. If you are doubtful of your ability to out-think or outwit the market, but find long term investment boring, following trends could suit you. But remember that you are always likely to be two steps behind the professionals, so it is only worth jumping aboard serious trends. Don't be the mug whose entry shows that the game is over. Chartism demands skills and imposes disciplines of its own. (See Chapter 2.)

Most of these strategies deserve the epithet contrarian. And as we said earlier beating the stockmarket normally involves spotting a mismatch between the market's expectations and what is actually likely to happen. But naive investors sometimes make the mistake of assuming that they can make money just by disagreeing with the market. Alas, as Benjamin Graham pointed out: 'The fact that other people agree or disagree with you makes you neither right nor wrong. You will be right if your facts and reasoning are correct.' Intelligence, not pure cussedness, is what's needed.

Market Analysis

IN A NUTSHELL

1. Shares have been a more profitable long term investment than alternatives such as gilts. But price fluctuations make them dangerous. All investors try to buy
   when prices are low and sell when they are high.
   Share prices already discount what the majority of
   investors expect to happen. But analysts look for cases
   where the majority has got it wrong.

2. Academic theories, such as the Random Walk and the
   Efficient Market Hypothesis argue that trying to beat
   the market is a waste of time. Share price movements
   are unpredictable, and all relevant information is
   rapidly incorporated into share prices. But most
   academics and investors nowadays accept that there
   are chinks in the efficient market: anomalies do exist.
   And even if short term market movements are unpredictable, longer term stockmarket performance tracks
   company profitability closely. Interest rates are more
   important in the short term.

3. Private investors can copy professionals and use long
   term forecasts when deciding how to divide their
   money between different types of investment, such as
   shares and gilts. But this is only an occasional
   exercise, and such sums should be treated only as
   back of the envelope exercises.

4. The short term performance of the market depends on
   a lot of different factors. But there is no set recipe for
   putting the different ingredients together to predict
   market movements.

5. Company profits are affected both by long term
   economic growth trends and by the ups and downs of
   business cycles. Investors can try to profit from

business cycles either by timing their market purchases cleverly or by switching from one sector to
another at the right time.

6. Falling interest rates are broadly good for both gilts
and shares, and rising rates bad. Correctly anticipating the effect of interest rate changes on the economy
and stockmarkets can provide good opportunities for
profits. But spotting the turning points at the time is
hard.

7. Tax changes affect the whole economy but are particularly important to consumer sectors. But the market
has usually factored changes into share prices before
the politicians act.

8. Major changes in the value of sterling can have a big
effect on the market both at the time and for months
afterwards.

9. Much of the stockmarket's reaction to elections takes
place in the run-up, rather than after the result is
known. The UK market is also influenced by US
elections.

10. Gilts are the main alternative to shares in the UK. The
most popular yardstick for comparing their relative
attractions is the gilt-equity yield ratio.

11. Wall Street is still the major overseas influence on the
London stockmarket, though the linkage is not constant.

12. Every private investor needs to have a strategy to cope
with the stockmarket's gyrations. The best one for you
will depend on your own tastes and talents. Are you a
stockpicker, a fundamentalist, a market timer, a
trader, or a trend follower?

Chapter 2
How to Use Charts

Technical analysis, or charting, uses price charts to analyse prospects for whole stockmarkets, individual shares, groups of shares, currencies, commodities and interest rates. The basic technique was developed by Charles Dow (of Dow Jones) in the US, although the Japanese used so-called candlestick charts in the rice trade several centuries earlier. Many professional investors treat charts as a valuable source of extra information, to be used in conjunction with fundamental analysis.

A company and its share price are two different things. Fundamental analysts study the company's business and its prospects and then work out where they think the share price 'ought' to be. Technical analysts ignore the 'ought' and concentrate on the actual share price. They argue that what matters in markets is the balance between supply and demand, and that this is accurately reflected in investors' purchases and sales of shares. So, for those who believe that history repeats itself, charting is a better guide to what is likely to happen to the price than the most painstaking analysis of the company's business.

Charting is more concerned with investment timing than investment choice. A technical analyst accepts that he will never catch a share or market right at the bottom or sell it right at the top. What he aims to do is to buy soon after the bottom, run his profits as long as it is safe, and sell soon after the top.

Chartists see markets as a never-ending uphill-downhill battle between buyers and sellers. Every time one side scores a notable victory, it fortifies that bit of the battlefield, which makes it even harder next time for the other side to force its way through. A pocket of **resistance** from sellers tends to stop a price rise, a pocket of **support** by buyers tends to stop a price fall. But neither is always successful. (The BTR chart in Fig 2.1 on page 33 shows a good example of prolonged periods of resistance and support.) Of course, like fundamental analysts, chartists often get it wrong and they often disagree. This is partly because they all have their favourite methods of interpreting charts.

The basic concepts are the **trend** and the **trendline**. Markets do not rise in a straight line: they zigzag. Moreover, major long-term trends are often made up of several shorter trends. The chartist tries to determine where the price is on what sort of trend. What laymen find easy to ridicule are the classic **patterns: head and shoulders, double and treble tops and bottoms, triangles, rectangles, flags**. The names refer to shapes made by share prices and the patterns are still used as indicators.

But many chartists spend more time using comparatively homely tools, such as **moving averages** and **relative strength** charts. (See charts for BTR opposite, Glaxo Wellcome on page 38 and Sainsbury on page 280.) Moving averages are, in effect, a variant on trend lines, calculated mathematically rather than drawn by eye. The shorter the period over which the average is calculated, the more closely the average tracks the price. Relative strength and weakness charts show how a particular share or sector is performing relative to some broader yardstick such as the FT-SE-A All-Share index. Many of the indicators are just a different way of analysing the same price pattern.

Trends and patterns

Chartists squabble as much as members of any other group. But belief in trends is at the heart of the technical analysis movement. The jaunty slogan 'Make the trend your friend' is its unofficial credo. As long as a price trend is intact, the investor can relax. The moment of truth comes when the price trend breaks, for that is when decisions to buy or sell may need to be taken.

The trend shows you the main direction of the share price or market. Long term investors and short term traders are united in their need to know when a trend is going to change. Most technical analysts work on the assumption that a trend moves along inside a channel: like a drunk

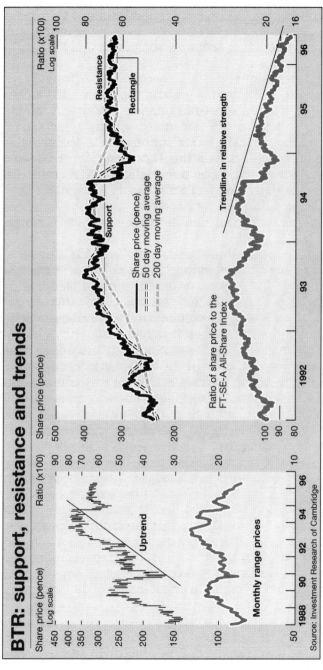

Source: Investment Research of Cambridge

Fig 2.1 BTR provides some excellent patterns. Once the uptrend was broken, the price kept bouncing back up from the support level until late 1994. But once the price broke down through the support, the former floor turned into a ceiling, as a rectangle took shape.

rolling home from the pub, it lurches from one side of the road to the other, but, provided it does not actually turn down a side street, it keeps heading in broadly the same direction.

Different techniques define the channel in different ways. The simplest is to draw a parallel line each side of the zigzag. But every channel has one key retaining wall, the **trendline**. This is the line underneath a rising trend and on top of a falling one. (The BTR chart on page 33 shows both a rising and a falling trendline.) A trend is considered established once the price has bounced off its trendline three times. Many analysts still like to draw their own trendlines on to a chart by hand, but nowadays some use computers to search out the line which best fits the price data.

If the price breaks through the trendline, it is a signal to investors to pay close attention. This may be the moment at which the trend is broken, or the price could be dithering before getting back into its channel. The difference is crucial, and most analysts emphasise that it is dangerous to second guess the price when it is hesitating.

There are many alternatives to the simple trendline. One variant uses moving averages instead, sometimes within a channel of their own, with walls that are a certain percentage above and below the moving average. A refinement of this method is the temptingly named **Bollinger bands**, with elastic walls that bulge as the share price movements become more frenzied and tighten when it sobers down.

But, whatever the technique used, all the analysts are hunting the same prey: the **breakout**. Once the price has broken through its trendline, channel wall or band, the obvious question is 'Where next?'. Many in the older generation of analysts answer this question by identifying recurring price patterns, and saying: 'If it looks like this, you can expect the price to do that'. These patterns are ignored by some analysts nowadays, partly because they occur so seldom. But they remain a reasonable way of understanding how chartists think.

Shares and markets often spend as long moving sideways as they do going up or down. These sideways hesitations are conventionally divided into **continuation patterns** and

reversal patterns. (Some of the standard patterns are shown in Fig 2.2 on pages 36 and 37.) This sounds more helpful than it is. For, although some of the continuation patterns always imply that the price is going to carry on in its original direction, some may equally well end with a reversal as the price heads off in the opposite direction. In either case, the price may well have a brief **pullback** into the area of the pattern before it starts its serious journey along the trendline.

Some analysts argue that you can predict how far the price will fall (or rise) when it breaks out by measuring the relevant bit of the preceding patterns. The commonsense explanation for this is that, once the battle between buyers and sellers has been decisively won, many investors on the losing side will want to reverse their positions. And, since nothing succeeds like success, doubters on the sidelines may also join the victors.

The most interesting patterns are those which reverse major trends: **reversal patterns**. At peaks they include the **head and shoulders, double and triple tops**, and smoother patterns with names like **saucers**. All have their mirror images when a downtrend gives way to an uptrend: the **reverse head and shoulders, double and triple bottom** and so on. (The Glaxo Wellcome chart in Fig 2.3 on page 38 has a classic double bottom. The Sainsbury chart on page 280 shows a rather unconventional head and shoulders. The surge up through the 500 level in August 1993 should have meant that the pattern aborted, but it did not.)

A couple of points worth noting are that a reversal pattern is important only if it follows a marked uptrend or down-trend, and that the patterns count only if they are complete; many abort.

The main **continuation patterns** are **triangles, rectangles** and **flags**. (There's a good rectangle on the Sainsbury chart on page 280.) **Flags** are the easiest. They occur only in very minor (tertiary) trends, they last for a few days or weeks at most and they always end in a continuation of the previous trend. They are a short but frenzied spasm halfway up, or down, the trend. **Triangles** and **rectangles** are both ambiguous periods of hesitation in primary and secondary trends, and can last for months. They can result in a breakout in the same direction as the original trend, or in the reverse

Trendlines

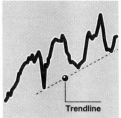

Trendline

Any long term chart contains several different trends for varying time periods. The trendline is drawn underneath a rising price and above a falling one, and should have at least three points of contact with the price. When the price breaks through the trendline, it may be a signal that the trend will be reversed, but this does not always follow. A trend is only reversed when the price breaks decisively through the last level at which a major struggle took place. A downtrend is broken when the price goes through the peak reached in the last upwards rally; an uptrend is broken when the price falls through the low point touched in the last downwards reaction. Stay with the trend until it is broken.

Head and shoulders

The head and shoulders top is considered a relatively reliable sign that an uptrend has been broken. The uptrend first has a slight check as a few investors take some of their profits. Buyers regain the upper hand, but though the price temporarily rallies even higher, there is not usually much volume behind the rally, and down goes the price again. The third and final rally is pretty pitiful with very low volume and ends with a

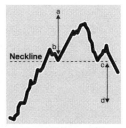

conclusive victory for the sellers as the price collapses through the neckline. Once the price has gone through the neckline, its next downwards move (c to d) is likely to equal the distance between the top of the head and the neckline (a to b).

Double tops

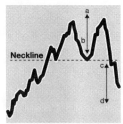

The stockmarket action which produces a double top is similar to what happens in a head and shoulders - but the buyers lose heart earlier. The neckline joins up the bottom points of the earlier reactions, and once the price falls through the neckline, its next stopping point is likely to be the same distance below the breakout level as the distance between the price peak and the neckline: (c to d) should equal (a to b). Both head and shoulders and double top patterns have their mirror images at the bottom of downtrends: reverse head and shoulders and double bottoms. The Glaxo Wellcome chart (fig 2.3) shows a good example of a double bottom.

Source of all charts: Investment Research of Cambridge

Fig 2.2 Some standard chart patterns

Triangles

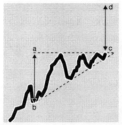

These hesitations occur in both uptrends and downtrends. They are usually just a temporary pause, but can mark the end of the trend if the price breaks out of the triangle in the opposite direction to the previous trend. Triangles can have flat tops, flat bottoms or be more regular, but in all cases the price should touch both sides at least three times. If the price gets too close to the apex without a breakout, the pattern may be aborting. Best results come when the breakout occurs between the halfway and three quarter points. If the price breaks upwards in an uptrend, expect it to rise the same distance as that between the top and bottom of the triangle : (c to d) should equal (a to b).

Rectangles

Many share prices spend much of their life in rectangles. Again what you are looking for is a breakout, which can be in either direction. And again the initial move after the breakout is expected to equal the distance between the top and bottom of the rectangle. As with other chart patterns, the price sometimes makes a brief pullback inside the rectangle after its initial breakout, but don't count on it: sometimes the move into

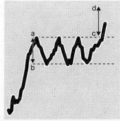

new ground can be very rapid. Like many chart patterns, rectangles are easiest to identify with hindsight. The BTR chart (fig 2.1) shows a good example of a rectangle. So does the Sainsbury chart (fig 12.2).

Flags

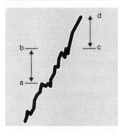

These are short-lived flurries in a short term trend, lasting anything from a few days to at most four weeks. They occur when profit takers move in during a rising trend or when there is a rush of despairing sellers in a falling trend. The rise or fall in the share price immediately before the flag forms is usually sharp, but the volume of dealing also picks up sharply while the flag is forming. Once the flag is out of the way the price should rise the same distance as it had risen immediately before the pattern developed: (c to d) should equal (a to b). More important for the long term investor is that a flag normally signifies that an uptrend has plenty of energy left.

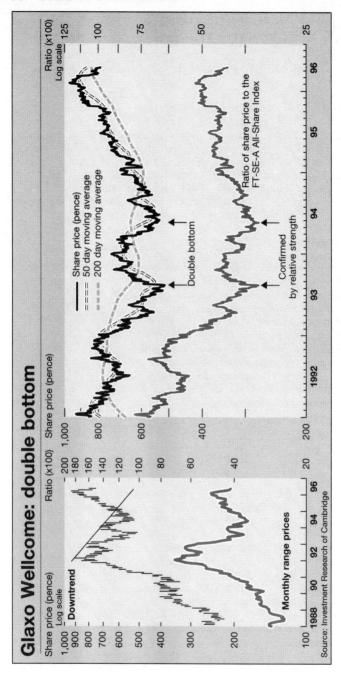

Fig 2.3 Glaxo Wellcome provides a textbook example of a double bottom. What analysts find particularly comforting is that the relative strength chart was giving the same message as the price itself. Chartists believe in having both belt and braces.

direction, but are equally valid whichever way they go. Other continuation patterns include **wedges**, **pennants**, and **gaps**.

Mathematical indicators

The trouble with pattern recognition is that its predictions are often misleading. Investors relying exclusively on charts of price movements to predict future trends would frequently lose money. Some chart patterns give false signals, others are useful only with hindsight. So, chartists have developed a range of other techniques to supplement pattern recognition.

Most involve mathematically-based indicators derived from the price itself. Others analyse price movements in the light of related factors, such as the volume of dealings, or charts of other prices. These supplementary indicators are normally used in two ways: to confirm (or negate) signals given by the primary price patterns or to provide early warning of an imminent change in the existing price trend. The fact that so many of them are mathematically based makes them appeal strongly to novice investors who hope for an infallible way of making money. But professional analysts warn, first, that different indicators tend to work in different types of market and, second, that no indicator should be followed blindly.

Charles Dow emphasised the importance of **confirmation** when he calculated a Railroads index – now Transportation, and still used as a measure of contemporary activity – as a supplement to his original Industrials index. If the Industrials hit a new high but the Railroads did not, this divergence undermined the validity of the bullish signal given by the Industrials. Modern analysts still use this approach when looking to sector indices for early warning that a whole market could be topping out.

Two popular indicators used to confirm trends in the underlying price are **relative strength** charts and **moving averages**. A relative strength chart considers the movement of a particular share price in the context of the market as a whole or of the relevant sector. A 10 per cent rise in a share price is not impressive if the market as a whole has risen 20 per cent. And if a share starts to show weakness relative to the market, even though its price is still rising, chartists take that as a warning signal. A change in the relative strength trend can be the prelude to a change in the trend of the underlying price. (The Glaxo Wellcome chart on page 38 shows the relative strength line confirming the double bottom traced out by the actual share price. The Sainsbury chart on page 280 shows that in late 1995 the share price uptrend was not confirmed by the relative strength chart which was in a downtrend. This divergence was a warning sign, soon justified.)

Moving averages are what they sound like. The price is averaged over a certain number of days. On each successive day, one new figure is taken into the calculation, while the oldest figure in the previous day's calculation drops out. Moving averages are most useful in a market where a strong uptrend or downtrend is in place. When used together with the share price they are also an indicator of momentum. Since they necessarily follow rather than lead the price, averages can never be used to predict a movement in it; they are used to confirm such movements.

Weighted moving averages, which give greater emphasis to the latest figures in the series, reduce the time lag. Some moving averages, such as the Coppock Indicator, a weighted average of a market index, are used to give automatic buy signals in their own right.

The Coppock Indicator, invented by a Texan called Edwin Coppock, is meant to give buy signals when the worst of a bear market is over. It was never intended to give sell signals, though some investors use it in this way. The original version was based on a 12 month weighted moving average. The 12 month period was deliberately chosen to match the typical period of mourning after a family bereavement. (The bear market equates to the bereavement.) The *Investors Chronicle*, which publishes Coppock Indicators for most world markets, used a calculation for only 10 months. Mourning is obviously briefer in the UK than in Texas.

But most analysts use two or more moving averages for different time periods in conjunction to produce automatic buy and sell signals when the averages cross each other. If the averages are both moving in the same direction when they cross, it is considered significant.

For example, if the short term moving average crosses up through the longer term moving average, when both have recently started to rise (a configuration known as the Golden Cross), this confirms that a falling market has turned into a rising one. (When the averages cross on the way down, it is known as a Dead Cross. There's a suitably grisly one on the Glaxo Wellcome chart in January 1993.) Unfortunately, such crosses only give a confirmation of a trend already under way.

Many investors, however, are more interested in indicators that give early warning of a price movement. Most early warning indicators measure the speed at which a share price is moving. They are known as **momentum indicators** or **oscillators**, and are used to identify short term turning points.

Oscillators are most efficient in a sideways market, when the price is zigzagging but not trending up or down. The turning points tend to coincide with times when the price has been rising or falling unusually fast. So, measuring its acceleration can provide early warning of a change in direction. One popular momentum indicator, the Relative Strength Index (RSI),* developed by an American called J. Welles Wilder Jnr, has been refined so that it always oscillates between 0 and 100. In a sideways market, chartists talk of the price being overbought when the RSI reaches 70 and oversold when it falls below 30. (If the RSI is used when the market is trending, the parameters need to be adjusted: in an uptrend 80 indicates overbought, in a downtrend 20 counts as oversold.) But a price can stay overbought or oversold for quite a long time.

Many analysts use momentum indicators simply as vetoes: never buy when a share is overbought, never sell when oversold. Others analyse the trend in the indicator

---

* Often confused with charts of relative strength for fairly obvious reasons. Some chartists have rechristened the Welles Wilder **relative strength indicator** the **rate of change indicator** in a brave attempt to dispel confusion. It doesn't.

itself. If, for example, the rate of acceleration is slowing, this can provide confirmation that an uptrend is running out of steam. But even those who use them in this way warn they can be dangerous in inexperienced hands.

Candlesticks

Japanese rice traders were using candlestick charts to predict price movements centuries before Charles Dow constructed the Dow Jones Industrial Average. Now, they are catching on in the City.

Like western chartists, analysts using candlesticks believe that similar price patterns recur in similar situations. And, by identifying patterns which occur at important market turning points, they hope to predict changes in price trends. (Our example of a candlestick chart in Fig 2.4 opposite uses the Hang Seng index simply because so many different patterns appear clearly on it. But candles are equally suitable for occidental markets such as the Footsie or international ones like gold.) Some of the patterns they use are similar to those found in western textbooks. These relate to trading for relatively long periods and signal the reversal of a major trend. But candlestick aficionados also believe that patterns produced by just two or three days trading can give important signals. This makes the technique potentially helpful to short term traders in markets such as foreign exchange.

Candlestick charts use four different prices from each day's trading: open, close, high and low. The wick of each candlestick runs between the high and the low, and the wider rectangular **candle** or **body** runs between the opening and closing prices. If the closing price is lower than the opening price, the body is shaded black. If the closing price is higher than the opening, the body is coloured white – or red in the original Japanese version. The thin bar emerging above and below the rectangular body is known either as the upper and lower **shadow** or as the **wick**.

A conventional western line chart, like those used in the *Financial Times* and the *Investors Chronicle*, is based on closing prices for each day's trading. Giving one to an

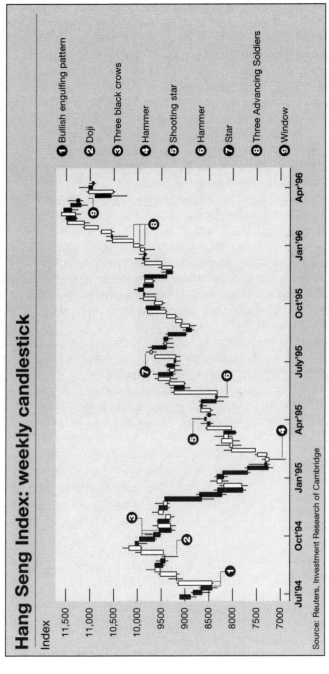

Hang Seng Index: weekly candlestick

Index

1 Bullish engulfing pattern
2 Doji
3 Three black crows
4 Hammer
5 Shooting star
6 Hammer
7 Star
8 Three Advancing Soldiers
9 Window

Source: Reuters, Investment Research of Cambridge

Fig 2.4 One reason candlestick charts are popular with many currency traders is that some of their signals result from the interpretation of just a few days' trading. As in Western charts bullish formations have their mirror-image bearish counterparts.

analyst is like telling a football enthusiast the result of a series of matches – but not providing any details of the play. A candlestick chart is equivalent to a brief report of the highlights of each match. And the differing colours make it immediately obvious whether buyers or sellers won.

A long white body shows that the buyers were in the ascendant throughout the day. A long black body shows the opposite. But some of the less blatant results can be more interesting. A small body at the bottom of the day's trading range with a very long upper shadow shows that buyers made a sortie halfway through the day but were roundly defeated and slunk back home with their tails between their legs. That is not an encouraging portent for the next day's trading. (Look at the **shooting star** in April 1995 on the Hang Seng chart on page 43. If, however, the body is at the top of the day's trading range and there is a long lower shadow beneath it, a formation known as a **hammer**, that is far more bullish. The sellers did their best to push the shares further down and, indeed, they succeeded, but not for long since there were still enough confident buyers around to leave the price back at around its opening level.

The one-day snapshot becomes even more useful when set against the background of trading in the previous few days. If there has been a sequence of black days, with prices moving down steadily, a white candlestick will always be important. But it is particularly important if the body is at the top of the trading range, and the price itself plumbs new lows. For what that shows is that sellers attempted to drag the price to new depths but failed to keep it down.

Analysts have drawn up a number of rules of thumb to help investors interpret the relationships between successive days' trading. If the body of a black candlestick covers both the top and bottom of the body of the previous day's white one (or vice versa), that is interpreted as a convincing victory which is likely to be followed through in subsequent days' trading. And if the white body covers the three preceding black ones it is even more significant. (The **bullish engulfing pattern** near the start of the Hang Seng chart marked a convincing victory.)

The objective is to analyse what is going on in the market and see through the dealings to the emotions of the buyers and sellers. The names Japanese candlestick analysts give to their patterns are suitably evocative. **Morning star** (a bullish sign that a downtrend is likely to be broken), **evening star** (the opposite), and **hanging man** (another warning sign) turn technical analysis into poetry.

Cycles and waves: Elliott and Gann

All technical analysis aims to predict future price movements by studying past movements. But most types of charting are relatively pragmatic, and can be rationalised in terms of underlying investor behaviour.

Cycle theories are dogmatic, with lengthy creeds which the faithful have to swallow whole. The two most common ideologies are Elliott wave theory, and Gann's raft of theories. Elliott's theory is intended to apply to equity market indices, not individual securities. Even its fans agree that it works better in some situations than in others. It is, for instance, very good for newly emerging markets. Gann is used primarily for individual stocks and commodities, though some analysts also apply it to markets. Both theories incorporate some magic numbers: mathematical relationships which recur time and again. But the two theories use different numbers.

● **Elliott waves.** Ralph Elliott, a telegraphist, based his theory on that originally enunciated by Charles Dow. Dow had noted that a bull market in shares tends to have three distinct upward movements. The initial recovery takes place against a background of public scepticism. The second surge is far more vigorous, with heavier volume reflecting increased interest from professional investors and speculators. The third is when everybody has turned bullish, particularly laymen, and only a few professionals are beginning to get worried. Then comes the bear market.

Elliott stuck to the basic Dow shape, but considered that a bull market had five waves, not three. For he included not only the **three upward impulses**, but also the **two downward corrections** in his count. The bear market which followed consisted of three waves: down, up, down. That

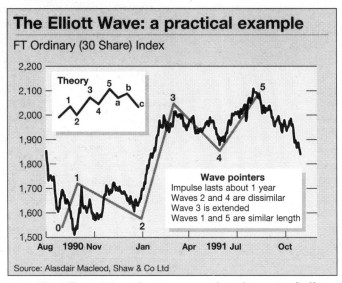

The Elliott Wave: a practical example

FT Ordinary (30 Share) Index

Wave pointers
Impulse lasts about 1 year
Waves 2 and 4 are dissimilar
Wave 3 is extended
Waves 1 and 5 are similar length

Source: Alasdair Macleod, Shaw & Co Ltd

Fig 2.5 The Elliott Wave theory argues that the major bull market advance is developed in five waves and corrected by a 3 wave decline. It can be applied to any timescale: periods of hundreds of years or less than an hour.

completed the cycle, and a new bull market was set to begin. (See Fig 2.5 above for both a theoretical and a practical example of an Elliott wave.)

This cyclical pattern is applied to all markets, and a wide variety of time periods. Elliott himself identified nine different time periods over which his theory applies. The longest was the grand supercycle, lasting 150–200 years and consisting of five supercycles. Then came the supercycle, cycle, primary, intermediate, minor, minute, minuette and finally the sub-minuette, which could last less than a day.

He set out a series of rules concerning the relationship of different waves in a cycle to each other. These rules do not tell the investor how long particular waves will last. But they do allow him to make some pertinent deductions about the probable length of future waves from the actual length and character of those immediately preceding them.

But, not yet satisfied, Elliott then sprinkled some medieval mathematics into his detective game. The **Fibonacci numbers** can be traced in many relationships of the natural world, from the rate at which rabbits can breed to the leaf arrangement of plants. They are also the basis of the golden numbers used by ancient Greek and Egyptian architects. The Fibonacci series of numbers starts with one and grows by adding the next lowest whole number to the latest number in the series: 0+1=1; 1+1=2; 1+2=3; 2+3=5; 3+5=8 and so on. Thus the sequence begins with fairly small intervals between the numbers but they rapidly widen: 0,1,1,2,3,5,8,13,21,34,55 and onwards and upwards. The relationship between any two successive numbers in the higher echelons is 1.618 or (inversely) 0.618. And the ratio between alternate numbers is 2.618 or (inversely) 0.382.

Fibonacci ratios are used by Elliott to calculate price objectives for the different market waves. Some analysts say that they knew that 1987 would probably be a major turning point, because it was 55 years after the start of the Wall Street bull market that followed the 1929 crash!

● **Gann.** William D. Gann was a market trader whose extensive writings make Elliott's theories look pellucid. He, too, studied market waves and looked for standard relationships between them. His conclusions, termed **Quantum theory**, were that moves of 25 per cent, 50 per cent and 100 per cent were common, and moves of one third and two thirds also occur, though less frequently. Both rises and retracements tended to conform to these proportions, though not always exactly. He also concluded that there was a relationship between the extent of a price movement and the time the price took to achieve it. If the share moved up one unit of price for every one unit of time, the resulting trendline was at an angle of 45 per cent, and the trend could be expected to continue.

Gann described this 1:1 relationship as **the squaring of price with time**. If, however, the price broke up or down through this trendline, its new rate of acceleration would have a mathematical relationship with the old one. It might for example rise twice or three times as fast, or just half as fast. A Gann chart has a series of horizontal lines, and series of trend-lines fanning out at an angle from the start of the trend. The horizontal lines act as price targets, or as support levels during corrections. The fan of trend-lines provides investors with a reserve trendline, whenever the price breaks through the existing one.

A small number of addicts base their entire trading strategies on highly detailed rules extrapolated from Gann's or Elliott's theorising. A larger number of investors use Elliott, or Gann numbers, or both, when setting price targets for rises and corrections.

Both theories also find an echo in pure mathematics. Fourier analysis breaks down complex wave patterns into the sum of a series of simple waves, just as Gann and Elliott have attempted to in the stockmarket.

Tools of the trade

What many novices find daunting about technical analysis is that it embraces so many different highly complex techniques. But most working analysts tend to use only one or two techniques, often the simpler ones. They find out what works for them and stick to it.

Analysts also differ in the way they like their basic information presented. Some stick to simple **arithmetic line** charts, some prefer **semi-logarithmic** scales. Others always use bar charts. And a third school insists, equally firmly, that only **point and figure** charts give them a real feel for what investors are doing.

Line charts are everybody's idea of a chart. The horizontal axis represents time and the vertical one price. The share price line connects each day's closing price with the next one. Normally, these charts are drawn on an **arithmetic scale**. Whatever the grid size used, it remains constant: any one day or month occupies the same space on the paper as any other day or month. And one rise or fall of 100p or 100 index points looks the same as another. So, if a price rose from 100p to 500p over a four-month period at a steady rate of 100p a month, the share price line would run straight from the bottom left-hand corner to the top right-hand corner.

Many investors, however, prefer charts drawn on what is known as a **semi-logarithmic** scale, particularly for longer periods of time or when the price is rising or falling very sharply. A semi-log scale follows the same convention for time as an arithmetic linear chart: each day or month has the same space as any other. But it measures price movements from a relative point of view.

When the share price in our earlier example moved from 100p to 200p, that was a 100 per cent rise. But when it moved from 200p to 300p, that was only a 50 per cent rise – and the semi-log chart would show the second 100p rise occupying only half the space occupied by the first 100p rise. In order to achieve this, the grid on the vertical scale gets steadily smaller as the numbers get bigger. So, instead of producing a straight line, the price sequence would show a sharp initial rise tapering off into a steadily flattening curve.

Semi-log charts have several advantages. They make it easy to compare two different charts with each other. They force the investor to put price movements into perspective. And they provide a handy substitute for more complex momentum indicators, designed to measure the speed at which a share price is moving, while also giving early warning if a trend is running out of steam. (The chart on page 220 shows how different the Body Shop price looks on arithmetic and semi-log scales. Peter Lynch bought some shares in January 1992. If he had looked at the semi-log chart, he might have hesitated.)

Many chartists prefer **bar charts** to linear ones. Most bar charts include each day's high, low and closing price on each vertical bar. The vertical line runs between the high and the low, and the close is shown as a crossbar. Normally, the closing price is towards the top of the day's range during a strong uptrend, and towards the bottom in a strong downtrend. So, a close near the bottom of the day's range when the price is moving up can be a warning sign; vice versa in a downtrend. (Turn to Fig 2.6 on page 50 for a bar chart of Footsie.)

Some bar charts also include the opening price. The opening price is shown as a short bar to the left of the high/low axis, the close as a short bar to the right. The information contained on an open/high/low/close chart is similar to that shown on the candlestick charts, but they lack the immediate visual appeal of candlesticks. Bar charts can use either an arithmetic or a semi-log scale, but they treat time conventionally.

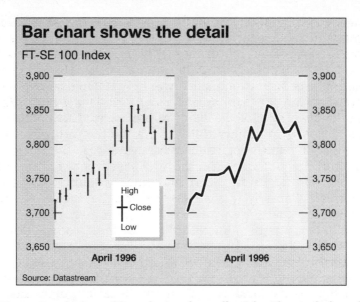

Fig 2.6 Bar charts are like rather crude candlesticks. They include each day's high, low and closing price on each vertical bar. The crossbar shows the close. Some bar charts also include the opening price.

Point and figure charts use a conventional arithmetic price scale on the vertical axis but consider time irrelevant. The number of plots depends not on the number of days or months which have passed but on the number of significant price moves which have occurred. They only include prices when they are moving, and omit what is regarded as irrelevant movement. (The point and figure chart of Footsie in Fig 2.7 on page 52 shows just what a ding-dong battle took place in 1995, before the buyers took control.)

When the price is rising, it is shown as a column of crosses; when it is falling, it is shown as a series of noughts. When it changes direction, the analyst moves to the next column and starts with the appropriate symbol. Thus, a price which moves very erratically for a month, and then stagnates for a year, would occupy a lot of space in both directions in the first month but none in the following year.

The point and figure analyst has two decisions to make which further influence the appearance of a chart. First, how big should each box – notifiable price movement – be? Does the analyst record each 1p movement, each 10p movement, or what? Second, what counts as a significant reversal? If the analyst moves to a new column every time the price hesitates, this over-sensitivity could make it harder to detect a genuine change in trend. Most point and figure enthusiasts use what is known as a three-box reversal system. They move to the next column and record a change in direction only when the price has moved three units or more in the opposite direction from the prevailing one.

Fans of point and figure charts argue that the price is interesting only when there is a change in the balance of power, as reflected in a sharp movement in the price. So, the point and figure system reflects everything of importance in its history.

How the pros use charts

A strict chartist looks only at the past behaviour of the share price and what it is doing now. He then interprets these patterns in the light both of an extensive collection of chartist theories, and his own experience of other price charts. And he refuses even to look at fundamentals. But many technical analysts use a combination of fundamental and chartist techniques. This is partly because they find the two complement each other, partly because they know that few of their clients are happy to take a decision purely on the basis of charts.

Some chartists talk as if they are behavioural psychologists, tracking the madness of crowds. Others sound as if they are the only true economic scientists left, focusing on supply and demand and screening out irrelevant factors. All regard themselves as pragmatists, studying what investors actually do – as reflected in their purchases and sales – rather than being influenced by what investors say. Those who refuse even to look at fundamentals argue that all knowledge about the company or market concerned has been discounted in market transactions.

The techniques used to interpret charts are still developing. And computers have made it much easier for analysts to employ a panoply of different tools at the click of a mouse. A modern City analyst will have a real time price feed for all

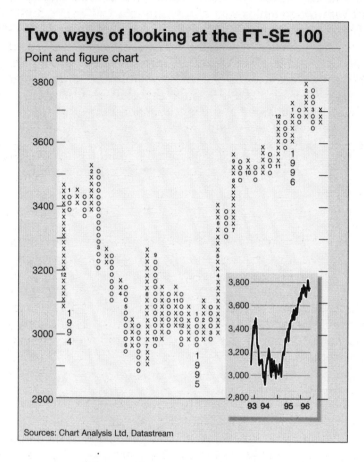

Fig 2.7 Point and figure enthusiasts argue that a price is only interesting when there is a change in the balance of power. Their charts only record significant movements and highlight the struggles.

When the price is rising, it is shown as a series of crosses. When it is falling, it is shown as a series of noughts. When it changes direction, the analyst moves to the next column and starts with the appropriate symbol.

These charts do not measure time. But in a nod towards convention, they do mark the beginning of each year. And the first significant movement in any month is recorded as the number of the month (January = 1, February = 2 etc) rather than as a cross or nought. Thus the first price fall in 1994 has a 1 in place of a nought.

the shares and markets he follows, plus a wide variety of
software programmes that allow him to apply half a dozen
different techniques to a chart in as many minutes. He can
draw in moving averages for various time periods, trend
lines or Bollinger bands (which surround the price's path
like an elastic bandage). He can add on volume and
momentum indicators, and carve the chart up according to
Fibonacci numbers or Gann retracement percentages.

Watching an analyst put his computer terminal through
its paces is like watching a conjuring show. But though the
diagnostic techniques have become infinitely more sophisticated, the problem to be solved remains much the same.
Charts do not give signals of their own accord, they need to
be interpreted. And any interpretation is only as good as the
interpreter.

Many technical analysts work for banks and brokers, with
foreign exchange traders generally being more enthusiastic
about charts than fund managers, perhaps because they have
fewer fundamentals to hang on to. But there are some
independent analysts, often one man bands, who sell chart
services. One of the best known in London is Brian Marber,
who concentrates on foreign exchange and stockmarkets,
not individual shares. He has no time for fundamental
analysis, but uses a wide range of different chartist techniques. His hand-drawn charts, based on daily closing prices,
have a scattering of relatively homely trendlines, classic
patterns, moving averages and momentum indicators. But
he will also turn to his Reuters screen for some of the more
fiddly charts: candlesticks inside Bollinger bands, for example. He uses semi-log charts when analysing stockmarkets
but arithmetic ones for currencies. His argument in favour of
semi-log charts is that they represent what is happening
more accurately, and are safer: the warning signals come
earlier when an uptrend is breaking, and later when a
downtrend is breaking.

Marber uses a particular technique so long as it appears to
work and sidelines it when it ceases to be effective. And he
recognises that some techniques work better in some markets than others.

One of his favourite indicators for stockmarkets is

Coppock (see page 40). He reckons, however, that it does not work in currency markets. It is the same story with momentum. But he has no time for Elliott's waves or Gann's theories. Occasionally, though, he might use some of Gann's retracement percentages when setting a price target.

David Fuller of Chart Analysis, a firm known for its point and figure charts, is the antithesis of Marber when it comes to technique, although the two quite often come up with similar predictions. Around a quarter of Fuller's analysis relates to fundamentals, mainly economics. He describes himself as a behavioural technical analyst and dismisses targets, patterns, and cycles as too theoretical and dogmatic.

He is nevertheless extremely interested in trends. Is the market **trending** (ie, moving up or down) or **ranging** (ie, moving sideways in a trading range)? How consistent is the movement? If trending, does it show any signs of an imminent reversal? To Fuller, a trend which is about to end will normally show at least one (and often more) of the three following characteristics: acceleration, a dramatic move against the prevailing trend, and highly volatile churning. He tends to start with the long term picture, using a three-box point and figure chart with at least five years' data. Then he will switch to a more sensitive one with a more detailed price scale. For the very short term, he uses bar charts. All his charts are arithmetic rather than semi-log.

Investment Research of Cambridge, which has been operating for 50 years, publishes a host of different chart services and also manages portfolios. Like Fuller, Investment Research analysts tend to pay attention to fundamentals as well as charts. Unusually, they even pay attention to the views of fund managers. If they like a market, but the unit trust managers are bearish, they wait. Their charts always show a long term price chart as background. The more detailed price chart will have a couple of moving averages and a relative strength chart for individual shares. (The BTR, Glaxo and Sainsbury charts are all adapted from their main Chart Book.) Momentum is another favourite tool. When they are buying for clients they use both fundamentals and chartist techniques, but decisions to sell are sometimes based purely on charts.

How easy is charting for an amateur?

Charts have always been popular with private investors for both good and bad reasons. The bad reasons are similar to those of punters searching for a formula which will crack the lottery, the gaming table or the race-course. Such people are looking for a magic way of picking winners: the alchemist's secret. Private investors who approach charts in this spirit are often drawn to Elliott and Gann, and too often adopt their teachings with the uncritical zeal of a new convert. But there are plenty of good reasons why private investors may find technical analysis attractive. Probably the most important is that it is a technique where the individual investor can compete on level terms with the pros, without spending a fortune.

An individual investor hoping to enjoy some new fundamental insight into a major company ahead of the professional analysts has the odds stacked against him. He is unlikely to have as much time or as good equipment. He will not be able to talk to either the company or other market participants. So he is almost bound to have less idea of what people are saying. The attraction of charts is that they ignore what people are saying in favour of what they are doing, and argue that their actions are all in the price. That price is equally available to everyone. Who needs to be an insider if he can see what the insiders are doing?

Some of the specific tools used by chartists, such as point and figure charts, can be drawn by anyone with some squared paper. And it is worth noting that many of the pros continue to use a paper and pencil even though they have an on-line screen service at their elbow. Computer enthusiasts can also get a variety of relatively inexpensive programs which will allow them to manipulate price data in much the same ways as the pros: this is particularly useful for people attracted by some of the mathematical indicators. (See Appendix B.)

Charts also impose some useful disciplines on the individual investor. Used in conjunction with fundamental analysis, they can provide a second opinion. They are also helpful on timing, always tricky. Investors who do not like drawing their own charts and are not computer-friendly may well find a subscription to a chart service gives them all the ideas they need.

One caveat from several professional analysts is that using too many different chartist techniques can be self-defeating.

Where to get charts

The best known supplier of charts for UK private investors is Investment Research of Cambridge (01223–356251), which sells a number of different services. Its monthly UK Equity Chart book, with charts on over 650 companies, can be supplemented by a daily market fax, a fortnightly service covering the traded option stocks, a monthly market leaders update of the firm's views on the 200 leading shares in the UK market. Most charts are based on daily high/low figures for over three years, plus moving averages, market relatives and a longer term chart as background. Investors who prefer point and figure charts should try Chart Analysis (0171–439–4961).

Most of the leading investment software houses (see page 374 for details) include technical analysis packages. Some, such as MetaStock support a wide variety of different types of chart formats others are tailored to a particular technique such as Gann or Candlesticks.

How to use Charts

IN A NUTSHELL

1. Technical analysis, or charting, uses charts to analyse price prospects for whole stockmarkets, individual shares, groups of shares, currencies, commodities and interest rates. Charting is the analysis of supply and demand, and is more concerned with investment timing than investment choice.

2. The basic concepts are the trend and the trend line. The chartist tries to determine where the price is on what sort of trend. A price will normally continue moving along its trendline until it breaks decisively through it. But it will often hesitate for lengthy periods when it meets resistance or support.

3. Past investment decisions of people who have bought and sold a stock are reflected in the chart patterns, and they help analysts work out where to expect a trend to meet resistance or support in future. Resistance from sellers tends to stop a price rise, support by buyers tends to stop a price fall. But neither is always successful.

4. Analysts have identified certain recurring hesitation patterns which end with the price either reverting to its existing trend or reversing direction. These price formations are conventionally divided into continuation patterns and reversal patterns. But patterns are only valid if they are complete; many abort. And it is dangerous to take investment decisions on the basis of an incomplete pattern.

5. Chartists have developed a range of other techniques to supplement pattern recognition. Most involve mathematically-based indicators derived from the price itself. Others analyse price movements in the light of related factors, such as the volume of

dealings, or charts of other prices. These supplementary indicators are used either to confirm (or negate) signals given by the primary price chart or to provide early warning of an imminent change in the price trend.

6. Candlestick charts, an old Japanese technique for predicting price movements, are becoming popular in the West. They look at the pattern of trading within each day as well as the closing level of the price.

7. Cycle theories are based on the belief that all markets follow certain long term sequences. Elliott and Gann are the two best known exponents of cycle theories. Elliott's wave theory applies to all markets, but not to individual shares. Gann's theories are applied mainly to individual stocks and commodities.

8. Different types of chart record the same price information in different ways. The main choices are between linear and bar charts; arithmetic and semi-logarithmic scales. All use the horizontal axis to measure time conventionally. Point and figure charts disregard time and only record a price when there is a significant movement.

9. Some professional chartists use fundamentals as well; some stick to charts. Most use more than one type, though their choices differ. Many analysts argue that different types of chart work for different types of market, and that once-valid techniques may cease to work for particular markets.

10. Private investors who thoroughly understand charts are on an equal footing with professional technical analysts. Many chart services and computer programs are relatively inexpensive.

Chapter 3
Directors' Dealings

One of the advantages of charts is that the information they provide is objective. They tell the investor what happened to the price, and he can see from the volume figures whether movements were made on the back of substantial trading. But the actual deals are anonymous. So the chartist does not need to decide whether specific deals are based on sound information or not. What matters is that a share trade took place, not who made it.

But some investors take the opposite view. They care more about the provenance of the deal than the fact that it was done. Like speculators who follow tipsheets, they are looking for tips, but their approach is more cynical. They want to know what the insiders are doing, not what they are saying. 'Follow the smart money' is their slogan. To a lesser extent, they are also interested in knowing where the mug money is going – so that they can head in the opposite direction.

The most popular source of such information is details of directors' dealings, which are widely available. A second source of more doubtful utility is activity by private investors. A third is speculative dealing. The information is mainly used as a pointer to the future movements in individual share prices, but can also be scanned for clues to the likely direction of the stockmarket as a whole. Many serious investors regard share dealing information with disdain – somewhat akin to ferreting round in dustbins. Others contend that, provided it is interpreted intelligently and used selectively, it can be a useful addition to the investor's armoury.

The unacceptable face of directors' dealings

Directors' share-dealings epitomise what many people think the City is all about: insiders taking advantage of their

position to make money at outsiders' expense. There is
some truth in this. But insider dealing and directors'
dealings are not identical, though they may overlap. Directors' dealings are the acceptable face of insider dealing.

'Insider dealing' is a criminal offence in the UK.* Its
essence is that someone who possesses unpublished price
sensitive information by virtue of his job (an insider)
wittingly deals or encourages someone else to deal in
securities likely to be significantly affected by this information if it were made public. Thus, if initial bid talks are
going on, both the companies' own directors and key
employees have price sensitive information, and so do their
advisers. And if one of the bankers involved in the deal tips
off a broker who tips off a friend who deals in the shares and
is found out, the insiders are in trouble.

But additional European Union (EU) regulations introduced in 1994 have widened the net. For it is no longer
necessary for the inside information to come from the
company in whose securities the dealing takes place. If, for
example, a quoted (but not an unquoted) retailer told an
analyst that it had started buying goods from a particular
supplier, and the analyst told a friend to buy shares in that
supplier, that would seemingly count as insider trading
under the EU regulations.

The obvious target of the law is company directors
themselves and City slickers trying to make a fast and
nefarious buck for themselves and their friends. But it also
puts a spoke in one of the City's favourite wheels: the
regular cosy chats between quoted companies and stockbrokers' analysts. (See Chapter 10.)

Nowadays neither company directors nor analysts are
sure how far these chats are allowed to go. In 1993 a Scottish
analyst was convicted of insider dealing (though the conviction was subsequently quashed) because he passed on to his
clients bad news a company called Shanks McEwan had
given him about its current trading. In the same year
London International was reprimanded by the Stock

---

* See Section V of the Criminal Justice Act 1993.

Exchange for selectively briefing 13 analysts and four institutional investors about its falling profits.

The Stock Exchange also has a model code of conduct, which explicitly bans share dealing in certain circumstances. For example, company directors and senior executives are routinely banned from dealing for a specific period ahead of the company's announcement of its results – normally two months for a company which reports twice a year. Dealings are also prohibited in any period when there is something price sensitive afoot at the company which is likely to necessitate a stock exchange announcement – even if the director concerned knows nothing about it. Directors have to get clearance from the chairman or a stand-in for any dealings in a company's shares, and clearance is seldom given during the 'close period' ahead of results.

Some companies have gone to considerable lengths to publish and be saved. Some have started issuing statements of what they have told analysts, or even saying in advance that they will be trotting analysts round a factory. Others have abandoned the practice of individual briefings, on the grounds that it gives the advantage to the first one through the door. All highly commendable. But, like original sin, insider dealing will always be hard to eliminate totally.

Tips from the horse's mouth

At the other extreme are routine dealings by directors. Many companies, for example, insist that all directors should have a token shareholding. And some investors, such as Warren Buffett, are reluctant to invest unless the company's top executives have significant share stakes. He argues that it is easier for them to think like owners if they are in fact at least part owners of the business. It is certainly usually sensible to steer clear of new issues in which all the shares come from directors and none of the issue proceeds will be available to expand the company's business.

There are, however, many greyer areas. Who, for example, decides whether particular information is price sensitive or not? Common sense suggests that the executive directors of a company ought always to have a better idea of the company's prospects than other people, insofar as those prospects depend on the company itself. That does not, of course, mean that they are equally well equipped to judge the effect that knowledge would have on the stockmarket if it were generally known. But it does mean that, although the majority of directors' share-dealings are perfectly legal, they always have a potentially insiderish whiff to them.

All dealings by directors have to be reported to the Stock Exchange within five days, and they are published in the *Stock Exchange Weekly Intelligence*, a publication crammed full of such statistics. Unsurprisingly many investors pay attention to such dealings. The trouble is that it is hard for the outsider to know which of the dealings are likely to be worth following, and which are routine.

Several firms which provide information on the Stock Exchange monitor these dealings, and sell the information to their investment clients. For example, *The Inside Track*, part of Edinburgh Financial Publishing, publishes a service for institutional clients which includes charts showing all recent dealings by directors in a particular company, together with a commentary on their significance. It produces a retail newsletter based on this information, also called *The Inside Track*, with the alternatives of a weekly service, a hotline and a fax service.

The same company produces a comprehensive list of recent dealings for the Weekend Money section of the *Financial Times* which is published, together with a chart of one of the more interesting companies concerned, every Saturday. A check in early 1996 on the subsequent performance of shares in these charts showed that overall the 'buys' did slightly better than the market, and the 'sells' slightly worse. The buys seemed to be rather better indicators than the sells. But the survey also showed that investors needed to be very selective about which dealings they paid attention to. Over the course of more than a year there were only a handful of outstanding signals from directors' dealings. These buoyed up the averages.

Directors sometimes explained share sales by saying that institutional investors had been asking for more shares to be made available, or that they wanted to buy a little retirement home in Florida. Sometimes the shares did notably badly afterwards. There can be more than one explanation for a deal.

The *Investors Chronicle* also publishes each week three charts of companies in which there have been recent dealings.

How to interpret directors' dealings

Many people argue that directors' purchases are more useful than their sales for two reasons. First, more investors can take advantage of a 'buy' signal than a 'sell' signal. Second, few people buy shares unless they expect them to go up. There are many personal reasons why directors might decide to sell shares – perhaps they need the money to buy a house or for school fees.

The Inside Track provides its customers with a checklist of points to consider when deciding whether a particular share deal is significant.

- Pay attention only to purchases which are meaningful in relation to the director's existing stake. As a rule of thumb, that means deals amounting to 10 per cent or more of his holding.
- Pay particular attention to several directors dealing at the same time or close together. This is probably the strongest single indicator that something is about to happen. But do be aware of other circumstances. If, for instance, three new directors have just joined the board, you may well find all three buying their token share stakes on the same day: nothing significant about that.
- Don't take one deal in isolation. If a director has made large sales at the top of the market, and makes some minor purchases lower down, that does not necessarily mean that the turning point has come.
- Watch what happens when a company has a rights issue. If the directors don't take up their rights, there may be a reason. But it had better be a good one. Otherwise follow their example. And it might be appropriate also to

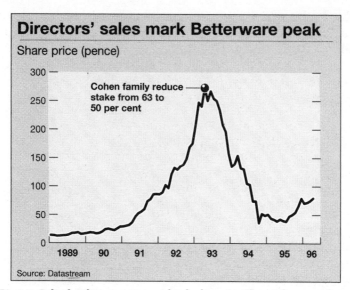

Directors' sales mark Betterware peak

Share price (pence)

Cohen family reduce
stake from 63 to
50 per cent

Source: Datastream

Fig 3.1 Sales by directors are said to be less significant than purchases –
but that's not always so. Anyone who copied the directors of Betterware
got out at the peak.

consider whether you are happy with your existing
shareholding.
● Pay attention to what directors do a couple of months
before the results. This is their last chance to deal before
the company enters purdah. So their dealings may well
give a good clue as to whether those results will be good
or bad.
● If a single director is the only buyer in sight, watch out.
He may be trying to support the share price in defiance of
the market's general gloom. In such cases the market's
gloom is usually justified in the end.
● If you spot a director who seems to have a good track
record in buying and selling at the right time, pay
particular attention to him.

Anyone interested in this subject will probably soon be able
to add to this list. For example, deals by executive directors
are more significant than those by non-execs; most significant of the lot are those by the chief executive or the finance
director.

Share sales which are consequent on the director exercising an option should be treated a little differently from sales of shares already held. Few directors can afford to keep all the shares on which they have options. But they are still likely to exercise the options and sell the shares when they reckon the share price is relatively strong. It is worth trying to find out whether there was any particular pressure on the director – for example, his option was near expiry. Be careful also of share sales near the end of the financial year. Many directors routinely bed and breakfast a few shares in order to reduce their eventual capital gains tax liability.

A study by the London Business School suggested that 'shares purchased by company insiders perform abnormally well over a considerable period following disclosure of the transaction.'

There are plenty of concrete examples of directors' dealings providing valid signals. Betterware was one of the most amazing little growth companies of the early 1990s. (See Fig 3.1 opposite.) But, like so many rapidly expanding companies, it eventually ran out of puff. Anyone who followed the controlling family when it slimmed its holdings in 1993 would have got out at the peak.

Carpet company Harris Queensway was doing badly in 1987. Four directors sold shortly before the stuffing was knocked out of the share price. But while it was still bumping along the bottom, Sir Philip Harris and a couple of his co-directors bought heavily. In 1988, along came a bid from a company which subsequently renamed itself Lowndes Queensway. This bid gave Harris and his fellow directors a handsome profit. So while Lowndes Queensway went bankrupt in 1990, Harris survived to launch a second carpet company, Carpetright.

Another interesting example was the sale in May 1994 of a large line of shares in the Telegraph by Hollinger, a company controlled by the Telegraph's Canadian-born chairman Conrad Black. The following month the *The Daily Telegraph* newspaper cut its price in retaliation against price cutting by other newspapers, notably *The Times*. The price of Telegraph shares plunged. (See Fig 3.2 on page 66.) The Stock Exchange cleared the sale because it found no evidence that a price cut was contemplated at the time of the share sale.

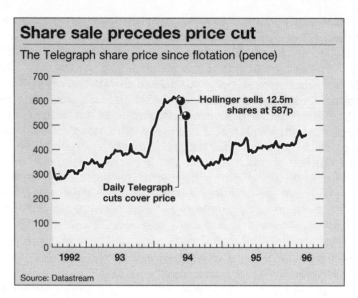

Share sale precedes price cut

The Telegraph share price since flotation (pence)

Hollinger sells 12.5m shares at 587p

Daily Telegraph cuts cover price

Source: Datastream

Fig 3.2 The Stock Exchange investigated Hollinger's sale, and found no evidence that the price cut was contemplated at the time of the sale. But Cazenove resigned as broker to the Telegraph.

Most investors use directors' dealings in relation to particular shares. But *The Inside Track* also calculates a buy/sell ratio for aggregate directors' dealings (See Fig 3.3 opposite.) This shows a rough correlation with the stock-market. As a general rule, when purchases outweigh sales by more than 2.5:1 it is a 'buy' signal for the market. When the ratio dips below one it is a sell signal. The ratio's record is rather better on the buy side than the sell side. Again, this is reasonable enough. A company's directors will have a very clear idea when their business is being valued at well below its real worth.

Beware the mug money

Private investors have always had a reputation for inept investment timing. Like most generalisations, this one is undoubtedly unfair to many individual investors. But it has been broadly true that private investors have shown an increased interest in the stockmarket only after a bull market has become mature, and their interest often peaks at roughly the same time as the market.

It is easy to see why this is so. The number of serious private investors who have an ongoing interest in the stockmarket is relatively fixed. Many keep their portfolios through thick and thin. But when the market is buoyant, the long term individual investors are joined by a crowd of fair-weather fellow travellers. They are the people who buy because they have read in their newspapers and seen on the television that the market has gone up. But stockmarket rises only become the stuff of newspaper headlines when big rises and new records have already occurred. So mass public interest in the stockmarket is by definition too late to get in near the bottom of a stockmarket rise.

The belief that the public gets aboard right at the end of a bull market is actually part of the original Dow theory. This (see Chapter 2) argued that the first wave of a bull market takes place against general scepticism, the second is when professionals and habitual speculators jump aboard, the third is when everybody has turned bullish, particularly

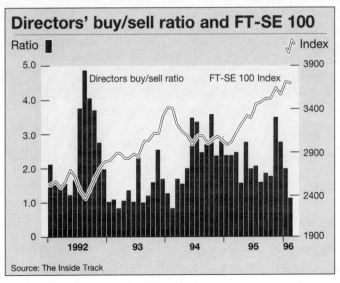

Fig 3.3 The rule of thumb is that when directors' purchases outnumber sales by more than 2.5:1, it is a 'buy' signal for the market. It worked in 1992 and 1994.

laymen. The third wave occurs shortly before the bear market sets in.

There are plenty of signs to look out for to gauge whether the public at large is buying shares:–

● **Unit trust sales.** These are the traditional way of measuring public involvement in the market: sales peak with the bull market, and the bottom of the bear market is often marked by net sales of units. The Association of Unit Trusts and Investment Funds publishes a variety of different figures. The ones to note are net new retail sales, which are published each month in the *Financial Times*. But nowadays they are slightly tricky to interpret. The introduction of personal equity plans (PEPs) means that unit trust PEPs tend to be marketed and bought most heavily in the final quarter of the tax year, that is in the first quarter of the calendar year. An investor trying to work out what the underlying trend in retail sales is needs to allow for this seasonal bias. (See Fig 3.4 opposite.)

One investment trust analyst uses net sales of specialist unit trusts and investment trust savings schemes to gauge the underlying demand for that type of trust. If, say, net sales of Japanese unit trusts are rising sharply, he argues that the discount on the shares of investment trusts specialising in Japan is likely to narrow.

● **Advertisements for tipsheets.** Sales of tipsheets tend to be very highly geared to stockmarket swings. Existing tipsheets enjoy large increases in sales, and new ones are often launched when a bull market is mature. Since sales are by subscription only, customers normally join up in response to advertisements in newspapers or mailshots. The marketing departments of tipsheets are skilled at knowing when the stockmarket background is encouraging enough to pull in new punters, and spend relatively freely at those times.

The *Investors Chronicle* itself used to reckon that it put on 10,000 sales in a bull market and lost them in a bear market. A sure sign that the market was close to topping out was when villains started trying to steal the magazine in order to buy its tips before publication. Such attempted theft and skullduggery was rife in the autumn of 1987.

● **Penny share frenzy.** This is an extension of the previous point. When the stockmarket is in the final frothy stages of a bull market, tipsheets and their clients often force the price of penny shares (those quoted at just a few pence each) to ludicrous levels. Most penny shares belong to companies which have fallen on hard times. Some are shells, companies with virtually no trading activity left but a clean balance sheet, and potentially attractive to entrepreneurs wanting to buy a company with a stockmarket quotation rather than go through the hassle of a new issue. But many are the ghosts of companies which have failed to deal with their problems.

Since there are often not many shares in issue, a recommendation from a tipsheet, followed by a wave of buying from its customers, can have a dramatic effect on the price. This is sometimes self-reinforcing: a particular share will be recommended because it has gone up in response to an earlier recommendation. In late 1987 a spot check showed that on one day there were as many dealings in one penny share, called Rotaprint, as in some of the Footsie companies. Many erstwhile penny shares were by then trading at well

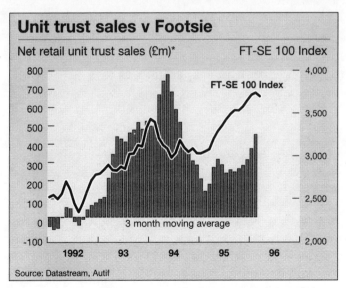

Unit trust sales v Footsie

Net retail unit trust sales (£m)*   FT-SE 100 Index

3 month moving average

Source: Datastream, Autif

Fig 3.4 The cliché is that unit trust sales boom when the market is at its peak and collapse when it is poised to recover. Note the way unit sales continued to climb after the market peaked in early 1994.

over 60p: often they had trebled in a few months for no fundamental reason. Then came the collapse. Rotaprint subsequently went bust.

● **New issue frenzy.** New issues are on average bad buys. This has been clearly demonstrated in both the American and the British stockmarkets, and the new unit and investment trust markets in Britain. The public at large has, however, always liked and bought new issues.* New issues are normally most frequent when the stockmarket is mature, though not necessarily at its peak.

Issues are a tricky signal to interpret. A general increase in the number of new issues at fancy prices can be merely a sign that companies and their promoters are cashing in on public gullibility, not that the market as a whole is overblown. A spate of issues in a particular sector tells you that sector is in favour; it does not tell you whether this local boom has yet reached the bubble stage. (See Chapter 4.)

But a bevy of new launches of unit and investment trusts can still often provide a useful pointer to incipient peaks in particular sectors or markets. The enthusiasm for emerging market trusts in 1993 and early 1994 was a classic third Dow wave.

Dealings by unknown speculators

The final source of information, dealings by traders not known to the private investor, can be highly dangerous. For professional investors may well know precisely who is behind a large deal, and be able to evaluate its significance. Trading on the basis of inferior knowledge is a recipe for losing money. But used sensibly day to day changes in prices and dealing activity can provide a poor man's chart service.

* It is not yet clear whether the Stock Exchange's decision that private investors should no longer have an automatic right to participate in issues over a certain size will induce more sobriety in the new issue market. (It could just mean that issues open to the public get swamped, and that the chances of private investors finding good value among new issues fall even further.)

The second section of the *Financial Times* (FT) during the week contains several useful bits of tabular information. The list of new 52 week highs and lows on the back page provides fodder for chartists trying to measure the breadth of a market movement. Some use a ratio of the two, some chart the actual numbers. But investors can also get inspiration from the actual companies involved. Any company notching up new lows in a rising market or new highs in a falling one is obviously showing relative weakness or strength. What the table does is prompt the investor to ask why; it does not provide the answer.

The analysis of trading volume of major stocks, also on the back page of the FT, is another source of questions. It is an up-to-date one day version of the volume figures used by many chartists, and makes most sense to the regular reader who has a good feel for the normal level of dealing in the shares.

What the investor is looking for is abnormally high volume. There are a few obvious traps. Corporate activity and the release of corporate information always generates a high level of activity. For example, if the volume of trading in the shares of one of the clearing banks increases tenfold on the day its results come out, that is nothing to get excited about. As we explain in the chapter on stockbrokers' analysts, the release of new information provides one of the best opportunities in the year for brokers both to reassess a company's merits and to generate some dealing commission. But if there is a sharp rise in volume for no obvious reason, it may be worth investigating. Often the reason will be apparent from comment elsewhere in the FT. For example, trading volume in Hanson was consistently heavy after it announced its demerger plans, and the FT market report explained that a broker was recommending its clients to reduce their holdings.

A supplementary check to the volume in the shares themselves can sometimes be the volume in the associated options. This is not published in the FT but in the Hanson example a brief comment on the futures and traded options market did point out that option trading in Hanson had been very heavy. Only a limited number of the most active shares have traded options, but the FT also notes a handful of the deals in traditional options. The most any private investor can sensibly do is observe this kind of activity and brood on it. But if you already hold a share and notice unusual activity, such intermittent brooding is all part of managing your portfolio.

Directors' Dealings

IN A NUTSHELL

1. Insider dealing is a criminal offence in the UK. Its essence is that someone who possesses unpublished price sensitive information by virtue of his job wittingly deals or encourages someone else to deal in securities likely to be significantly affected by this information if it were made public.

2. Directors' dealings are the acceptable face of insider dealing: purchases and sales of shares of the company of which the shareholder is a director in circumstances which are OK with both the Department of Trade and the Stock Exchange.

3. Such deals have to be reported to the Stock Exchange within five days, and information about these dealings is widely available, either through specialist services, or in newspapers.

4. Some directors' purchases and sales provide useful pointers to the shares' future performance. But investors need to be extremely selective in following these pointers. There are some rules of thumb on how to tell which deals are significant.

5. Private investors' sales and purchases of shares are reputed to mark the bottom and top of the market respectively. Unit trust sales, tipsheet advertisements, penny share frenzy and new issue mania are all worth watching.

6. Overall rises in the volume of dealings in particular shares can be significant. But it is very hard for the private investor to interpret these signals correctly.

Chapter 4
Investment Psychology

Private investors are notorious for buying at the top and selling at the bottom of the market. Charles Dow said that they were the force behind the third wave of a bull market: the one that marked the final blow-off before the bear market set in. This may be true. But it doesn't have to be that way. Private investors are in a privileged position in the stock-market. Unlike professionals they usually have no need to buy or sell unless they choose to. And at least in theory they ought to find it easier to cast a sceptical eye on the follies of the market.

The market is irrational. It exaggerates both on the way up and on the way down, as investors swing between greed and fear. A series of past manias and panics display very similar behaviour patterns. Yet the majority of investors seem destined to go on repeating history. Successful investors emphasise the importance of taking an independent line. But group pressures make this very hard to do. This chapter explains why.

Group psychology

There are two different points for the investor to consider. First how does the market behave? Second, how should he himself behave in relation to the market and individual shares? Psychology has some pointers on both issues. For it is concerned both with individuals and with groups.

Interest in crowd psychology goes back to Gustave Le Bon: 'Crowds are somewhat like the Sphinx of ancient fable: it is necessary to arrive at a solution of the problems offered by their psychology or resign ourselves to being devoured by them.'* He argued that when an individual enters a

* See *The Crowd* by Gustave Le Bon.

Fig 4.1 Mary Evans picture library.

crowd, he 'descends several rungs in the order of civilisa-
tion'. Still worse, crowds act like a woman.

Modern psychologists say broadly similar things, though
they package the message more tactfully. Groups of people
demonstrably behave differently from individuals in isolation. And although the behaviour of any particular group
will depend on a host of different factors, such as its
function, size, and who is in it, typical group processes and
group behaviour have been identified. For example:–

● **Group processes.** Some of the behaviour in any group
relates to the way members cope with the strains of
proximity. Such behaviour is relevant to the group as a
group, not to its members' overt objectives.*

A British psychiatrist called Bion identified a number of
underlying emotional patterns in all group life. Members
squabble or find excuses not to do their job. They form
factions. They look for an outside saviour.

Individuals are generally agreed to have subconscious
motives and hidden agendas. What Bion and his successors
argue is that groups do too, even though individual members are often unaware of them. To take an obvious example,
the apparent objective of a group discussion may be choosing a date for its next meeting; but the real issue may be a
covert power struggle between rival factions.

Group emotions have been found to affect their members'
actions in several common ways.

● **Group decision-making.** Many people perfectly capable
of making correct judgements on their own will agree with
an incorrect judgement presented in a group context. When
most groups make decisions they tend to polarise towards
the average of earlier individual decisions. If the shift is the
result of an open discussion, members are influenced by
novel and cogent arguments. But if a particular decision-
making group is both highly cohesive and very cut off from
the rest of the world, it has the capacity to make spectacularly bad decisions. One of the symptoms of this kind of
'groupthink' is an illusion of invulnerability.

The stockmarket has always had a clubby atmosphere:

* See *Group Processes* by Joseph Luft.

Fig 4.2 Mary Evans picture library.

very large amounts of money are handled by a small number of 'experts'. Any boom tends to produce rationalisations about why this one really will reach the sky.

● **Size and leadership.** Morale tends to be lower in large groups. The larger the group the more attention members pay to leaders. But new leaders need to win acceptance from the group before they can acquire followers. For established groups have their own behaviour patterns and rules. So when joining an existing group, even a potential leader has to learn and abide by the existing rules for a bit. But once he has acquired enough authority he can start changing the rules.

Think how much attention the stockmarket pays to the actions of successful investors. When George Soros expresses an interest in gold or property, his interest alone can create a mini-boom.

But the stockmarket can also be slow to accept change. When derivatives were first introduced to London, the 'not invented here' response meant they were slow to catch on. But once it became clear that the foreign-owned banks who used them had a technical advantage, investors without a clue what derivatives were happily employed them.*

● **The effect of anxiety.** Anxious individuals waiting for a threat to materialise choose to associate with others in the same position – in order to check whether their own responses are appropriate. People appear to form ad hoc groups as a way of coping with their own level of anxiety.

Think of any historic market crash or bank collapse and what do you remember? Pictures of people thronging the streets waiting for the bad news.

● **Rumour and humour.** Rumours are particularly prone to develop in groups when there is a strong need to know what is going on, but information and communication are

---

* In the early 1990s one highly respected UK fund management group launched a derivative-based unit trust which soon turned sour. Asked afterwards why the management had felt happy to introduce such a complex product, one director explained that none of the individual directors had fully understood the derivative mechanism behind the trust, but between them they reckoned they had grasped all the essential aspects.

limited. For example, they are particularly prolific in wartime. Silent members of a group tend to stimulate rumours. So do particular members or subgroups that exert a strong influence on the group. Group humour tends to focus on themes or processes which are particularly important to the group. It provides relief for anxiety and can also sometimes aid decision-making.

Every day the *Financial Times*' stockmarket page reports dozens of rumours. Any well-known predator is invariably linked with new bid rumours, and the words 'no comment', so beloved of the Hanson camp, serve merely to inflame the rumour-mongers. Base rate cuts, American investors buying or selling, financial collapses: they are the equivalent of the Russian troops 'with snow on their boots' spotted near Aberdeen in 1914. Jokes often cluster round the same topics.

● **Interaction and awareness.** The way particular individuals behave in groups or one-to-one encounters is unsurprisingly influenced by their individual psychological make-up. One of the more practical models of interaction is known as the Johari window. (See Fig 4.3 page 80.)*

It is based on the idea that different aspects of the same individual are perceived by different people. An individual's relations with others are divided into four 'quadrants'. The 'open quadrant' includes those of his feelings, behaviour and motivation which are known both to the individual and to other people. The 'blind quadrant' refers to those perceived by others of which the individual is unaware. The 'hidden quadrant' refers to those known to the individual but hidden from others. And the 'unknown quadrant' refers to feelings, behaviour and motivation known neither to the individual nor to others. The name of the game is trying to find out more about one's own blind and hidden areas, which have strong links.

Private investors often have emotional and irrational reactions both to the whole stockmarket and to individual shares. You think you are a rational investor? So why did you sell that dud share the moment it got back to your buying price? Investment writer John Train once compared

* Named after Californian psychologists Joseph Luft and Harrington Ingham. See *Group Processes*.

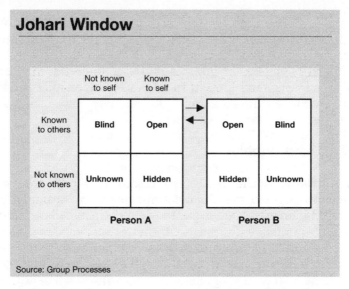

Fig 4.3 Top speculator George Soros argues that self-awareness and awareness of others is vital to investment success. The Johari window points out the limitations of awareness of both.

the situation with that of a woman whose faithless lover is trying to insinuate himself back in her affections. 'Take that you cur,' she says, as she bashes him with her handbag. It is perfectly possible that the share which has let you down is only at the start of a major recovery. Don't let your desire to get equal with it prevent you from benefiting.

Chartists are great practitioners of group psychology. They note the clashes of rival tribes at resistance and support levels. They happily admit that prices can at times reflect solely the emotions of people in the marketplace. And one of the fathers of British chartism used to talk about every share having its own 'crowd', like a football club.

Some investors will dismiss all this as psychobabble. Others may find it both amusing and useful to look at the stockmarket as an example of group dynamics at work. For every investor has to decide how to deal with the market. Does he join the existing group – the herd? Does he make specific alliances or join a sub-group? Or does he remain a loner?

Learning to understand yourself, and in particular your

attitude to investment, should help you decide on the most suitable strategy for you. It should also help you to be more realistic in making your investment decisions. Top speculator George Soros says that his superior understanding of both the market and himself in relation to the market is the main reason for his success.

Booms and bubbles

Long before psychologists had begun to study groups, historians decided that financial markets were particularly susceptible to manias and panics. One of the most pleasing stories tells of the tulipomania which infected the sober Dutch in the seventeenth century. At one point a single rare tulip bulb was worth 12 acres of prime building land, or more than a new carriage and pair – the Rolls-Royce of the time. Of course the speculative fever ended in tears. But that didn't prevent new manias.

In the early eighteenth century the French succumbed to enthusiasm for the Mississippi development scheme at virtually the same time that the British chased the South Sea bubble. In both cases company promoters got government backing for schemes which effectively privatised the national debt. The promoters were given important overseas trade and development concessions. Their companies then offered the public the chance to exchange their existing claims on the government for shares in the exciting new companies, or simply to buy shares for cash. In London bubble mania was so rife that one promoter pulled in a lot of money for 'A company for carrying on an undertaking of great advantage, but nobody to know what it is'. Unfortunately neither the Mississippi development scheme nor the South Sea bubble had any commercial reality. Both eventually collapsed, ruining thousands of people.*

What is significant about these examples is that investors' enthusiasm for the shares appeared rapidly to lose touch with the reality of the company or concept they were

---

* See *Extraordinary Popular Delusions and the Madness of Crowds* by Charles Mackay.

buying. In these cases the reality was sadly deficient. But similarly irrational enthusiasm can equally well occur when the concept is valid.

The emerging markets boom of 1993 and the mania for Internet shares in 1995–96 were both based on new concepts which were grounded in reality. South East Asia is growing very rapidly. The Internet does create a new dimension in communications. But the prices put on these new concepts still seems arbitrary. It was determined by the extent of investor enthusiasm, not by any rational attempt to assess the value of the markets. One reason new issues as a class are so dangerous is that they are so often bought for emotional reasons.

Modern historian Charles Kindleberger argues that there is a consistent pattern to financial manias and panics.* He cites Hyman Minsky's theory that the events leading up to a crisis always start with a shake-up to the system. This creates new opportunities for profit in some areas, and closes down some existing ones. Businessmen and investors scramble to get a stake in the sunrise industries, and a boom develops. Prices rise, positive feedback develops, and euphoria leads to overtrading. Speculation breeds emulation. And soon the bubble is ripe for bursting.

Kindleberger suggests that the relationships between rational individuals and the irrational whole are more complex than commonly believed. Different processes include:–

- People change at different stages of a continuous process. They start rationally and, gradually at first, then more quickly, they lose contact with reality.
- Rationality differs among different groups of traders, investors and speculators. And groups formed in the early stages differ from those formed in later stages.
- All succumb to the fallacy of composition. Each individual buying decision can be rationalised, but the boom as a whole cannot. For individual rationalisations fail to take account of the fact that others are behaving in the same way.

* See *Manias, Panic, and Crashes* by Charles P. Kindleberger.

- The market may have the right reaction to a particular development, but it may still wildly overdo the size of that reaction.
- The market may get its basic reaction wrong. Either it starts off in the wrong direction, or it ignores crucial bits of information, or it even suppresses information that does not fit its chosen model of what's happening.

Kindleberger instances a wide variety of different objects of speculation: banks, foreign bonds, foreign mines, land, railways, foreign exchange, commodities, new issues. Similar psychological characteristics can be detected time and again.

The 1929 Crash on Wall Street and the 1987 Crash both on Wall Street and in London are instances of speculative manias affecting the whole market. But local manias are a regular feature of most stockmarkets. Sometimes conglomerates are in vogue, sometimes property companies or banks, sometimes concept retailers. Or technology stocks, nickel mining companies, European privatisation stocks, penny shares. The opportunities are endless. Sometimes local booms and busts lead the whole market up, or down. Sometimes they remain parochial.

Trading against the market

Private investors aiming to beat the market at its own game have the odds stacked against them. Keynes argued that most professional investors and speculators are simply trying to keep one step ahead of their rivals. 'They are concerned with how the market will value an investment under the influence of mass psychology, three months or a year hence.' As mentioned earlier, he compared it with a beauty contest in which each judge chose the contestant he thought likely to be judged most beautiful by the others. Amateurs are unlikely to know the market's taste in beauty queens as well as do those who work there.

Here are two models of what makes a successful market trader.

● **George Soros.** This successful speculator (see also Chapter 9) argues that one precondition of success is to have a better understanding of what is going on in a market than do the other participants. But this means different things in different markets.

Some booms are essentially stockmarket phenomena. Thus, the idea behind the 1960s conglomerates boom was to acquire other companies with inflated paper; the idea behind the property trust boom of the 1970s was equity leveraging (gearing). To understand these boom/bust cycles all the investor needs to know is Soros's theory of reflexivity. This is essentially a psychological analysis of the interaction of fundamentals, stock prices and investor perceptions.

But to understand a boom/bust cycle in a sector such as technology stocks, the investor also needs to know something about the underlying trends in technology. Soros argues that two different types of investment analysis swing in and out of fashion in technology booms. The boom in technology stocks gets off the ground on the basis of fundamental analysis, but when it reaches the bubble stage only psychological analysis provides real insight into what is going on. By the time the technology market is near the bottom of the downswing, analysts are starting to become too sensitive to the importance of investor perceptions. And it is time for the fundamentalists to sound the charge for recovery.

Soros's analysis bears a strong resemblance to Kindleberger's. Some booms have their roots in fundamentals, but the extent of the boom is not related to the strength of the fundamentals: they have a bubble dimension. Other booms are mainly bubbles, particularly those created by financial engineering.

Soros also sounds as if he would feel eminently comfortable with the idea of Johari windows. You could well rephrase his own description of his investment 'edge' thus: Soros has above average awareness of other investors' blind quadrants, while his own blind and unknown quadrants are unusually small. Soros admits that one of his (rare?) character flaws is the urge to reveal himself. But as yet few of his imitators appear to have got the alchemist's formula quite right.

● **The psychologist's supertrader.*** One American psychologist does believe that successful trading can be taught. Dr Van K. Tharp aims to improve his clients' performance by teaching them the winning traits of top traders. He is also trying to turn his most successful clients into supertraders. He compares himself to a sports coach.

Clients go through an eleven point test. He checks five psychological factors: a well-rounded personal life, a positive attitude, the motivation to make money, lack of conflict and responsibility for results. Then there are three decision-making factors: a solid knowledge of technical factors, the ability to make unbiased decisions, and the capacity for independent thought. Finally come the management-discipline factors: risk control, the ability to be patient and intuition.

His identikit picture of a losing trader is someone who is highly stressed, has a negative outlook, lots of personality conflicts, and blames others when things go wrong. The luckless man also lacks a proper framework of working rules, and is disorganised and impatient. For example, one of the prime rules for successful speculation is to cut your losses short and run your profits. Most people do the opposite. Most people are also bad at dealing with stress; they bring their personal conflicts to the trading floor; and they allow their emotions to control their trading.

Tharp argues that to become a successful trader you have to duplicate the beliefs, mental states and mental strategies of top traders. His sample of top traders shared these beliefs:

● Money is not important.
● It is OK to lose in the markets.
● Trading is a game.
● Mental rehearsal is important for success.
● They've won the game before they start.

His successful sample had all begun by studying the markets extensively. They had highly developed models of

* See *Market Wizards* by Jack Schwager.

how to trade. And they rehearsed what they planned so often, that they went into the fray believing that they were going to win. This self confidence was not shaken by minor setbacks. Long term they knew they were winners.

It's a tall order.

Alliances and dependencies

Many private investors create new alliances and dependencies, without having heard of Bion's labels for these group phenomena. And perfectly sensible too, provided they go about it the right way. Private investors often feel like second class members in the large and amorphous group of UK stockmarket investors. They want to exchange ideas with someone who is on their side. But alliances often work better than dependencies.

● **Stockbrokers.** Some private investors depend heavily on their stockbroker for advice. In some cases their trust is totally justified. They have a treasure: someone who is on their wavelength, can give and receive ideas, and has enough time and interest to keep the investors' portfolios constantly in mind. But such treasures are rare.

Most advisory brokers make their money from their more active clients. It would take superhuman qualities for a broker to continue to phone up a client who regularly spent half an hour discussing an idea, but then decided to do nothing. But most successful investors agree that inactivity often pays.

Jim Rogers, Soros's erstwhile partner, once commented: 'One of the best rules anyone can learn about investing is to do nothing, absolutely nothing, unless there is something to do . . . I don't think of myself as a trader . . . I wait for a situation that is like the proverbial shooting fish in a barrel . . . I may make three decisions a year, or five decisions a year, and I'll stay with them.'

But you do not make your broker rich by waiting until you see the fish swimming round in the barrel. So although he may well remain friendly and efficient, he is hardly likely to save all his best ideas for you, is he?

● **Tips.** Novices sometimes rely blindly on newspapers

and tipsheets for advice. In the 1987 boom some people bought shares on the basis of five line recommendations at the front of the *Investors Chronicle*, without bothering to look at the discussion on which that recommendation was based. That kind of 'investment' makes backing red look rational.

● **Investment clubs.** An alternative, long popular in the US and beginning to catch on in the UK, is forming an investment club.* One called the Beardstown Ladies Investment Club gained cult status in the mid-1990s when a bunch of small-town Mid-Western amateurs managed to beat the market.† They did their research, invested in companies they liked, and ran their portfolio on common-sense lines.

But what was arguably just as important as their investment strategy was that their club seems to have worked as a social entity. Members shared the research work. No member claimed guru status. Decision-making could be based on open discussion with new and cogent arguments given suitable weight. No groupthink for them as they swapped recipes amid the share tips. Establishing a strong group culture of their own made it easier for them not to get swept away by the emotion of the stockmarket crowd.

For the record, the ten points the ladies looked at when choosing a stock were: industry ranking, timeliness (a predictive rating from US investment service Value Line), safety, debt, beta, sales and earnings, absolute price, PE ratio, upside-down ratio (relative odds of potential gain versus risk of a loss), and management.

Each new investment was recommended by a stock selection committee of three members, who served until a transaction was executed. The committee started by looking for industries which would add diversity to the portfolio and then scouted around for appealing companies using

* ProShare, the sponsored private investor lobby group, sells a manual on starting up an investment club. Tel: (0171) 600–0984.
† Beardstown is a small town in Illinois where 'it's not only safe to leave your car unlocked, but you can leave the keys in the ignition'. The *Beardstown Ladies Common-sense Investment Guide* records the 23.4 per cent annual return the club made in its prime.

relative comparisons to help fine down their choice. The committee presented its recommendations to the whole club, which had a thorough discussion before voting. Often recommendations were accepted unanimously; if not, a majority vote prevailed.

The number chosen for the research committee is well suited to achieving a result. 'Two-person and three-person groups have unique characteristics with reference to closeness of feeling and power as interaction factors,' says one group psychologist.* The worry might be that such a closely-knit unit could go off the rails. But at Beardstown it had to report to the whole club. Another textbook option is having a group of five discussing the whole question from beginning to end. But this might be a touch small for a fully fledged investment group.

Less formal associations may well suit some investors better. What matters is having someone you respect to bounce ideas off.

Staying aloof

Many of the greatest investors both stay aloof from the market and operate as one man bands. (See page 6 for Benjamin Graham's advice on how to deal with 'Mr Market'.) Some even stay physically aloof. Sir John Templeton, for example, who built up the Templeton fund management organisation, ran it from Nassau. Warren Buffett notoriously seldom moves far from Omaha, Nebraska.

But what matters is mental aloofness and toughness: 'To buy when others are despondently selling and to sell when others are greedily buying requires the greatest fortitude and pays the greatest reward,' argued Sir John.

Keynes said his 'central principle of investment is to go contrary to the general opinion, on the grounds that if everyone agreed about its merits, the investment is inevitably too dear and therefore unattractive.' And he talked about how tough it was to be an equity investor.

* Joseph Luft again.

'Adam Smith', as so often summed it up pithily. The one absolute requirement of a money manager is emotional maturity: 'If you don't know who you are, this [the stockmarket] is an expensive place to find out.'*

Putting it all together

Investment psychology is a much fuzzier subject than company accounts. The basic message from this chapter is reminiscent of Kipling's *If*. Be suspicious of others' folly, and keep your own head.

- Do not expect the market to behave rationally. It is likely to over-react both at the top and at the bottom. Beware of being sucked into the crowd's emotion.
- If you aim to outwit the crowd you need to stay clear-witted and flexible. And remember that, although market booms may be psychologically similar, some have their roots in reality, some are financial phenomena. They need to be analysed differently.
- When people are anxious they have a natural tendency to join the herd. But does it make sense in difficult times to join a group likely to make more irrational decisions than you would yourself?
- Investors are always short of information. So they are particularly prone to rumour-mongering. But that does not make the rumours any more likely to be true.
- Most successful traders study their market closely and have a game plan in mind before they start.
- Because investors are not perfect, they often do the opposite of what they should. For example, they run their losses and cut their profits. Stick to your strategy.
- Charts can be a good way of checking the psychological state of the market.
- If you need support in making your decisions, you may be better off in a formal or informal investment club rather than relying on experts or tips.
- Most investors trade too frequently. Save your fire power

* See *The Money Game* by 'Adam Smith'.

for dead certs. Successful investors concentrate on getting a few things right.

Investment Psychology

IN A NUTSHELL

1. Private investors have the reputation of always selling at the bottom and buying at the top.

2. Psychologists believe that groups have their own emotional patterns which influence members' behaviour. For example, people will agree to incorrect decisions. Isolated groups are prone to groupthink which can produce spectacularly bad decisions.

3. Financial markets are particularly prone to manias and panics. They all show broadly similar behaviour patterns, although several different types of irrational behaviour can be identified.

4. Beating the market at its own game is extremely hard for the amateur investor. George Soros argued that it required the investor to understand both the market and himself better than anyone else.

5. Many private investors form defensive alliances, such as investment clubs, in an effort to fight back against the pressures of the stockmarket herd. The right small group can help rational decision-making.

6. Most really successful investors are lonely contrarians.

Section Two:
Investment Tools

Chapter 5
How to Use Company Accounts

Investors use company accounts to put hard numbers on information the management reveals, and to find out facts the management conceals. They have several different objectives when reading them. They are assessing the company's recent trading record; checking its financial fitness; estimating its future earnings potential; and working out whether the current share price is a fair reflection of that earnings potential.

Earnings estimates and investment recommendations are based on several different factors. If a company is healthy, investment analysts often pay more attention to the business outlook than to the accounting ratios when weighing up its prospects. Accounting checks come into their own when investors are worried about the company's financial fitness. But a clean bill of health is like a vet's certificate: it states that the horse is fit to run; it does not predict that it will win.

A quoted company's annual report and accounts normally gives more information about it than any other document it publishes, after its initial prospectus.* The accounts contain three major financial statements. The profit and loss account summarises the result of the year's trading. The balance sheet is a snapshot of everything the company owes and owns at the end of its financial year. And the cash flow statement records how much hard cash was paid in and out during the year.

Professional investors use accounts to work out a number of business ratios. Operating ratios, such as profit margins,

* The correct term for what most people refer to as a 'quoted' company is a 'listed' company ie one which has gone through the scrutiny required to obtain a listing on the London Stock Exchange. The prospectus is based on the 'listing particulars'. The 20-F document published by UK companies which get a listing in the US is even more informative.

return on capital employed and stockturn, help them assess the company's recent performance and compare it with its peers. Financial ratios, notably gearing and liquidity ratios, help them test the company's health and strength. All these are calculated from the annual accounts, supplemented by the interim statement half way through the financial year. And many investment yardsticks, such as the price earnings ratio, the price cash flow ratio, dividend cover and asset value are also based on figures in the accounts.

Unfortunately company accounts can be used to conceal as well as reveal. Investors who never look at accounts often have a touching belief in their objectivity. Accountants and professional analysts know that most accounts are full of gaps, guess-work and grey areas. Accounting techniques are far less cut and dried than laymen expect. They leave company managements considerable discretion on how to treat a wide range of items. And the treatment chosen can make a big difference to some of the key figures in the accounts.

Accountants and analysts insist that it is not possible to distil the performance of a complex organisation, such as a company, into a single measure, such as earnings per share. But company managers know that many investors favour companies which produce steady earnings growth year after year. So, if the managers see that profits and earnings are heading for even a short term dip, they sometimes prop them up. No great harm in that perhaps, though it can be dangerous if investors are misled about the true volatility of profits. But if profitability has taken a serious turn for the worse, prolonged cover-ups can aggravate the problem. The next chapter (6) explains how to spot some of the more common types of camouflage.

What accounts contain

Most published accounts contain a mixture of hard and soft information.* The hard information is a series of detailed

---

* The term accounts is nowadays used as shorthand for 'Annual report and accounts'.

financial statements and reports from the directors and auditors; the soft information, usually based around the chairman's statement, consists mainly of text seasoned with pictures, graphs and statistics.

The hard information is the **directors' report**, the **profit and loss account**, the **balance sheet**, the **cash flow statement** and the **auditors' report**. These four key elements are supplemented by a **statement of total recognised gains and losses**, which highlights important items which would otherwise be tucked into a footnote, a note explaining how **shareholders' funds** have moved over the year, notes giving additional details about items appearing in the primary statements, a **statement of accounting policies**, and nowadays a report from the **remuneration committee**.

● **The directors' report** tells you what the company does, who its directors are and what their stake in the company is, whether there have been any significant business or financial developments during the financial year or subsequently, and provides a brief review of the year's trading. But many directors nowadays keep their report terse and refer investors to other parts of the accounts, such as the **chairman's statement**, the **operating and financial review** (OFR) (if there is one) or the notes for further information. Some accounts buffs recommend the OFR as the best place for a non-professional to start.

● **The profit and loss account** (p&l) summarises the result of the latest year's trading in figures. It tells you what the company sold, what its costs were, how much profit it made, what the tax charge was, what was left for shareholders, and how much of this is being paid out to them and how much ploughed back into the company. It also shows you the comparable figures for the previous year, so that you can see whether the company is growing and whether it is more profitable – not necessarily the same thing.

● **The balance sheet** is a snapshot of everything the company owes and owns at the end of that particular financial year.* It tells you what its assets are and how it

* Well, up to a point anyway. Some assets, such as brand names are normally omitted, others can be costs which have been shunted out of the p&l. And as we explain in the next chapter, most assets are not included at their true worth.

finances those assets. Again, the accounts provide comparative figures for the previous year, so that you can monitor
changes. The p&l tells you about the latest performance, but
the balance sheet reveals the company's fundamental financial health. If the company is having problems, the balance
sheet will tell you whether it should be able to stand the
strain.*

Investors can use the p&l and balance sheet in combination to check whether the company is earning a reasonable
return both on their money and on the total capital
employed (including borrowed money). They can also
check whether the book value of the assets backing their
shares is rising or falling.

● **The cash flow statement** is the most pragmatic of the lot.
It first compares the amount of cash coming into the
company – from trading profits, investment, more efficient
debt collection and so on – with the amount flowing out – in
trading losses, tax, dividends and so on. Then it adds or
subtracts the cash produced by capital raising or spent on
capital repayment.

Like individuals, companies need to be able to pay their
bills when they fall due. Companies which steadily haemorrhage cash end up having to sell the family silver for a
knock-down price. If a company starts making losses, it may
well recover; a company which runs out of cash seldom gets
a second chance.† The cash flow statement tells you what
happened last year and warns of trouble on the way.

● **The auditors' report** tells you whether the directors
have obeyed the rules in drawing up their accounts to
shareholders. The auditors do not themselves calculate the
figures in the accounts; they check whether they provide a
'true and fair view' of the state of affairs and whether they
meet the legal and professional accounting requirements.

Publication of all this information is a legal requirement

---

* Fans of cash flow argue that it provides a more reliable health
check. The assiduous investor will use both.
† The attitude of its bankers is of course crucial, as Eurotunnel
demonstrates.

upon companies, and the form in which it is published is closely controlled by the Companies Act and a series of mandatory accounting standards, put out by the **Accounting Standards Board** (ASB) and policed by the **Financial Reporting Review Panel**. Companies quoted on the London Stock Exchange have to include additional information on matters such as significant share stakes, potential conflicts of interest and the reasons for shortfalls on published forecasts. They also have to say whether the accounts comply with the 'best practice' recommendations of the **Cadbury report** on corporate governance.

The auditors already have to report on whether their client has toed the Cadbury line on disclosure. They also have a Cadbury obligation of their own: to give a view on whether the company is likely to go bust – euphemistically described as whether accounts drawn up on a **going concern basis** are appropriate. But as yet this obligation is honoured mainly in the breach, for nobody has decided how to go about it. It is an understandably hot potato, since auditors are paid by the company they are reporting on. And the public expression of concern by an auditor could turn into a self-fulfilling prophesy.

The purpose of accounts is to enable users to make financial decisions. Many users, such as investment analysts, have long argued that the format of the various financial statements needed to be revised to make them more informative. Accounts developed with the stewardship function to the fore: telling existing shareholders how the managers had looked after the resources entrusted to them. But in today's active secondary markets, potential investors want to be able to weigh up the managers' ability, not just their honesty. And they are more interested in where the company is going to than where it is coming from.

The way UK companies present their accounts has changed substantially in the last few years, thanks to a steady stream of exposure drafts (FREDs) and financial reporting standards (FRSs) from the Accounting Standards Board. But there is more change to come, since the ASB is preparing to embrace international accounting standards in 1998.

How to calculate some common ratios

Good investment analysts always warn that number crunching alone will not help you pick good shares. What matters most is whether the underlying business concept is sound and the company well-managed. But calculating some basic ratios is a useful way of checking whether shareholders' money is being used efficiently. They can also reveal problems the management omits to mention. Below we explain how to calculate some of the main ratios mentioned in the chapter. We have used a simplified version of Marks and Spencer's 1994–95 accounts to provide some practical examples. The remainder of this chapter explains how to use the ratios to find out more about a company's health and strength.

Operating ratios provide a score-card for the company's latest year's trading. They can be used both to compare its performance with that in earlier years, and to rank it against its competitors. Most involve looking at the balance sheet as well as the profit and loss account.

• **Profit margin:** trading (or operating) profit as a percentage of sales (or turnover). Trading profit is calculated before taking account of interest charges or tax. So profit margins reflect the underlying profitability of the company's trading activities, not whether it is making money for its shareholders. Typical margins vary considerably from one type of business to another.

For M&S the sum is:

$$\frac{897 \times 100}{6,806} = 13.2\% \text{ Profit margin}$$

• **Return on capital employed:** trading (or operating) profit as a percentage of capital employed. This takes all the assets employed in the business – both those representing shareholders' funds and those financed with borrowed money – and measures the annual return the company made on them. If a company has a low return on capital, it is using its resources inefficiently, even if its profit margin is high. An attractive return on capital needs to be higher than the return on gilts (the yardstick for a risk-free investment return). And unless it is higher than the cost of borrowing, any increase in the company's borrowing or the general level of interest rates will reduce shareholders' earnings. A ROCE of 20 per cent or so is generally admitted to be good.

Marks and Spencer plc
Simplified profit and loss account
Year ended 31 March 1995

	1995 £m	1994 £m
Turnover	**6,806**	**6,541**
Cost of sales	(4,417)	(4,247)
Gross profit	2,389	2,294
Other expenses	1,493	(1,440)
Operating profit	**897**	**854**
Property loss	(6)	(17)
Net interest income	33*	14
Profit before tax	**924**	**851**
Tax	(300)	(272)
Profit after tax	**624**	**579**
Minorities	(1)	(1)
Dividends	(288)	(256)
Undistributed surplus	**335**	**322**

* Total interest received was £181m of which £119m is excluded because it related to the finance activities, leaving £62m relating to the trading activities credited to the p&l. The total interest paid was £66m, of which £37m is excluded because it related to the finance activities, leaving £29m relating to trading activities charged against the p&l. The £33m credit shown in the p&l is the difference between the £62m credit and the £29m debit.

Marks and Spencer plc
Simplified balance sheet
At 31 March 1995

	1995 £m	1994 £m
Fixed assets		
Tangible Assets	3,297	3,095
Investments	43	16
Total fixed assets	**3,340**	**3,111**
Current assets		
Stocks	377	355
Debtors		
Short term	578#	480
Over 1 year	482	404
Investments	193	264
Cash	736	551
Total current assets	**2,366**	**2,054**
Current liabilities		
Creditors (short term)	1,364*	1,181
Net current assets	**1,002**	**873**
Total assets		
(less current liabilities)	**4,342**	**3,984**
Creditors (over 1 year)	569	599
Provisions	38	40
Net assets	**3,735**	**3,343**
Capital and reserves		
Called up share capital	699	696
Share premium account	190	162
Revaluation reserve	455	457
Profit and loss account	2,370	2,009
Shareholders funds	**3,714**	**3,324**
Minority Interests	21	19
Total capital employed	**3,735**	**3,343**

* Current liabilities include £274m of short term borrowings, and £175m of trade creditors.
# Short term debtors of £578m include £33m of trade debtors.

Critics argue that to be meaningful the stated figure for capital employed should be adjusted upwards for any goodwill write-offs (see Chapter 6 page 141.)

In the M&S example the calculation involves first working out total capital employed. Many investors would happily use the £4,342m figure for Total assets less current liabilities given in the balance sheet. We have added in the short term debt of £274m shown in a footnote, although with M&S its addition does not make much difference. This gives a total capital employed of £4,616m. The sum now is:

$$\frac{897 \times 100}{4,616} = 19.4\% \text{ Return on capital employed}$$

● **Sales as a multiple of capital employed:** sales (or turnover) divided by capital employed. A supplementary yardstick. The appropriate level depends on profit margins. If margins are high a figure of 1 to 2 is acceptable, but not if margins are low. If the figure is unusually low, it suggests that the low ROCE stems from insufficient volume, not excessive costs. Remedy: either increase volume or reduce capital employed, preferably by galvanising or getting rid of divisions which do not earn their keep.

For M&S the sum is:

$$\frac{6,806}{4,616} = 1.5 \text{ Sales as a multiple of capital employed}$$

● **Stockturn:** there are two ways of expressing this. First, sales (or turnover) divided by year-end stocks. Second, stocks divided by sales and expressed as a percentage. Both show how fast the company shifts its goods. Money tied up in stock reduces the return on capital. If stockturn is presented as a percentage, the lower the figure, the leaner and more efficient the company. If it is a multiple, the higher the figure the leaner the company. Again a figure where the norm varies according to the business. It is particularly relevant for manufacturers and retailers. Typical percentage for a manufacturing company: 15 to 20 per cent; typical multiple 5 to 6.

An alternative yardstick is stocks in relation to the cost of sales or operating costs. Some analysts argue that this measurement is more realistic since stocks themselves are valued at cost rather than selling price.

For M&S the sum to calculate the stockturn multiple is:

$$\frac{6,806}{377} = 18$$

In other words the stock is turned over 18 times a year.

To get a stockturn ratio the sum is:

$$\frac{377 \times 100}{6,806} = 5.5\%$$

In other words year-end stocks are equivalent to just 5.5 per cent of annual turnover.

A third way of expressing stocks is as the number of days that goods stay in stock on average. Here the sum is:

$$\frac{377 \times 365}{6,806} = 20 \text{ days}$$

Whichever way you calculate it, stocks are obviously pretty low. One of the joys of being a large retailer is that stocks are usually someone else's problem.

● **Debt collection:** trade debtors as a percentage of sales (or trade debtors divided by sales multiplied by 365 to give a collection period in days). This shows how long it takes the company to get paid for what it sells. The longer the period of free credit given to customers, the lower the real profit margin on the sale. Not relevant for cash businesses, including most retailers. Typical target for a manufacturing business might be 50 to 70 days. An abnormally high or rising collection period suggests inefficiency, potential bad debts, window-dressing of the sales figures, or deliberate bullying by large customers trying to improve their own cash management.

Working out the sum for M&S requires a quick flip to the footnote to the short term debtors, which shows that trade debtors are a mere £33m. The sum which gives the percentage is:

$$\frac{33 \times 100}{6,806} = 0.5\%$$

In other words trade debtors are a minuscule 0.5 per cent of turnover.

The other calculation is:

$$\frac{33 \times 365}{6,806} = 1.8 \text{ days}$$

In other words M&S collects its trade debts in less than 2 days on average. Again what this very low figure really shows is that debt collection is not a useful statistic for a business such as M&S. (The balance sheet notes also included some debts relating to customers, which have been excluded from these sums, since we are not looking here at M&S's credit card business.)

● **Trade creditors as a percentage of sales:** the other side of the coin. The higher the figure, the more free finance the company is getting from its suppliers. Provided the amounts owed to creditors outweigh the amounts owed by debtors, a high creditor/sales figure will reduce a company's need for capital and increase its return on capital employed. An alternative here is creditors in relation to purchases or operating costs.

The creditor/sales relationship can also be shown as a collection period in days.

Again with M&S you need to look to the footnote to the short term creditors to find that trade creditors account for £175m of the £1,364m total. The sum to calculate a percentage is:

$$\frac{175 \times 100}{6,806} = 2.6\%$$

In other words trade creditors account for just 2.6 per cent of sales.

If you want the payment lag in days the sum is:

$$\frac{175 \times 365}{6,806} = 9.4 \text{ days}$$

Unlike some big retailers' such as the supermarket chains, M&S is nearly as prompt at paying as it is at getting its money.

● **Trade creditors as a percentage of stocks:** another way of looking at the same point. Supermarkets, for example, get all their stocks financed by their suppliers.
  For M&S the sum is:

$$\frac{175 \times 100}{377} = 46\%$$

In other words nearly half M&S's stocks are financed by its creditors. But since its stocks are so low, this is not a big deal.

● **Cash-to-cash cycle.** This shows how long the company has to finance its own stocks for: the period between the initial cash outflow (to the supplier) and the final cash receipt (from the customer). Cash-to-cash days = stock days + debtor days − creditor days.
  For M&S the sum involves manipulating figures already calculated:

Stock days	20
Debtor days	1.8
Creditor days	(9.4)
Cash-to-cash	12.4 days

Yet another confirmation that stock finance is not a problem.

Financial ratios provide a health and fitness check. They measure the company's financial structure; show how this is likely to affect trading results; and how likely the company is to break down under strain. Most of these ratios are calculated from the balance sheet.

• **Gearing:** either borrowings as a percentage of shareholders' funds, or borrowings as a percentage of capital employed, preferably adjusted for goodwill write-downs. High gearing can be very beneficial to shareholders' earnings or very dangerous. Provided the company's return on capital remains consistently higher than the cost of its borrowing, and profits are rising, gearing ensures that pre-tax profits will increase faster than operating profits. But high gearing is dangerous, if the cost of borrowing rises above the return on capital, or if operating profits or profit margins are naturally erratic. A few bad years can easily eliminate shareholders' funds in a highly geared company.

Taking M&S as an example shows just how many ways there are to calculate gearing. The first decision to make is whether to use gross borrowings, or whether you net them off against any cash holdings. The former is obviously more severe. The second decision is whether to look at borrowings in relation to shareholders' funds or total capital employed. The former will usually produce the more alarming percentages. We will start by working out the two percentages on gross borrowings, then do it on net borrowings.

Calculating the figure for gross borrowings involves delving into the footnotes to the two creditors items. The £569m longer term creditors include £526m of borrowings. The current liabilities include £274m of short term borrowing: a total of £800m. Shareholders' funds include minorities (£3,714m plus £21m = £3,735m).

So the sum to work out gross debt as a percentage of shareholders' funds is:

$$\frac{800 \times 100}{3,735} = 21.4\%$$

The equivalent calculation to work out gross debt as a percentage of total capital employed uses a different definition from the one on M&S's balance sheet. The widest definition of capital employed starts with shareholders funds (£3,735m), and adds in both long and short term debt (£843m) and even provisions (£38m). So the end figure is a lofty £4,616m (see above page 103).

So the sum to work out gross debt as a percentage of total capital employed is:

$$\frac{800 \times 100}{4{,}616} = 17.3\%$$

But many people would argue that it is more realistic to use net debt. M&S has £736m of cash in its balance sheet. Set that against the gross borrowings of £800m to get a net debt figure of only £64m. Now repeat both the earlier calculations replacing gross debt with net debt.

For net debt as a percentage of shareholders funds the sum is:

$$\frac{64 \times 100}{3{,}735} = 1.7\%$$

And for net debt as a percentage of total capital employed the sum is:

$$\frac{64 \times 100}{4{,}616} = 1.3\%$$

Many analysts would argue that even these figures are a bit unfair. The balance sheet shows investments of £193m which could easily be sold to raise more cash. Add those into the equation and the net debt of £64m is transformed into net cash of £129m.

It is worth calculating the gearing figure a number of different ways to see whether any give grounds for alarm. It is also worth making comparisons with gearing ratios for similar companies worked out on the same bases.

• **Interest cover:** the percentage of the operating profit absorbed by interest payments on borrowings. Shows the impact of gearing on the p&l. If the percentage is high, a small reduction in operating profits, or a rise in the cost of borrowing, can wipe out pre-tax profits. (Turn to page 143 in the next chapter to see how capitalised interest can muddy the calculation.)

M&S's profit and loss account shows net interest income

rather than a payment. Interest cover is normally worked
out on the net figure. So on that basis there is no sum to do.
But it is often worth working the figures out on the gross
interest payment. If, say, the interest credits relate to a fixed
rate deposit and the charges to variable rate borrowing, a
rise in interest rates could increase charges with no compensatory rise in credits.

The full M&S footnote makes it clear that the bulk of the
interest charges and receipts relate to M&S's financial
activities. This in itself is worth knowing, since it suggests
that much of the borrowing mentioned above also relates to
the financial side. So gearing on the trading side is probably
even lower than the calculations above suggested.

The part of the footnote relating to interest expenditure
shows total expenditure of £66m with £37m of it relating to
the financial business, and only £29m to M&S's trading
activities. The quick and dirty way to work out the interest
cover is simply to set the interest charge against the
operating profit shown in the profit and loss account.

$$\frac{29 \times 100}{897} = 3.2\%$$

A more correct way, which assumes that interest credits
are a given, starts with pre-tax profits and adds in the
interest charge and the property loss: (£924m + £29m + £6m
= £959m). The sum then is:

$$\frac{29 \times 100}{959} = 3\%$$

With M&S both figures are negligible. But if, say, a
company is capitalising a large part of its interest charges
(adding them to the cost of the asset financed by the relevant
borrowings), this sort of calculation can help highlight a
hidden problem.

● **Current ratio**: current assets divided by current liabilities. A popular liquidity yardstick. How easily could the
company pay its bills if all its creditors converged at once?
In theory this figure should be at least 1; over 1.5 suggests

excessive caution. But some companies, notably supermarkets, happily survive on current ratios of less than 0.5.

For M&S the calculation is simple since both figures are included in the simplified balance sheet shown. The sum is:

$$\frac{2,366}{1,364} = 1.7$$

● **Quick ratio** (also known as the **acid test**): current assets minus stocks divided by current liabilities. A more drastic version of the current ratio, which assumes the creditors are hammering at the door and there is no time to hold a fire sale.

Another easy sum for M&S, since again the figures are all there. First remove stocks from current assets: (£2,366m – £377m = £1,989.) Then the calculation is:

$$\frac{1,989}{1,364} = 1.5$$

No worries about either figure.

What to look for in the p&l

The p&l account is the first place most investors turn to for information on a company's recent trading performance. Unfortunately many of them never get any further. Professional analysts normally use the p&l in conjunction with the balance sheet to measure a company's performance. And they use the p&l in conjunction with the cash flow statement to see whether the profits reported were translated into hard cash. For, as explained in the next chapter, ways of inflating profits are legion.

Some of the standard ratios analysts use to measure performance were defined above (page 100 onwards: How to calculate some common ratios). Which ones are most relevant and what the norms are depend on the company's business.

Here are some typical questions investors ask when studying the p&l, plus suggestions of where to find the answers. But remember that the relevant information may be lurking in the footnotes.

● Is the business thriving? Are sales increasing and is the company making a good profit on those sales? Check the latest sales figure against the previous year's, and work out the **profit margin** on sales. Make sure that you are comparing like with like: adjusting for acquisitions and disposals is easier than it used to be because of the additional detail provided at the end of the relevant year.

● Are all the divisions doing well, or are there any problem areas? Turn to the footnote providing a **segmental analysis** of sales, profit and assets. This allows you to work out margins and the **return on assets** for the company's different activities. A geographic analysis is also provided if relevant. But it is often difficult to discover whether a specific activity in a specific country is doing well.

● How volatile are pre-tax profits likely to be? High fixed overheads and high borrowings can both produce unusually volatile profits. If a large proportion of capital employed consists of borrowings, a small change in trading profits or interest rates will have a disproportionate effect on pre-tax profits and earnings.* Erratic profits can jeopardise dividends. Look at the **interest cover** in conjunction with the balance sheet **gearing**. But remember that seemingly skimpy cover or high gearing are less dangerous if the company's basic trading profits are steady, as in most utilities.

● How safe is the dividend otherwise? Is the company paying out most of its earnings in dividends – in which case a profit downturn could provoke a dividend cut – or is the dividend well covered? Precise calculations of **dividend cover** are often complicated by tax.† But you can get a

---

* Companies with high operational and/or financial gearing usually have high 'betas'. (See Chapter 7 page 180.)

† If the company gets a high proportion of its profits from overseas, it may not pay enough mainstream corporation tax to use up the advance corporation tax it has to pay on dividends. Thus the actual dividend cover is smaller than a simple comparison of dividends and earnings suggests. But nowadays companies can elect to make part of the payment through a **foreign income dividend**, which does not carry the tax credit. Low taxpayers and investors holding shares through a personal equity plan should be wary of companies paying foreign income dividends.

rough idea just by seeing how much of its earnings the company pays out in dividends, how much it retains.

• Was the growth 'organic', produced by making more out of the existing business, or was it the result of an acquisition? If so, that acquisition may well have increased the number of shares in issue, so earnings per share may not rise in line with the profits. Nowadays companies have to segregate the profits of businesses recently bought, sold or discontinued in the p&l. So it is easy to spot acquisition-based growth in the first year after the deal, less easy in subsequent years. The **earnings per share** figure at the bottom of the p&l (see below) is based on the average number of shares in issue during the year. Always investigate if trends in profits and earnings diverge.

• Is the company making a good **return on the capital employed** (ROCE) in the business? The fact that profits are improving does not imply that return on capital is also improving or that it was satisfactory in the first place. Perhaps the managers should be doing something else with shareholders' money. Return on capital employed is particularly relevant to private investors, since they have no need to invest in any company or industry unless they think it will use their money well.

Unfortunately, the ROCE is often grossly distorted by accounting techniques such as write-downs of purchased goodwill, which reduce capital employed to artificially low levels. (See Chapter 6 page 141.) What's more, inflation means that the book values of long life assets are often ridiculously low compared with their current worth.

• Is the company making a good return compared with its direct competitors? If a retailer's sales margins and return on capital are both half the level of a competitor's, it is at least worth checking whether there is some fundamental difference between the two businesses. It may be a bad sign: the management is getting it wrong. Or it may be a good sign: the management has the scope to double its return if it starts getting it right. This kind of relative assessment is particularly popular with stockbrokers' analysts, since their clients usually want to know which retailer to pick, not whether to invest in retailers at all.

• Does the **statement of total recognised gains and losses** throw up any additional questions? It itemises capital gains and losses recognised (though not necessarily realised) during the year, such as revaluation deficits or surpluses and exchange adjustments. Polly Peck was one notorious example of a company which took a big capital loss on foreign currency deposits directly to reserves, while taking full credit for the investment income derived from the deposits in the p&l.

• Does the **reconciliation of movements in shareholders' funds** throw up any additional questions? This statement explains why the figure for **retentions**, at the bottom of the p&l, sometimes fails to tally with the increase in the cumulative balance sheet figure for the money transferred from p&l over the years. It provides a bridge between the p&l and the balance sheet. Items found in the reconciliation include goodwill write-ups or write-downs, and the proceeds of share issues. Any large sums found there are worth investigating further.

How to calculate earnings

The p&l relates to the past. What investors are interested in is the company's future capacity to produce profits, earnings and cash. So, if they think the latest year's trading was unusually good or bad, analysts adjust the actual numbers in order to calculate 'maintainable' earnings. They argue that this provides a more sensible basis for future earnings and cash flow projections.

The number of unusual, exceptional and extraordinary events which can distort the underlying trend in company profits is large. Until a few years ago, companies had considerable discretion on how to treat them: they could call an unusual profit 'exceptional', which meant it was included along with other profits in the calculation of earnings per share, but decide that an unusual loss was 'extraordinary', which meant it was excluded. Accountants' recent attempts to deal both with the genuinely ambiguous areas and with the abuses of earlier accounting loopholes have produced a slightly perverse situation.

The latest accounting rules on reporting financial performance (contained in **Financial Reporting Standard 3**, known as **FRS3**) require that companies itemise abnormal profit items separately, which is useful. But they also insist that the companies include virtually every profit or loss, no matter how abnormal, in the p&l account and stated earnings. So many companies now show a far more erratic profits record than they would have done under the old rules. What is more, and this is the seemingly perverse bit, investment analysts have responded in a way which almost nullifies the accountants' decision: they go through the accounts stripping out all the capital profits and losses again.*

The **Institute of Investment Management and Research (IIMR)**, the analysts' club, has developed a set of standard adjustments to reported profits, which excludes all capital transactions from a company's earnings. Thus a trading item, such as bad debts, will be in earnings, however large and exceptional; but the profit on the sale of fixed assets will not be in earnings, however large and regular.

The IIMR standard produces what are known as **headline earnings**. These exclude: profits (or losses) on the sale or closure of part of the business; profits (or losses) on the sale (or expropriation) of fixed assets; amortisation of goodwill; bid defence costs; reductions in the value of fixed assets; profits (or losses) on the capital reorganisation of long term debt; profits (or losses) on the sale of trade investments.

Most stockbroking firms broadly adhere to the IIMR adjustments. But headline earnings are designed for use in statistical services and newspapers, which need inflexible criteria. Analysts are paid to exercise judgement. And in

---

* In other words, the analyst and not the company now decides what is above and what below the line. Analysts find this extremely sensible. The general public may beg to differ. What are now published are accounts which everybody agrees are often not much use without adjustments: a DIY kit. Undoubtedly the world would be a finer place if all shareholders had a thorough grounding in investment analysis and could assemble this kit for themselves. But they do not.

their search for maintainable earnings, they often refine the
IIMR adjustments to exclude some additional one-off costs
or credits. Stockbrokers' circulars use **normalised earnings**,
but these may vary from one firm to another, since individual analysts have their own little quirks.

The result is that company accounts now try to please
everyone. Although they usually (but not invariably) publish only one pre-tax profit figure (which follows the FRS3
accounting standard), many companies publish a plethora
of different earnings figures. For example:

- earnings per share (the accountants' version, following
  FRS3)
- adjusted earnings per share, alternatively described as
  earnings per share before exceptional items (the analysts'
  version, following the IIMR adjustments)
- fully diluted earnings per share (the accountants' version, but assuming that any shares which the company is
  liable to issue in future – on the exercise, say, of
  directors' share options or a convertible stock – already
  rank for dividends)
- adjusted fully diluted earnings per share (the analysts
  version, diluted as explained above).

Most newspaper statistics are based on undiluted
adjusted earnings per share, that is the IIMR headline
earnings. But a private investor wanting to relate these to the
rest of the published p&l account, or the profit figures
published in the same newspaper, has to make his own
adjustments to numbers higher up the p&l.

The Byzantine complexity of even fairly simple profit and
loss accounts nowadays does much to enhance the mystique
of accountants and investment analysts, little to assist the
private investor.

What to look for in the balance sheet

Investors use balance sheets to check two different aspects
of a company. First they look at the balance sheet together
with the profit and loss account to refine their assessment of

the year's trading. Second, they use it to check the company's financial strength.

A routine profitability and efficiency audit might cover some of the following points. Which ones are most relevant will depend on the business. Remember that the balance sheet date will have been chosen to put the company in a flattering light. And do not forget that the p&l and the balance sheet are a partnership to be used in tandem. The fact that they sometimes pull in different directions is one of life's little challenges.

● How has the return on assets been achieved? Is the asset figure stated in the balance sheet a fair reflection of the money originally invested, or has capital employed been slimmed by purgative write-downs? Is the capital structure potentially risky? Ratios to calculate include the **return on capital employed**, and **sales to capital employed**. And check **interest cover** and **gearing**, to discover whether returns have been increased by using a large proportion of borrowed capital.

It is also worth looking at the company's accounting policies and history to see whether it has reduced its stated capital employed. Return on capital employed is one of the most important investment yardsticks, but also one of the easiest to manipulate (see Chapter 6).

● If it is a manufacturer, is it keeping its stocks in line with its sales? Keeping too much money tied up in stock is expensive. What's more, as explained on page 137, manufacturing for stock can be a device to prop up profits. The ratio to check is **stockturn**.

● Are its trade debtors rising faster than its sales? Apparent sloppiness in collecting debts can conceal bad debts to come and always costs money. Check whether the **debt collection period** is increasing unduly.

● Does the company get reasonable credit from its suppliers? If not, maybe you should be worried about it too.*

---

* An individual supplier may have particular reasons for limiting credit; a blanket restriction is worrying. When Rolls-Royce ran into difficulties in 1971, the factoring companies were quick to refuse it further credit, despite its famous name. Collapse resulted.

The normal size of trade creditors' balances varies enormously according to the type of business. Companies such as supermarkets manage to finance all their trading stock at their suppliers' expense. Check both the level and changes in **trade creditors as a percentage of sales** and as a **percentage of stocks.** An alternative guide is the **cash-to-cash cycle**, which takes the two together.

Then come routine checks of the company's financial strength. Again, the norms will vary according to what the company does.

● First, gearing. How much of the company's capital employed comes from borrowing, how much belongs to shareholders? There are two reasons for checking this. As explained above, it helps you work out the likely volatility of profits. But it also helps you test the company's solvency. A company with very high borrowings in relation to its shareholders' funds could be heading for trouble. That's particularly true if the goodwill element in shareholders' funds is significant. Check **gearing, and borrowing as a percentage of shareholders funds,** or **of capital employed.**

Most companies have set limits on the amount they can borrow in relation to shareholders' funds under their articles of association: twice shareholders' funds is fairly typical. Debenture and loan stock covenants often impose additional limits. But few healthy companies normally get anywhere near these limits. Borrowing of around one third of shareholders' funds is a fair benchmark for a normal company, less for one in a volatile business such as commodity trading, more for one in a steady business such as electricity supply. But borrowing is only worthwhile if the return on assets outstrips the cost of borrowed money. And interest rates, alas, do change.

Remember too that gearing ratios depend on asset valuations. So you need to check what the assets are and how they have been valued. If most of shareholders' funds are deployed in clapped-out manufacturing plant which needs substantial new investment, the true gearing level may be both understated and set to rise sharply.

● Second, liquidity. Now you are checking how easy the company would find it to keep paying its bills, if times got tough. How do its current assets stack up against its current liabilities? Try this one both including and excluding stock among its current assets. That is the **current ratio** and the **quick ratio**.

Now turn to the **cash flow statement**, especially if the company's finances are at all worrying. This complements the p&l with details of changes in borrowings and cash pulled in by additional financing.

It is also worth checking both the footnotes and the Statement of Accounting Policies for additional information.

● **Capital commitments.** These explain how much money the company plans to spend, but not when it plans to spend it. Worth noting if it is rising or falling sharply, and if it looks disproportionate to the company's existing activities or financial strength.

● **Contingent liabilities.** Normally obligations the company hopes it won't have to meet but might have to if events go against it. Often they point to items such as guarantees of associates' borrowings. Sometimes they mention a legal dispute. They are usually as uninformative as the company can make them.

● **Statement of accounting policies.** Read this in conjunction with any relevant footnotes to the accounts. If the company has changed any of its accounting policies, ask yourself why and what the effect is likely to have been. Revaluations of stocks and both tangible assets (such as property) and intangible ones (such as brand names) affect the balance sheet, and can have a big knock-on effect on profits.

Cash flow statements in flux

Cash flow is the newest of the main financial statements contained in accounts. It was introduced in 1975 in the rather unsatisfactory form of a 'statement of source and application of funds', and changed to a cash flow statement under **FRS1** in 1991. Revisions were suggested in late 1995. Its twin functions are to provide information on cash generated and absorbed by the company, and to explain changes in liquidity. It can be used in conjunction with the p&l to assess the trading results; or it can be used in conjunction with the balance sheet to assess liquidity, solvency and financial flexibility.

The statement's introduction followed investors' increasing appreciation of the extent to which companies could play tricks with the traditional p&l and balance sheet. The new rules for the p&l mean that earnings are either extremely volatile, or misleadingly bland, while profits can still be considerably influenced by the accounting method chosen. And critics argue that traditional liquidity ratios, such as the current and quick ratios, are unreliable if used in isolation and can be made to look better than they normally do.*

The accounts already include a bridge between the p&l and the cash flow statement (the footnote described below). And, if the current proposals are adopted, they will soon also include a formal bridge between the cash flow statement and the balance sheet.

The original accounting rules (FRS1) require companies to list inflows and outflows of 'cash and cash equivalents' under five headings:

- Net cash inflow from operating activities
- Returns on investments and servicing of finance
- Taxation
- Investing activities
- Financing

This statement is supplemented by an important footnote, **reconciliation of operating profit to net cash inflow from**

---

* Of course, many year-end figures are untypical, because companies with seasonal businesses often choose an accounting date which puts them in a flattering light. Companies, like women, wish to be admired.

But a company which wishes to improve its current ratio overnight can sometimes put a temporary corset on its liabilities. If, say, a company with net current assets uses most of its spare cash to pay creditors off unusually promptly, its liabilities will fall proportionately more than its assets and its current ratio will rise. Thereafter, of course, it can relax and allow its figures to resume their normal proportions.

operating activities, explaining why the net cash inflow at the top of the cash flow statement does not tally with the operating profit shown in the p&l. It reconciles the difference by itemising non-cash charges against the p&l, such as depreciation, and showing how assets and liabilities, such as stocks, debtors and creditors, have moved over the year. It also shows (as a credit) charges allowed for in the p&l but not yet actually spent – which will, therefore, hit future cash flow.

But companies complained that the accounting requirements of the standard were not an accurate reflection of the way they actually ran their finances. First, the definition of 'cash equivalents', to include only investments with an original maturity of less than three months, and repayable on demand, forced them to make an artificial distinction between these and other equally liquid investments with a slightly longer original maturity date. Second, the 'investing activities' category lumped together items resulting from short term investment with those from long term portfolio and fixed asset investment. And third, the statements were not helpful to investors trying to assess the company's liquidity.

The late 1995 revision to FRS1 (contained in **Financial Reporting Exposure Draft 10**, better known as FRED 10) suggests several ways in which the presentation of the cash flow statement can be altered to meet these criticisms. These suggestions are based on the belief that where the original accounting standard had gone wrong was in trying to use one financial statement to meet two different needs. The revisions try to make the existing cash flow statement more useful as an alternative measure of prosperity, and suggest an additional footnote to help investors concerned about liquidity and solvency. This new footnote would link the cash flow statement to changes in net debt in the balance sheet, in the same way that the existing footnote links it to the p&l.

FRED 10 responds to criticisms about FRS1's arbitrary treatment of cash equivalents by limiting the items eligible for inclusion in most headings in cash flow statements strictly to cash, and introducing a new heading 'liquid resources' for a wider range of cash equivalents. And it deals with complaints about lumping short and long term investments together by increasing the number of different headings in the statement to eight:–

- Net cash inflow from operating activities.
- Returns on investments and servicing of finance.
- Taxation.
- Capital expenditure (formerly part of investing activities).
- Acquisitions and disposals (formerly part of investing activities).
- Dividends paid (formerly part of returns on investment).
- Management of liquid resources (formerly part of investing activities).
- Financing.

The new note reconciling the cash flow statement with balance sheet changes in net debt starts with the net cash increase or decrease at the bottom of the cash flow statement. It then itemises first those elements in the cash flow statement which relate to changes in net debt, such as increases or decreases in debts and liquid resources, and then adds debt brought in with acquisitions and other new non-cash liabilities such as finance leases. A footnote to this footnote shows how these items tie in with the aggregate figures in the balance sheet. And another explains the impact of acquisitions.

How to use cash flow statements

Two types of investor study cash flow statements. First, traditional investors wanting a cross check on a company's profitability, and on its liquidity and solvency. Second, those who consider that cash flow multiples and cash flow projections are the only useful form of investment analysis.

Even those analysts still obsessed with earnings use the new cash flow statements as a check on the veracity of the p&l. If the p&l shows substantial and improving profits, but the cash flow statement shows a net outflow, it is time for some detective work. Companies which are expanding rapidly through acquisition often show a net cash outflow, made good by additional financing. That can be the prelude to problems unless the new businesses start producing profits fast.

Some of the points worth checking will be found in the cash flow statement itself; others in the note reconciling it with the p&l.

• Use the cash flow as a lazy man's guide to points worth checking in the rest of the accounts. The depreciation charge and changes in stocks, debtors and creditors (all discussed earlier) are summarised here.

• Does the trend in cash flow match the trend in profits? If not, there could be an important shift in the company's financial position taking place such as a refinancing. Is this a one-off, or part of a continuing improvement or deterioration?

• If there was a cash outflow, was it steady or was it accelerating as the year progressed? A good question, though the answer may be hard to find. Check back on the interim statement. A handful of companies provide cash flow projections – but they are seldom those with cash flow problems. Look at a share price chart to see what the market thinks.

• Do the cash outflows for one-off costs such as reorganisations match earlier provisions against these costs? If not, watch out for further cash outflows in future years.

• Are there large items for interest receivable as well as interest payable? If so, the company probably has an active cash management programme. Does the board explain what its policy is? And would you understand it if it did?*

• Are there any big changes in dividends from associates or cash invested in associates? Both are possible alarm bells.

The other traditional use of cash flow statements is in

---

* One leading investment analyst has argued the inevitable increase in the use of derivatives by companies will make company accounts far harder to analyse; and that financial analysis is likely to become almost as specialised as heart surgery. And presumably as lucrative for the top "surgeons".

analysing solvency and liquidity, in conjunction with the balance sheet. The new footnotes reconciling the cash flow statement to the balance sheet should make the investor's task easier. For they will enable him to see at a glance why net debt has risen or fallen over the year.

Even the enhanced cash flow statement will have limitations. It will not tell you whether borrowings have risen since the year end, how close they are to the agreed limit, and whether the management has got the company's bankers on its side.

A fashionable analytical approach treats cash flow as the basic building block in what is called 'shareholder value analysis'. This technique is based on the belief that whereas profit is a matter of opinion, cash is a matter of fact. It argues that earnings – derived from profits – are junk: they are intrinsically subjective and of very little use as a share price predictor. Shareholder value analysis attempts to look forward, by projecting cash flow several years into the future, and then discounting those future flows back to arrive at a present value. Shareholder value is defined as the total return to the shareholder in terms of both dividends and share price growth. (See page 175.)

What to look for in the auditors' report

An auditor's report is noteworthy only if it is qualified. Qualifications are of three types. First, the auditors may say that they were unable to check some of the information in the accounts. If the limitations on their audit are very important the auditors may abnegate their normal responsibility and say that they cannot form an opinion on the accounts. Second, they may disagree with the accounting treatment of some item in the accounts, for example whether a debt is collectable. Third, they may disagree so violently with some item in the accounts that they feel the accounts as a whole do not give a true and fair view of the state of affairs.

If the auditors reckon that there is fundamental uncertainty relating to an important element in the accounts, but that this uncertainty is adequately flagged, they will mention it in their report but not qualify that report – unless it could have far reaching implications.

Cash flow and Enterprise Value

The rising popularity of **cash flow analysis** reflects both increasing cynicism about manipulation of the profit and loss account, and the search for internationally valid yardsticks. But unfortunately there are several ways of calculating cash flow. Most are based on a profits number long favoured by Americans, now catching on internationally, known as **EBITDA**: earnings before interest, tax, depreciation, and amortisation.* But different analysts knock different items of expenditure off EBITDA, arguing that this gives a better idea of the cash actually at the company's disposal.

For example, **free cash flow** starts with EBITDA and deducts the tax paid and (usually) capital expenditure. **Gross cash flow**, the measure traditionally used in the UK, starts with EBITDA and deducts both net interest paid and tax paid. **Net cash flow** starts with gross cash flow and deducts dividends paid and (sometimes) capital expenditure.

Cash flow was traditionally calculated from the p&l account. The introduction of cash flow statements allows analysts to refine the calculation. Whichever cash flow figure is chosen can then be used as a substitute for profit in measuring the return on sales or capital, or for working out interest cover.

Investment analysis conventionally looks at a company from the point of view of **Shareholders' Interests** ie excluding debt. But some analysts nowadays argue that you get a better reflection of the company's trading performance by measuring it against its **Enterprise Value** rather than just Shareholders Interests. Enterprise Value is the combined

---

* Amortisation is a method of writing off assets, such as goodwill. The mechanics work much like depreciation

market value of the equity and the net debt. Those using Enterprise Value have cash flow yardsticks of their own, which in several cases differ from those used in Shareholder Value calculations. Investment bank BZW uses no less than eight measures of cash flow.

	Shareholder Only	Enterprise Value
Operating Profit	xx	xx
+ Depreciation and amortisation	xx	xx
= EBITDA	XX	XX
+ (−) Movements in working capital	xx	xx
+ (−) Provision creation/spending	xx	xx
+ (−) Other operating items (eg profits on asset sales)	xx	xx
= OPERATING CASH FLOW	XX	XX
− Net interest payments	xx	na
− Preference & Minority divs paid	xx	na
+ Dividends received from associates	xx	xx
− Tax paid	xx	xx
= CASH EARNINGS	XX	XX
− Capital expenditure	xx	xx
+ Proceeds from asset sales	xx	xx
= POST CAPEX CASH FLOW	XX	XX
− Ordinary dividends paid	xx	na
= FREE CASH FLOW	XX	XX

These cash flow figures can be used in calculating various investment ratios, such as the price to cash flow ratio and Enterprise Value to cash flow ratios. (See Chapter 7 pages 172 and 175.) Enterprise Value is growing in popularity as the basis of several yardsticks for weighing up companies. (See Chapter 7 page 178–79.)

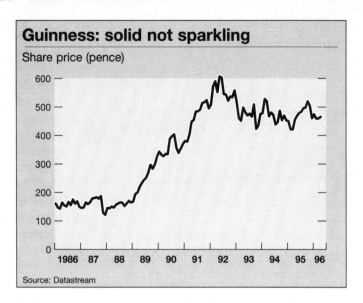

Fig 5.1 Fundamental analysts will go right through a set of accounts before they begin to consider whether the shares are worth buying. Even a simple chart tells you what other people think about the company.

How the pros use accounts

The clearest guide to using accounts is a textbook called *Interpreting Company Reports and Accounts*, by Geoffrey Holmes and Alan Sugden. Holmes was the editor of *Accountancy* for more than 20 years; Sugden spent 20 years in the City as an analyst and fund manager and was a director of Schroder Investment Management, a fund management firm respected for its disciplined approach to investment. The chapter called 'Putting it all together' in the fifth edition shows a step-by-step analysis of the 1993 accounts of drinks group Guinness.

● What does the company do? Most analysts and accountants emphasise that you will get more out of the accounts if you think about the company's business and financial structure before looking at the numbers. The structure of a supermarket group is materially different from that of a whisky manufacturer. Guinness is a big international drinks group. All four words in the description matter.

● What is interesting in the p&l? This leaves the authors with outstanding questions about falling profit margins, an important European associate called LVMH, some large exceptional items, high interest charges, the reason for the low tax charge and a reorganisation.

● What is interesting about the balance sheet? Points noted here include: brand values given a substantial capital value in the balance sheet; some large but slightly mysterious investments; massive stocks; a negative goodwill reserve; and a large reduction in borrowings.

● Does the cash flow statement help? Although profits were down, cash flow was up because of a fall in working capital. The cash spent on reorganisation falls well short of the provision made a year earlier. Like most big international groups, Guinness is using derivatives as a financial management tool. It is paying back its borrowings rapidly.

But there are some new queries. Foreign exchange losses, reported in the statement of total recognised gains and losses, are substantial. Retained earnings are under pressure because dividends rose while profits fell, and the foreign exchange losses increase the squeeze. LVMH continues puzzling.

The analysis proceeds steadily through the segment analysis (a big variation in profit margins), the reorganisation costs (part of the reorganisation related to a write down which does not affect cash flow) and pension costs (the company will soon come to the end of its pensions holiday). It considers the reorganisation of the group's French interests, centring round LVMH, after the balance sheet date. It highlights the balance sheet's dependence on brand values, and the fact that roughly a third of the value attributed to whisky stocks relates to finance costs.

On again to the financial review (not published by all companies). This provides a forecast of free cash flow in the coming year, explains how the board plans to deploy it, and outlines the management's attitude to foreign exchange and financing.

When the jigsaw is complete the authors recommend the

investor to make a one page summary of his conclusions. This covers:

First, what the company does.

Then the story. Turnover is rising, though profits are under pressure. But profits should improve next year and the company is well placed to benefit from improving market conditions. Operating costs are being reduced. Outside forecasts predict an expansion in the spirits market as sales to developing countries increase. The LVMH deal makes sense.

Third, the risks. The rise in sales to developing countries may not come off. The group remains exposed to currency fluctuations. Own brand competition is growing. Is Guinness hooked by the reorganisation bug?

The final assessment. This weighs up the pros and cons for the business. Then, and only then, should the investor look at the recent performance of the share price, and decide whether the shares look good value at their current level.

How easy is it for an amateur to analyse accounts?

Some professional analysts argue that private investors are wasting their time trying to analyse accounts. Pragmatists point out that most short term price movements occur in response to information contained in preliminary or interim profit statements, other trading news announced by the company, or outside events. Purists argue that in an efficient market any additional information in the accounts will be reflected in share prices long before the private investor has sussed it out. Pessimists predict that the introduction of derivatives as an everyday management tool in large companies means that even professional analysts will become increasingly incapable of interpreting accounts.

But private investors are normally more interested in investing for the long term than trying to catch short term movements. Many outstandingly successful individual investors, such as Warren Buffett, use accounts as an important tool in their selection process. Smaller companies – those outside the largest 350 listed on the stockmarket – are often relatively neglected by professional analysts, and far less likely to use complex derivatives than the majors. Since these are exactly the companies that many private investors find most interesting, they will find analysis of accounts well worth the considerable effort involved.

Their biggest problem is likely to be finding anyone at the company to answer questions raised by the accounts. Professional analysts tend to find that accounts may arm them with the right questions, but it is only the company which can provide the answers. Amateurs are unlikely to be given half an hour of the finance director's time.

Where to get accounts

Most companies will happily send investors a free copy of their accounts. Find out where the registered office is and phone up. Some of the larger companies have an investor relations department; some still leave this kind of job to their registrars. Expect to make at least two telephone calls before you find the right person.

The *Financial Times* offers a free annual reports service for a number of major companies. Turn to its London Share Service (inside the back page in the second section during the week, and in the same position in the first section at weekends). Any company there annotated with an ace of clubs belongs to the service. A note in the bottom right hand corner of the right hand page gives both a telephone number and a code number.

Both the *Financial Times* and the *Investors Chronicle* also sell *Company Focus* reports for a few pounds per company These provide supplementary information on City profit forecasts, five year share price and financial reviews, balance sheet and p&l data and recent Stock Exchange announcements. Worth considering if the annual report has aroused your interest, but go for the free information first.

Interpreting Company Reports and Accounts by Geoffrey Holmes and Alan Sugden is published by Prentice Hall/ Woodhead Faulkner in both hardback and paperback. At £21.95 the paperback is a sound investment.(See Appendix A for additional sources of information.)

How to Use Company Accounts

IN A NUTSHELL

1. The purpose of accounts is to provide information which will enable users to make financial decisions. Investors use accounts to assess the company's recent trading record, check its financial fitness and flexibility, estimate its future capacity to generate wealth, and decide whether its shares are good value at their current price. The analysis of the past is carried out only as a basis for assessing the future.

2. Accounts are not as cut and dried as laymen imagine. They leave managements wide discretion on how to treat certain items. This means accounts can be manipulated through creative accounting.

3. Accounts contain three major financial statements and two subsidiary ones. The profit and loss account summarises the result of the latest year's trading. The balance sheet is a snapshot of everything the company owes and owns at the balance sheet date. The cash flow statement shows how much cash flowed in and out during the year. The statement of total recognised gains and losses supplements the p&l account. Another statement reconciles the p&l with the balance sheet. The note on accounting policies and the auditors report are also vital. The presentation of accounts is changing rapidly ahead of the adoption of international accounting standards in 1998.

4. The function of the p&l account is to provide information on the company's performance, particularly its profitability. It enables investors to check the latest year's performance against the previous one, calculate profit margins, and check on the potential volatility of profits and dividend cover.

The return on capital is calculated using both the p&l and the balance sheet.

5. FRS3, the accountants' rules for reporting financial performance, has considerably altered the presentation of the p&l. FRS3 says that companies should include all profits and losses, even abnormal ones, in their stated profits, but provide detailed analysis of the source of the profits. This means that the profits of many companies are now considerably more volatile than they were when companies were allowed to strip out extraordinary items.

6. The Institute of Investment Management and Research, the analysts' professional society, agreed a method of calculating 'Headline Earnings' which involves stripping out a number of one-off items from FRS3 profits. These are the earnings used by statistical publications such as newspaper prices pages. But the IIMR decided there was no standardised way of calculating maintainable earnings and left further adjustments up to the individual analysts.

7. The function of the balance sheet is to provide information about the company's financial position. Used in combination with the p&l it enables investors to refine their analysis of its performance. Relevant operating ratios include the return on capital, stockturn, and debtor and creditor ratios. It is also the key statement used in assessing the company's financial strength and adaptability. Relevant financial ratios are gearing and the current and quick ratios.

8. The function of the cash flow statement is to give information on cash generated and absorbed by the company and on changes in liquidity. Investors use it to check how closely the profits stated in the p&l are matched by the net cash inflows. They also use it to supplement balance sheet information relating to liquidity, solvency and financial adaptability.

9. Many analysts regard cash flow projections as the basic building block of financial analysis. They argue that it is a better predictor of prices than earnings, and that cash is a matter of fact not opinion. Shareholder value, the total return to the shareholder including both income and capital growth, is calculated as the present value of future free cash flows.

10. Some professional analysts argue that private investors cannot understand modern accounts, and that even if they do, the market price will already have adjusted for all the information in them. But many very successful investors use accounts as one of their tools. And small companies in particular are comparatively neglected by professional analysts.

11. Most companies will send investors copies of their latest accounts free.

Chapter 6
Creative Accounting

Creative accounting can damage your wealth. When companies tinker with the p&l, they can turn losses into profits. Attempts to massage the balance sheet often conceal a desperate need for additional finance. When the underlying problems are revealed, as they almost always are in the end, investors in companies which have indulged in creative accounting can lose some or all of their money. Spotting creative accountants at work may not help you pick winners, but it can help you avoid losers.

The profit and loss account is the most popular subject for cosmetic treatment, because it is the source for earnings per share, the yardstick most investors use. Despite the best efforts of accounting pundits to encourage more catholic tastes, even professional investors remain unhealthily obsessed with earnings. But a minority of companies massage their balance sheets. This is usually because the balance sheets would otherwise look worryingly over-stretched, and might scare off investors and bankers alike.

Since the profit and loss account and the balance sheet are interdependent, a boost to one tends to weaken the other. So it is difficult for any company consistently to massage both. But cynics argue that the only part of the accounts which cannot readily be manipulated is the cash flow statement. Cash flow projections could yet replace earnings in investors' affections, though even cash flow statements are not totally tamper-proof.

Ways of enhancing profits are legion. Some techniques boost operating profits – the raw trading profit at the top of the p&l account; some reduce depreciation, the annual provision for wear and tear of assets, which is a major charge against operating profits in manufacturing companies; some increase interest receivable or decrease interest payable to the benefit of pre-tax profits; some reduce the stated tax charge, which flatters earnings.

Rather fewer options are available for companies which want to make the balance sheet look stronger than it is. A weak balance sheet is normally one with too little capital to support the company's expansion; one where too much of the capital employed is borrowed; or one where the company does not have enough cash to pay its pressing bills. An undercapitalised company cannot take advantage of trading opportunities; an over-borrowed company is likely to produce erratic profits and can easily become insolvent. An illiquid company can find the receivers at the door even though it is still in one sense solvent.*

If shareholders' funds can be increased at a stroke, the company will appear stronger and will also be able to borrow more without looking over-borrowed. If the company can issue more of its own shares at a high price, well and good – for the company, though not necessarily its shareholders. Failing that, it may announce that its tangible assets (properties, equipment, vehicles and so on) are worth more than their book cost (cost less cumulative depreciation). Or it can argue that its 'intangible assets', reflecting the excess cost of buying another company or the cost of brand names, should be given a monetary value in the balance sheet.

Until recently, there was also a clutch of ways in which companies could push some of their borrowings off the balance sheet and out of sight through techniques such as leasing and factoring. This is now harder. But, although the new accounting rules insist that more relevant information is disclosed, there are still some loopholes. And even if the information is contained in a footnote, many investors fail to notice it.

Companies without enough cash to pay their bills have no obvious panacea. Since accounts are simply a snapshot on one day of the year, juggling the timing of receipts and payments can provide a strictly temporary pain-killer. But

* Solvent remains a slippery word. It is used both to describe a company whose assets exceed its liabilities, and as a near synonym for liquid. An illiquid company, which cannot pay its bills when they fall due, is technically insolvent.

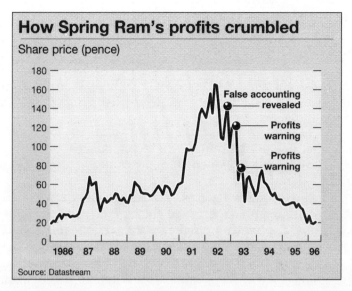

How Spring Ram's profits crumbled

Share price (pence)

Source: Datastream

Fig 6.1 Creative endeavours included overstating stock numbers, values and sales by £5.6m, earmarking for 1992 £5.6m of profits which belonged to 1993, and trying to classify £4m of development costs as an asset.

even the most optimistic accountant cannot manipulate a cash flow statement for long.

Beautifying the p&l

Different types of business offer different loopholes to creative accountants. But most ways of boosting profits do so at the expense of the balance sheet. And that is where you will often find the tell-tale evidence.

● **Sales.** These are hard to tamper with in most companies without resort to outright fraud. But always check the **debt collection** figures. If a company has pushed through a lot of sales just before the year end, the average collection period will lengthen.*

* But the average debt collection period itself is a fallible indicator with seasonal companies which make most of their sales at the end of the year for it assumes the debts are spread evenly

In some businesses it is possible to book sales at different stages in the sales process. When is a sale booked when made on a sale or return basis? Are warranty refunds deducted from sales or treated as a cost? At what stage does a leasing company book the revenue due under the leasing agreement, or a contractor the payments on a long term contract?

● **Cost of sales.** Manufacturers have most scope to increase trading or operating profits by reducing the cost of sales. A favourite tool is stocks (which appear under current assets on the balance sheet).

● **Stocks 1: valuation games.** Stocks can mean raw materials, work in progress or finished goods. Finished goods offer the greatest opportunities to the creative accountant (though work in progress also has its fans). First is the basic question of valuation method. Stocks have to be valued at 'the lower of cost and net realisable value'. But if manufacturing costs have risen over the year, their year-end cost is a moot point. If the products are standard items, companies have several choices. They can value their remaining stock on a 'first-in-first-out basis' (FIFO), which means sales are assumed to consist of the oldest items. This increases the value of the remaining stock, lowers the cost of sales and increases profits. In the US they can opt for 'last-in-first-out' (LIFO), which is not popular in the UK. This lowers the value of the remaining stock, increases the cost of sales, and reduces profits – although it may in practice give companies a good excuse for increasing selling prices early. Alternatively, companies can opt for some type of average or standard cost per unit.

Changes in a company's policy are worth noting. A company which used FIFO when prices were rising, and then had an exceptional stock write-down and switched to LIFO or average stock pricing when prices were falling, would be trying to eat its cake and have it.

over the year. If, say, a fireworks wholesaler made half its sales in the final month of a year ending on November 6, and payment for all these sales was still outstanding at the year-end, its debt collection period would appear to be 6 months. Not necessarily.

Most stock valuation systems make stock profits or losses possible, depending on the trend in prices. Oil companies, which carry large stocks, use replacement cost accounting, which recognises this. Profits are calculated on a replacement cost basis (which actually means valuing stocks on an average cost for the year), and the companies state stock profits or losses separately. Check year to year **changes in stock levels** against the rise in sales, and the **statement of accounting policies.**

● **Stocks 2: a dumping ground for overheads.** Another factor which affects the valuation of stocks, and has a knock-on effect on the cost of sales and operating profits is the treatment of overheads. Companies are required to include not just raw material and labour costs but a proportion of relevant overheads when working out the cost of their year-end stocks. (Indeed, they are even allowed to include interest costs on relevant borrowings, provided they mention it.)

Even if overheads are allocated fairly, the technique can be abused. If a company maintains or increases output volume beyond the level required by current sales – starts manufacturing 'for stock' – stocks will absorb more of the fixed overheads, reduce unit costs, increase profit margins and so prop up the p&l.

This is how it works. Some costs are variable: raw materials, processing costs such as electricity, heating, and some labour costs. But costs such as rent, and some finance and labour costs are fixed. The company pays out the same regardless of the level of production, unless it makes costly closures and redundancies. Since part of these fixed overheads is allocated to stock costs, the higher the number of units produced, the lower the overall cost per unit. So, the cost per unit actually sold is lower than it would be if the company cut production back in line with sales. The cost of sales for the year is lower than it would have been if production had been cut back, and the operating profit is higher. The snag is that the balance sheet will be stuffed full of unsold – and possibly unsaleable – stocks.

Only a masochistic management would be pessimistic enough immediately to cut the year-end stocks' value from cost to a (lower) realisable value.* But even if it did, that write-down would probably count as exceptional, and might be subsumed by some convenient provision.

Investors should always be wary of companies whose stocks, particularly of finished goods, rise much faster than sales. For unless the company is bailed out by a strong recovery in demand or divine intervention, the longer the day of reckoning is postponed, the nastier it will be. Check **stockturn**, particularly stockturn of finished goods, and the **accounting policies.**

The use of depreciation

Companies have considerable discretion over how much they charge each year for depreciation. A low charge increases profits and earnings.

This provision for wear and tear of company assets is not an actual cost – no money flows out of the company – just a charge against stated profits which recognises that most assets have a limited useful life. The cash outflow occurs at the time the asset is acquired; depreciation spreads the net cost over the asset's useful working life. The annual depreciation charge moves from the p&l to swell the cumulative depreciation provision in the balance sheet. (The annual charge appears in a footnote to the p&l, the cumulative provision in a footnote to the fixed asset section of the balance sheet.)

The lower the depreciation charge in any year, the smaller its bite on profits and the higher the stated profit figure. The annual charge is determined first by the value ascribed to fixed assets in the balance sheet, and secondly by the company's depreciation policy with regard to those assets. So once again decisions which appear to relate purely to the balance sheet can have a significant effect on the p&l.

Laymen often assume that the value at which assets appear in a company's balance sheet (book value) is meant

---

* It is the auditors' duty to insist on a write down if the net realisable value is patently below cost, but it is often hard to be categoric.

to reflect their current market value. Not so – or only if the accounts state that there has been a recent valuation and that book values have been adjusted in line with this valuation. Assets are usually included at their original cost less the accumulated depreciation since their purchase. Depreciation is based on original cost, or book value if the assets have been revalued upwards or downwards since purchase, and is calculated on a mathematical formula. Depreciation rates depend on the asset. A car or van is normally depreciated over five years, a freehold building over 50 years, a leasehold building over the life of the lease.

Some depreciation policies are loaded towards the early years of an asset's life, some (known as straight line methods) write off the same amount each year. But it is up to the company to decide what depreciation policy is appropriate. The cumulative depreciation provision in the balance sheet does not set out to cover the replacement cost of the asset.

Although companies deduct depreciation before they calculate pre-tax profits, their chosen depreciation figure has no effect on the tax charge they actually pay. This charge *is* affected if they qualify for any of the capital allowances made available by the government. But any overlap between the annual depreciation charge and the year's capital allowances is pretty incidental (see deferred tax below).

Other things being equal, then, companies that want to enhance their profits have every incentive to ascribe the lowest possible figure to the fixed assets in their balance sheet, depreciate them over the longest possible period of time, and avoid depreciation methods which are loaded towards the early years. A low book value for assets will also reduce the value of capital employed and so boost return on capital employed.*

But there are some opposing forces. First, companies with weak balance sheets may need to make their fixed assets appear as valuable as possible. This enhances shareholders'

* A variant on the theme is to ascribe a high residual value to assets at the end of their economic life. This cuts the annual depreciation charge without reducing shareholders' funds.

funds. The maximum amount a company can borrow is often set as a multiple of shareholders' funds. So, although a company in financial straits may desire to keep its depreciation charge down to enhance profits and please its shareholders, doing so could cause it to breach its borrowing covenants, upset its bankers, and ultimately give its shareholders more lasting cause for grief. Running a troubled company has some tricky moments.

Check changes in **depreciation charges, asset valuations,** and the **accounting policies**, both for the latest year and for earlier ones. Calculate too the **effective depreciation rate** for each asset class.

● **Depreciation: two types of write-down.** Companies which can afford it sometimes elect to **write down** their assets, that is they point out that their book value overstates their market value and that they intend to adjust the former to the latter. Most companies have two choices: write off the deficit at-a-blow through an exceptional charge against profits; or write the deficit off against profits over a period of years.* The impact on profits of these two methods is radically different.

The one-off write down has a big negative impact on profits in a single year, but it reduces the depreciation charge and so increases stated profits for years to come. This is because the new annual depreciation charge will be a proportion of the new (reduced) asset value. The write-down also automatically increases the return on capital employed. What is more analysts will sometimes almost disregard the profits hit, because it is exceptional, and concentrate on maintainable profits.

The gradual write down of a revaluation deficit is achieved by increasing the annual depreciation charge. Thus it has precisely the opposite effect to the one-off write down. It reduces stated profits throughout the period over which the deficit is being written off.† Unsurprisingly,

---

* A few already have a revaluation reserve in their balance sheet, dating from earlier upwards valuations of assets, and can simply write the deficit off against this reserve.

† Rival supermarketeers Sainsbury and Tesco adopted different

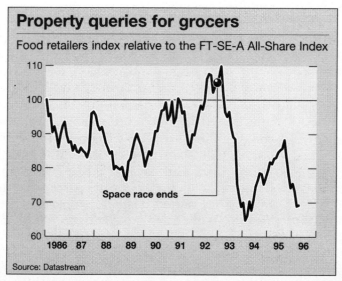

Property queries for grocers

Food retailers index relative to the FT-SE-A All-Share Index

Space race ends

Source: Datastream

Fig 6.2 During the great space race supermarket companies capitalised the interest on their developments and did not depreciate them. When the tide turned, the big grocers started depreciating.

many newly appointed chief executives prefer the one-off write down.

Check changes in **depreciation charges, asset valuations,** and the **accounting policies.**

● **Goodwill: a hot potato.** One related question is what write-down method is appropriate when dealing with the 'goodwill' element in acquisitions. If one company buys another and pays more for it than the value of the net assets (property, plant, machinery, vehicles, patents, trade-marks, brands, stocks and debtors less liabilities) it acquires, the

policies when they decided to write down the values of their properties in the early 1990s. Sainsbury opted for a relatively optimistic revaluation basis and one-off write down against the p&l; Tesco opted for a more conservative revaluation basis and decided to depreciate the deficit over 25 years. One investment analyst calculated that putting Tesco onto the Sainsbury basis would have increased its normalised earnings per share by 9 per cent. And the different treatments will continue to affect earnings for years to come.

remainder of the purchase cost, sometimes described as the cost of control, is classified as an intangible asset. This is the label normally put on things such as patents and brand names. Few companies ascribe any value to home grown intangible assets in their balance sheets, though one or two have included bought brand names in their balance sheets as intangible assets with hefty valuations.

Goodwill representing simply the cost of control is normally written off. These write downs are controversial. Some analysts argue that it is wrong to write this goodwill off at all – unless there has been a shock downwards reappraisal of the value of the company purchased: the phoenix was a pup. They suggest it should normally stay in the balance sheet under the label 'goodwill' or 'consolidation difference'.

But current accounting rules allow the purchaser either to write it off immediately against reserves, with no knock-on effect on the p&l, or to amortise (essentially another word for depreciate) it over a number of years against the p&l (the only system allowed in the US). The effects on the p&l are again totally opposite. The first method reduces the potential depreciation charge and the capital employed base to the benefit of stated profits and the return on capital employed in future years. The second reduces future profits for several years to come. Worry about the effect of such goodwill write-offs on the p&l can deter US bidders in a takeover battle.

The current accounting rules recommend the first method. And most companies happily adopt it. However, the rules are changing. In June 1996 the ASB published new proposals for dealing with goodwill in Financial Reporting Exposure Draft 12 (FRED 12). If accepted and implemented, it will deal with the main abuse: companies will no longer be able to write purchased goodwill off 'at a blow' against reserves. In most cases they will have to keep it on the balance sheets as an asset – like any other investment – and write it off gradually against the p&l over a period of up to 20 years. Companies taking this route will be in line with current international accounting standards.

But FRED 12 offers acquisitive companies an option –

which is not currently available under the international standards. If the value of the goodwill, or any intangible asset, is expected to be maintained indefinitely, it can stay on the balance sheet without being amortised. So purchased brand names, for example, can sit on the balance sheet in perpetuity, without impinging on reported profits. The accountants' only proviso is that such assets have to pass an annual 'impairment' test to check that value has not been leaking away. Cynics argue that companies will be tempted to attribute too high a value to purchased brand names in order to minimise the remaining goodwill – and the subsequent impact on the p&l.

The snag with the proposal is that it will institutionalise the disparate treatment of goodwill: companies which build up their own goodwill and brand names will not include them in their balance sheets as an asset; those that buy them will. And companies which have already made large goodwill writeoffs against reserves will not be asked to adjust the figures. So investors will still need to look at comparative return on capital figures with a sceptical eye.

Check **footnotes to the p&l and balance sheet** and see what the **accounting policies** say about **consolidation**. Look for the **cumulative goodwill** eliminated to date, usually found in a note to reserves.

Post acquisition write-downs were at one time considerably abused as opportunities to include provisions for many future costs not directly associated with the purchase. Again, this flattered future profits. Current rules prohibit this kitchen sink approach.*

Other ways of enhancing the profit and loss include the following.

● **Capitalised interest: turning costs into assets.** This is another method of shunting expenditure out of the p&l and into the balance sheet.

Interest on borrowings is charged before tax, and usually

---

* Companies have to include the assets of companies acquired in their consolidated balance sheets at 'fair values'. But it is still possible for a company to set up a catch-all provision, as long as it is charged against profits. The ASB is looking at this.

netted out against interest received on cash and deposits. But many companies treat the interest on borrowings to finance a project during construction as part of the capital cost. It then appears as part of the additions to fixed assets in the year-end balance sheet. This increases the stated pre-tax profit. The capitalised interest will then normally have to be depreciated in future years, like any other asset. But the additional charge will be relatively small, so this manoeuvre will also improve return on capital, at least in the early years of such a practice.

Capitalising interest on properties, which are then classified as 'investment properties', is even more effective. For investment properties are never depreciated. Capitalising interest on stocks of slow incubation products, such as whisky (see page 152) is also common. Capitalising interest on projects during construction is regarded as legitimate, but different companies adopt different practices. This complicates inter-company comparisons. Capitalising interest in the early years of trading after a project is complete is harder to justify.

Other items of expenditure which are sometimes capitalised are development expenditure (allowable only where the project is identified and the company is reasonably certain it can earn the money back) and start-up costs on a new venture. There have even been cases of companies capitalising marketing expenditure, maintenance costs and wages – not at all acceptable. All capitalised expenditure should be scrutinised very closely. Check the **accounting policies** and the **footnotes**.

● **Deferred taxation: beware time-bomb!** Some companies pay tax at well below the standard corporation tax rate because of generous capital allowances. Not all make compensatory provision for the abnormally high rate they may have to pay in future years. This boosts their current earnings in comparison with those of their more prudent competitors and may be a prelude to high tax and low earnings in future.*

---

* The existing accounting standard perversely restricts companies to providing only for tax likely to become payable.

Capital allowances are granted by the Inland Revenue to companies which purchase certain types of asset. They allow the company to offset the cost of the asset against profits over subsequent years. For example, if a company buys some new machinery for £4m, it can knock £1m off its profits before they are assessed for tax in the first year, £750,000 in the second year, £563,000 in the third year and so on. These allowances are a real benefit, which have a real effect on the amount of tax the company pays, and hence on the company's cash flow.

There is no direct connection between the size of a company's capital allowances and its depreciation charge. Company accounts state pre-tax profits after the depreciation charge. But tax is levied on profits after the capital allowances. So there is often a mismatch between the pre-tax profit stated in the accounts and the size of the tax charge which follows it.

Broadly speaking, capital allowances tend to be largest in the early years of an asset's life, because they are intended to encourage capital spending. So, if a company is spending heavily, its actual tax charge, based on the profits after capital allowances, may well be very small in relation to its stated pre-tax profits. For its taxable profits will be lower than stated pre-tax profits after depreciation, particularly if it uses a straight line method of depreciation. If in later years the company stops spending but continues depreciating its existing assets, its taxable profits may well be higher than its pre-tax profits after depreciation. Its tax charge will then appear high in relation to stated pre-tax profits. In the early years, earnings will benefit; in the later years, earnings will be squeezed.

The discrepancies between annual depreciation and capital allowances on the same asset are known as 'timing differences'. Companies are required to make some provision for timing differences in their accounts, because otherwise they might find themselves with an abnormally high tax charge in future years. Part of the total tax charge stated in the p&l is often described as 'deferred tax'. This tax is not paid out to the revenue, but transferred to the balance sheet where it forms a provision against future tax liabilities.

Full provision for deferred tax means that a company each year sets aside a sum equal to the difference between the corporation tax actually payable on taxable profits and the tax that would have been payable if the capital allowances had equalled the depreciation shown in the accounts. The actual and notional tax bills cross over at some stage in the asset's life. And the deferred tax accumulated in the early years is then available to pay the additional tax levied in the later years.

Conservative accountants and investment analysts would prefer full provision for deferred tax because it diminishes the chance of unpleasant shocks to come. But many companies make only partial provision, on the grounds that continued heavy capital spending means that the day of reckoning will never actually come. Current accounting rules require companies to provide only for deferred tax which they expect to become payable, although they have to note the total amount of deferred tax not provided for each year.*

Check the **notes to the tax charge** in the p&l and **notes to the provisions for liabilities and charges** in the balance sheet.

● **Pension costs.** A company whose pension scheme has a surplus can use this to reduce its costs and increase its profits for several years.

When the actuaries discover that a company has more money in a defined benefit (usually final salary) scheme than they reckon the scheme needs to meet its liabilities, they say it has a surplus. This surplus is often used both to improve benefits and to reduce the cost of funding the pension scheme. Amortising the surplus can allow the company to reduce its own annual contribution to the fund from the p&l for several years. Very large pension surpluses

---

* The description 'deferred tax' is a slight misnomer. Corporation tax is not deferred by capital allowances in the sense that the liability exists but payment is deferred; it is relieved. No liability exists in the year of the allowance, and a liability will only come to exist in future years if capital expenditure is reduced and taxable profits are earned. That future liability will not necessarily match the sums in the deferred tax kitty.

have been known to transform a pension charge in the p&l into a pension credit.

This is a complex and very sensitive topic. The size of the estimated surplus depends on a number of judgements about the future. Small changes in the actuaries' assumptions, about factors such as employment levels, wage growth or dividend growth, can have a huge effect on the size of the surplus and hence on profits. This means that investors comparing two apparently similar companies, which use different methods and assumptions in their pension fund valuations, are not really comparing like with like. But the accounts do not always allow even the informed reader to understand what is going on. The ASB is expected to have another go at this one. It plans to reduce the actuaries' options and improve disclosure.

Check the **footnotes** for details of **pension commitments**.
● **Currency mismatching.** One old trick, employed by Polly Peck, was to borrow money in a hard currency with low interest rates and deposit the proceeds in a soft currency with high interest rates. Net investment income

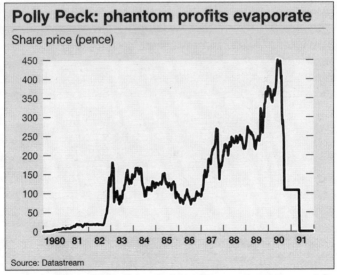

Fig 6.3 In 1988 Polly Peck took forex losses of £170m straight to reserves. It had borrowed in strong currencies with low interest rates and deposited the money in weak currencies with high rates.

soared and was credited to the p&l. The capital loss was taken straight to reserves, together with the increased sterling value of the hard currency borrowings. Nowadays most companies do take their currency losses through the p&l.

Check the new **statement of recognised gains and losses** which should include any currency translation differences. And check the **implied interest rate** for unusually high returns on deposits.

How to massage the balance sheet

Companies normally devote most attention to improving the appearance of the profit and loss account – since that is what investors usually pay most attention to. But there are a number of accounting techniques which can make the balance sheet look better than it is. Normally the objective is to reduce the apparent level of borrowings, because investors and bankers alike get worried when gearing is too high. The simplest reduce the level of debt just before the balance sheet is drawn up. Some try to remove a liability from the balance sheet altogether or distance it from the company by pushing the debt onto an associate.

Off balance sheet finance is the catch-all phrase used to describe ways companies used to borrow money without showing the debts on the balance sheet. They included leasing and running bits of the business through companies which were not consolidated with the main business in the accounts. Most of these dodges have now been stopped, and the additional finance has come on-balance sheet again. But details of the liabilities involved in leases and associated companies may still be confined to footnotes. They may either add to the company's liabilities or undermine the apparent solidity of its assets.

● **Cash management: now you see it ...** At the end of the year many companies pay bills slowly but demand rapid settlement from their debtors. This produces a very temporary reduction in their borrowings and an improvement in cash flow. It is particularly easy for companies with unusual year ends, or ones which differ from those of their suppliers. (Otherwise only big companies can get away with such a blatantly unfair practice on a regular basis.)

Check the **implied interest rate**. The best way to spot cosmetic cash management – and several other ways of reducing either the size or the cost of borrowing – is to check whether the interest paid seems to tally with the year end borrowings figure. If gross interest paid as a percentage of year-end borrowing looks higher than you would expect, year-end borrowing was probably untypically low. If the interest paid looks unusually low, that is also worth following up. It could mean some of the interest is being capitalised to the benefit of the p&l, or that the company has taken on a currency risk by borrowing in foreign currencies with lower interest rates than sterling.

● **Stock manipulation.** Cutting stock levels to the bone just before the year end will temporarily reduce the need for borrowings. The company may have chosen to draw up its accounts at an unusually favourable time of the year – for example, a cracker company which closes its books at the end of December. But not all companies can play this game, because it may hamper trading. And no company can use stock manipulation to improve both its profits and its balance sheet at the same time. Again, check the **implied interest rate** and compare its **stockturn** with its competitors'.

● **Debt posing as equity.** The game here is to borrow money through securities that have some claim to be classified as equity. This improves the gearing ratios by simultaneously reducing borrowings and increasing shareholders' funds. But new accounting rules have removed the benefit of this ploy, by insisting that such securities should be classified as debt.

Auction market preferred shares (AMPs) and convertible bonds of various types used in some circumstances to be classified as equity but (under FRS 4) are now debt. The litmus test on such convertibles is whether there is a genuine uncertainty whether the securities will be converted. If, for example, they allow investors to redeem early at a premium or have a steadily rising interest rate, investors may choose not to convert their securities into shares. So they are classified as debt.*

Some analysts ruthlessly treat all convertibles as debt in all circumstances, on the grounds that the only time the investor needs to pay attention to balance sheet gearing is when finances are stretched. And in those circumstances conversion would not be likely. Keep your umbrella waterproofed even when the sun is shining.

If securities can be redeemed at a premium, this premium has to be charged to the p&l as additional interest, spread over the life of the bonds. The additional notional interest charge is then transferred to the balance sheet each year to form a redemption reserve. The same procedure is followed for zero coupon bonds, where all the interest is rolled up until redemption. This rule, intended to ensure that future liabilities are adequately reflected in the balance sheet means that the p&l suffers from a notional charge which is not reflected in the cash flow statement.

Off balance sheet finance

The accountancy regulators have imitated the Inland Revenue in their efforts to find an effective way of stopping companies from pushing their borrowings off balance sheet. They have introduced the principle that it is the **substance of a transaction not its legal form** which should be reflected in the accounts.

This principle, embodied in FRS5, replaces rules with principles. This ought to mean that it is much harder to keep debt off the balance sheet. But principles have to rely on the judgement of the individuals applying them. Some

---

* Traditional convertible loan stocks continue to be classified as debt, even if the chances of their being converted are high. Convertible preference shares count as 'non-equity shareholders' funds', and have become the more popular alternative for companies for that reason. But if the company is doing so badly that conversion is unlikely, a cautious investor should probably treat them as debt, whatever the accounting rules say. Conversely, high gearing produced by a loan stock which is likely to be converted in the near future is not a threat.

individuals' judgement appears unduly swayed by the preference for an uncluttered balance sheet. It is then up to auditors and the Financial Reporting Review Panel, a quasi policeman, to keep companies from straying too far. But the Review Panel only looks at accounts which are drawn to its attention, and accounts of smaller companies in particular may not get extensive independent scrutiny.

Champions of FRS5 point out that the easiest way to keep debt off the balance sheet remains by the use of associates. These come under a different standard, which is due for an overhaul.

In theory, several of the following dodges are just history.

● **Leases.** These come in two varieties: finance leases, which are effectively a way of buying an asset instead of borrowing to finance the purchase; and operating leases, which are a far less onerous short term rental agreement. Until 1984 neither of these had to be mentioned in the balance sheet, although the interest charges were included in the p&l. But under **SSAP 21** finance leases do have to be included, operating leases do not.

A finance lease is defined as one where substantially all the risks and rewards of ownership pass to the company which is leasing the asset. The accounting rule's gloss on this suggests as a guideline one where the present (discounted) value of the minimum future lease payments required by the contract amounts to 90 per cent or more of the fair value of the asset. Companies leasing assets under finance leases have to include both the asset and the matching liability (the discounted value of minimum future lease payments) in the balance sheet. The annual lease payment is split into two elements: an interest element, which is charged to the p&l, and a capital repayment element which reduces the liability on the balance sheet. It works like a repayment mortgage.

The asset is depreciated (on whatever the company's normal policy for such assets is) over the shorter of the lease term or its expected future life, like any other. So finance leases do impair the appearance of both the balance sheet, by increasing borrowings, and profits – at least in the early life of the lease, since most of the lease payments in those years are treated as interest. (Again just like a repayment mortgage.) However, some companies have managed to twist the guidelines in such a way as to avoid their leases being classified as finance leases. By ensuring that the present value of the minimum lease payments is slightly less than 90 per cent of the fair value of the asset, they get leases classified as operating leases. The accountants are expected to have a second bite at this cherry.

● **Consignment stock.** Essentially this is a way for certain types of company to get their trading stock financed by their supplier without the debt appearing in the balance sheet. For example, if a car manufacturer supplies cars to a dealer, it may agree that the dealer only pays for them when it sells them. Normally the dealer would pay the manufacturer a deposit, which it might have to finance through borrowing. Instead the manufacturer agrees to accept a monthly fee from the dealer in lieu of the deposit. Effectively the dealer is paying interest on a loan to finance the standard deposit. But no loan appears in its balance sheet. (This practice and the two immediately below should have been affected by the introduction of FRS5.)

● **Stock finance.** A company whose products have a long incubation period, such as a wine or whisky manufacturer, gets a finance company to buy its immature stocks. But it retains the right, or may have an obligation to buy its stocks back when they are ready to sell. Neither the stock nor the effective loan appear in the balance sheet. The repurchase price is so pitched that the finance house gets what is effectively a rolled up interest charge when the company buys back its mature stock, and the wine or whisky never leave the company's vaults. This one is particularly dangerous in times of glut. Again the transaction should now be obvious.

● **Assignment contracts and performance bonds.** These are tailored for construction companies burdened by very long term contracts and patchy progress payments. The construction company effectively sells the future payments it is due to receive to a finance house and gives it a guarantee to finish the job. In return it receives a series of cash advances on which the finance house charges interest.

But the cash advances used not to count as a loan and were not mentioned in the balance sheet. This should have changed under the new rules.

● **Factoring.** This is a tried and tested way for a company to avoid the problems of debt collection, but the options vary. Sometimes the factor buys the debts and collects them itself, sometimes they remain the ultimate liability of the company. In the latter case both the debts and the loan from the factor should appear in the balance sheet.

● **Sale and repurchase.** This is a development of the familiar sale and leaseback arrangement which works a bit like the finance of whisky stocks. The company selling the assets, usually development land, has an option to repurchase it and develop it. Such deals sometimes involve a third party. But again the new rules mean that if the real ownership has not changed, the transaction should count as a loan and be put on the balance sheet. Giveaway signs are that the original owner has the right both to develop and to repurchase; that it continues to bear the risk of changes in the value of the asset; and that the nominal buyer receives what is effectively a market rate of interest.

● **Covert subsidiaries.** Companies have to include the borrowings of their subsidiaries on their own balance sheets. Hence the longstanding fashion for pushing borrowings into companies which were not classified as subsidiaries. This reduced borrowings at a stroke.

The new accounting rules together with the 1989 Companies Act substantially widen the definition of subsidiary. Nowadays voting control, control of strategy and participation in the risks and rewards of the junior company are all assessed in deciding whether it should be counted as a subsidiary.

There is still considerable scope for companies to push debt into associated companies or joint ventures, whose debt is not included in the balance sheet. However, if the parent company has guaranteed the debt of an associate, this should be mentioned in a footnote or under contingent liabilities. But such notes are often less than clear. A new exposure draft (FRED 11) will improve disclosures on associates when implemented.

How to burnish cash flow

Sadly cash flow's reputation as a sea-green incorruptible is not totally justified. In the short term a combination of delaying payments to creditors, shortening the credit given to customers, and running down stocks in the last month of the year can put a fine shine on the cash flow statement. Running stocks down too far can be a dangerous game. And successful manipulation of debtors and creditors in one year merely creates problems for the next year. However, to a company in trouble, a year is a long time.

How the pros tackle creative accounting

Spotting creative accounting techniques at work is the investment analyst's bread and butter. Analysts and their institutional clients are sometimes accused of failing to spot big company failures, such as British and Commonwealth and Polly Peck, in time. But one leading analyst argues that the only investors left in Polly Peck when it went down were index funds (who had no choice since it was a Footsie member) and private investors who did not understand what was happening.

Terry Smith was head of UK Company Research at UBS Phillips & Drew before he published *Accounting for Growth*, a guide to creative accounting. In it he listed six survival rules:–

- Read the accounts backwards. Don't expect the chairman's statement to point out that he's cooking the books. Read the footnotes.
- Read the accounting policies – and compare. Any change in accounting policies will have an effect on profits. And check current policies against earlier ones.
- Screen the accounts with filters. Use checks such as the implied interest rate or the tax charge as a way of highlighting anomalies.
- Watch out for transfers between the p&l and balance sheet. A quick way of checking whether reserves are being milked to prop up profits is to check whether the

net asset value (NAV) per share has risen in line with profits. (Most companies publish a five or ten year record which may well include NAV.)
- Cash is king. Profits are someone's opinion; cash is a fact.
- If in doubt, don't invest.

Can the amateur spot creative accounting?

No company is likely to use all the techniques mentioned here. And some techniques are relatively straightforward. Most intelligent laymen ought to be able to notice an unusual rise in stocks. Many will be able to work out the effect on depreciation and profits of a property write down. Fewer will feel comfortable with the intricacies of finance leases or interest rate swaps.

A major problem in identifying creativity is that, although most methods have knock-on effects which can be spotted, perfectly valid causes can have the same effect. For example, a rise in stock levels can mean that a company is deliberately postponing the day of reckoning by manufacturing for stock. But it could also represent a genuine gearing up to supply a growing market or follow through a successful marketing initiative. As always, the figures alone do not tell the full story; they need intelligent interpretation.

One of the most important lessons the layman can learn about accounts is that there is almost no figure that can be relied upon to be absolutely correct – all are affected by accounting policies or subjective judgements. There is a huge gulf between accounts and your bank statement. However, different figures have different degrees of flexibility. The range of acceptable values for sales, for example, is much smaller than for profits and earnings.

At the least, understanding a bit about accounting techniques enables the layman to get more out of newspaper comments. At best, if he sees a share price plunging for no obvious reason, he may be able to puzzle out where the problem is. One of the secrets of investment success is to avoid losers. The sign 'creative accountants at work' is normally a red light. Private investors have the great advantage that they do not need to invest in any company they do not understand. There are over 2,000 UK companies traded on the London stockmarket. Stick to the ones that don't use cosmetics.

Creative Accounting

IN A NUTSHELL

1. Many companies use cosmetic accounting to improve the appearance of the p&l account, because investors place so much weight on earnings. Those with weak balance sheets sometimes try to massage them into an appearance of greater strength. No company can prop up both at once for long.

2. The treatment of items in the balance sheet can be used to increase stated profits. And charges against profits can sometimes be transformed into assets on the balance sheet.

3. One of the easiest ways of increasing profits is by reducing the cost of sales. Choosing favourable stock valuation policies and manufacturing for stock are typical ploys.

4. Interest costs associated with capital developments can be capitalised: not charged against profits but added to the value of the asset in the balance sheet. This is legitimate, but can be taken to excess. It also makes inter-company comparisons difficult.

5. Companies which defer tax because of capital allowances are required only to provide for tax they expect to pay. Some companies' expectations are more carefree than others. A less conservative accounting policy will flatter profits in the short term.

6. Companies with surpluses on defined benefit pension schemes often benefit while the surplus lasts. Most take the opportunity to enjoy a total or partial pension holiday. This is legitimate enough. But some fail to distinguish clearly between ongoing profits and pension profits which are of lower quality because they will cease.

7. Cash and currency management can produce artificial investment income, which flatters profits, while the balance sheet bears the cost.

8. Companies worried about high gearing sometimes try to issue securities which count as equity even though they have many of the qualities of debt. This practice has been made more difficult.

9. Off balance sheet finance is the catch-all name for techniques which push some of a company's debt out of sight. It includes stock finance, factoring, sale and repurchase of property and the creation of covert subsidiaries. New accounting rules make it harder, but there are still ways round the rules.

Chapter 7
Stockmarket Tools

No single measure sums up the performance of a company. No single investment yardstick tells the investor whether its shares are worth buying. And whether a share is worth buying depends on his investment objectives and strategy. But provided the investor knows what he is looking for, investment yardsticks can help him choose among the 2,000 UK shares traded on the London stockmarket.

Companies can be categorised in several different ways: by size, by sector, by operating success, by the solidity of their financial structure, by the amount they spend on research, by the amount of money they have got in the bank or by the dynamism of their management. Investment analysts have yardsticks to measure all these things – except the management, which they often misjudge.

Some of these tools are the operating and financial ratios discussed in Chapter 5. But many are price-relative yardsticks. How much annual dividend can you buy for £1? How much earnings or how much cash flow? More sophisticated ones take account of earnings growth and make adjustments for risk. Another set of tools measures marketability – the ease and cost of buying and selling the shares.

All the yardsticks are relative: they can be used to measure one company against another. For the good reason that they were devised by investment analysts whose job is to measure one company against another. Analysts' clients are all professional investors running large portfolios of shares. These clients want views on which shares are worth buying or selling relative to the rest.

Most actual share selection is a compromise. Fund managers running income portfolios are looking for shares with at least a minumum yield but also capable of producing some capital growth. Those running a high performance fund are looking for short term growth without excessive risk. Recovery fund managers need to distinguish between high-yielding shares on the way back and those hesitating before the final plunge. Value investors, a rare breed in the UK, are looking for shares which are fundamentally under-priced but have some realistic chance of being revalued upwards.

So, although all managers normally apply several differ-ent screens in making their selections, their screens and their priorities vary according to their objectives and their idiosyncrasies. Each yardstick provides a different screen. Investors can approach these screens from two directions. Start with the company, and then see whether it gets past the screens. Or start with the screens and use them to produce a shortlist for further consideration.

A large number of successful growth investors start with the company. Peter Lynch, for instance, started with his wife's 'recommendation' of a firm selling tights called L'eggs in supermarkets, checked out the company making them, and made a lot of money out of the shares. And, as in staff selection, there is always a worry that initial screening will eliminate the unconventional superstar in the making.

Some value investors rely heavily on screens. Benjamin Graham's selection processes for bargain shares involve using several screens in conjunction to search out cheap shares, and then buying every share which qualifies. Using screens can also be a good way for the novice investor to find some investment ideas – provided he then treats them as simply the first step in the selection process.

Screening is also an essential part of monitoring a portfo-lio. All private investors need periodically to check their own performance. It is a necessary part of housekeeping exercises, such as bed and breakfasting shares to make the most of the annual capital gains tax allowance. This provides a good opportunity to re-evaluate shares already in the portfolio. Have they performed as expected? And do they still look relatively good value? These routine checks should sharpen the investor's stockpicking skills.

Active investors will probably want to re-screen their portfolios at regular intervals. Even buy-and-hold investors can use an annual MOT as an opportunity to cull holdings that no longer pass the screens. And since individual investors' objectives change as they grow older, their criteria are also likely to change. Someone five years off retirement may well want to apply a more cautious set of screens to the successful growth portfolio he bought when he was younger.

Screening is not always appropriate. The first recorded index fund screened out the riskiest shares in the index – which subsequently turned in the best performance. It can also be dangerous to attempt to cherry pick from a selection produced by scientific screening, particularly when buying high yielders, or any other class of high risk/high return shares. For arbitrary selection can miss the very shares that (with hindsight) gave the group their appeal in the first place. The *Investors Chronicle* high yield system, for instance, insists that it offers a take-it-or-leave it package, not a high yield buffet.

One general caveat about all investment yardsticks is that they are not carved in stone. The norms for even basic measures, such as PE ratios and yields, have changed substantially over time, and vary from one market to another. And different yardsticks work better at some times than others. The good gardener studies the state of the soil before going to his tool-shed.

What's in the tool-shed?

Many gardeners get by with a spade, a fork and a pair of shears. That is roughly what you are getting when you turn to the share price pages of the *Financial Times*: some rough but workmanlike tools which will give you a quick fix on a wide variety of shares.

On most days these consist of: share price, high/low, market capitalisation, gross dividend yield and PE ratio. All the shares are grouped in sectors.

Both the dividend yield and the price earnings ratio remain central to investment, though they are regarded as relatively primitive by professional analysts. The share price high and low provide an instant share price history, which can still be useful to investors without ready access to price charts. And the market capitalisation can be used both to calculate some investment yardsticks and as a tool

in its own right. Income, earnings, the share price history
and size: they are a good place to start. But first, the sectors.

Birds of a feather

The FT periodically infuriates its loyal readers by changing
the way in which it groups the shares in its share price
pages. There is a reason for the changes. The sector
groupings are devised by the FT-SE actuaries industry
classification committee to make it easier for investors to
compare similar companies. But the shape of British industry as a whole is constantly changing, and so is that of
individual companies. The sector groupings need to change
with them.

Twenty years ago the actuaries indices included rubber
and tea plantations, copper, gold and tin mining, discount
houses, shipping, toys, and machine tools. They did not
include distributors, electricity, gas, healthcare, media,
support services, telecommunications or water, all part of
the modern line-up. Grand Metropolitan used to come
under entertainment and catering; now it comes under
alcoholic beverages. Dalgety used to be an overseas trader;
now it is a food producer. Each sector has its own index,
with the shares in it weighted according to their market
capitalisation. And the All-Share index includes all the
shares in the sectors, again on a weighted basis.

Investors use sector ratings as a rough benchmark for
those of individual shares within the sector. The separate
FT table of FT-SE Actuaries All-Share indices lists the
dividend yield, net cover, PE ratio and the total return in the
year to date for every sector. (See table page 260 for a
truncated version.) Investors also often look at a share price
trend relative to the rest of the sector, rather than the rest of
the market.

This is partly because many fund managers divide the
money in their portfolios by sectors. A neutral portfolio will
be weighted to match that of the FT-SE 100 or FT-SE-A All
Share indices. If a manager is worried about a particular
share but happy with the sector as a whole, he may reduce

his holding in the company concerned but raise his weighting in other companies in the sector to compensate. If, however, the manager particularly favours electricity shares and dislikes construction, he will increase the proportion in electricity and decrease that in construction. If a particular sector is generally in favour with institutional investors, all the shares in it may benefit.

Sector rotation is the jargon name for the fact that different sectors come in and out of fashion, often at different stages of the economic and stockmarket cycle. Such re-ratings often last for several months and offer short term trading opportunities. Charts are useful for pin-pointing when a sector has begun to show relative strength and when that strength is in danger of petering out.

But even the actuaries' careful groupings are necessarily imperfect and incomplete. Insurance companies and clearing banks are rare examples of groups of companies which are virtually interchangeable as far as their customers are concerned. But many companies' activities do not fit neatly into a single sector, and there are often wide differences between companies in the same sector. A conscientious analyst evaluates each company's prospects individually and rates it accordingly.

Companies can be too large, too different or too small for sector comparisons to be relevant. British Gas dominates the gas distribution sector. So comparing British Gas with the sector is meaningless: their ratings will always be virtually identical.*

What's more, many of the companies included under sector headings in the FT prices page are not included in the actuaries classification system. This covers only those companies included in the All-Share index – 900 in mid 1996.

---

* The UK market as a whole is reasonably well diversified between different sectors. But investors considering other markets should be aware that in some cases a particular sector can dominate a market index in the same way that British Gas dominates the gas sector in the UK. In Mexico and New Zealand, for example, the telecoms sector represents 25 per cent of the index. In Spain utilities and financials dominate the index, which is accordingly abnormally sensitive to interest rate changes. Indexed funds are a bit of a misnomer in such markets.

Other companies which pay the FT to be included in its prices page are simply put under the most appropriate sector heading. But often they have very different characteristics.

Take food retailing, where the actuaries index includes 15 companies, but the FT lists 24. Supermarketeer Sainsbury sits just below Regina, which sells Royal Jelly products world-wide. But their differences are as obvious as their similarities. If supermarkets as a business are out of favour, Sainsbury and Tesco shares will both fall, though not necessarily at the same rate. But Regina's share price may well move in a different direction. The factors which affect its business are not the same. But the rating of Regina's shares will also be influenced by the fact that it is one of the smallest companies on the market.

Size does matter

The market capitalisation of a company (the market value of all its ordinary shares at the current share price) is important for several reasons. Fund managers and analysts pay most attention to shares which are members of the top 350 club: The FT-SE 100 index and the Mid 250. These are the shares which most managers buy and sell if they want to change their weightings. When analysts' circulars recommend switching, they mean switching between different members of the 350 club that fall within a particular sector.*

But although most professional investors concentrate on large companies, this does not mean that they are always

* Irritatingly the FT prices pages do not make it clear which shares belong to the Footsie or other market indices. But the market caps given there are of some help. The border between the bottom of the 100 index and the top of the Mid-250 comes at a market cap of around £1.5bn when the FT-SE 100 is in the 3,500 region. The border between the bottom of the Mid-250 and the top of the SmallCap comes at around £200m. Another check is the FT's table giving trading volume for around 170 major stocks. Any company in that list is pretty certain to belong to the 350 club, and it flags Footsie members.

more highly rated. Fashions change. But buying shares in a particular index because that index appears to be doing well can be dangerously simplistic. If the mid-250 is doing well because domestic companies are in favour, a mid-250 member with an overseas bias may not join the fun.*

One size-related trading manoeuvre which sometimes works is buying shares likely to be promoted to a higher index or selling those likely to be demoted. Index-tracking funds have to buy shares in companies in the index they track, and many other funds are closet trackers. Fund managers with some discretion over their purchases often buy before the move takes place; some trackers have to buy after the move has taken place.† This is normally a short term play, suitable only for active investors with low dealing costs. But sometimes, as when venture capital group 3i came to the market in mid-1994, a short term play can add zest to a long term investment.

Size can also affect both the ease and the cost of dealing in shares. The points to check here are the number of market makers, the normal market size and the spread or touch. The largest companies have the largest number of market makers dealing in their shares. Any companies with fewer than three market makers may be difficult to deal in. Each share also has a 'normal market size' (NMS) of between 500 and 200,000 shares traded in a single transaction, based on the average size of deals made over the previous 12 months. The smaller the NMS, the harder the shares are to deal in.

Private investors who are buying or selling small quantities of shares will usually be able to deal in any share. But the price may be disadvantageous because of the wide gap between buying and selling prices. The 'spread' is the gap between one market maker's buying and selling prices; the 'touch' the gap between the best buying price and the best

* Since investors tend to be undiscriminating when a fashion takes hold, the share may well benefit initially, but come down to earth with a bump when earnings disappoint.
† There was a pleasing incident in 1995 when several tracker funds were constrained to buy shares in an exceedingly illiquid investment trust called Dumyat, simply because it was an index constituent. The shares shot up, although there was hardly any dealing, before the actuaries expelled it from the index.

selling price for a share. The touch will often be less than
0.5 per cent on a FT-SE 100 share, but 15 per cent or more
on rarely-traded shares. This means that the shares have to
rise further before the investor shows a real profit: which is
why anyone interested in investing in very small companies
should only do so for the long term.

The small company effect

One reason so many successful investors prefer small
companies is that on average over the long term small
companies have done better than large ones. This has been
termed **the small company effect**. But the generalisation
needs to be treated with extreme care. There have always
been several periods in which small companies have done
worse than large ones. It is no longer at all clear that the
generalisation remains valid even in what used to be the
good times. And even when small companies have done
well, the good overall performance is influenced by the
stellar performance of a minority of high growth companies.

When the UK economy performs badly, smaller companies often do worse, because they are more likely to have
predominantly UK operations, they are often in businesses
which get squeezed hardest and they often have weaker
finances and less sympathetic bank managers. So their
shares will often be rated lower than the giants'. Come the
recovery, they bounce back further.

That is the truism, but it does not always work in practice.
The relative underperformance of small companies' shares
in the early 1970s and 1990s seemed to tie in reasonably
well with the rule. And in 1993 and 1994 the shares began
what fans hoped would be the start of a steady period of
above average performance, only to collapse again in 1995.

In 1995 the Hoare Govett Smaller Companies Index rose
by only 10.5 per cent compared with 20 per cent for the
Footsie. And in the first half of the 1990s it returned an
average 7.7 per cent compared with 12 per cent for the All-
Share index. As the London Business School, which
devised the Smaller Companies index, rather sadly put it:

the small company effect is still there but it has turned from positive to negative. (See Fig 7.1.)

Several reasons have been suggested for the change. As Benjamin Graham pointed out, market anomalies tend to be dissipated once they are widely accepted. Small companies became extremely popular in the 1980s before the 1987 Crash; and by the mid 1990s their ratings were again higher than those of larger companies. The mid-1990s takeover boom generally involved large companies, whereas in earlier booms small companies had often been scooped up at high prices. The fashion for small companies encouraged a large number of new issues, many of fairly unattractive businesses. International investors, who increasingly call the tune in London, are not interested in small companies. But even if they had been, the UK industries which made most of the running in the early 1990s, such as drugs and financial services, consisted predominantly of large companies, while a high proportion of small companies were in sectors such as construction and textiles which failed to participate in the recovery.

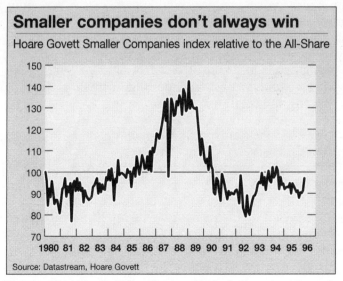

Fig 7.1 Like Yuppies small companies were in fashion during the 1980s economic boom, but fell out of favour during the recession. Even when small company shares are doing well, performance varies enormously.

But small companies may still have shorter term attractions. Some research by Capel-Cure Myers Capital Management discusses timing. CCM argues that the best period for smaller company performance is the middle and later stages of economic expansions and pin-points several factors which affect their relative earnings growth. They are more sensitive to economic upturns and downturns; more vulnerable to rising interest rates; suffer more when the longer leading economic indicator turns down; thrive in times of high inflation; and benefit relatively little from a fall in sterling.

There is a varying time lag before these factors affect the companies' share prices – from 3 months for leading indicators to 21 months for inflation. Overall the research concludes that the best time to invest in small companies is when growth is accelerating and the lead indicator and inflation rate are rising. For, although interest rates will also be rising, they will be outweighed by the beneficial factors.

The view from investment bank BZW is that it is simplistic to talk about the effect of the economic recovery on small companies: what matters is which bit of the economy is recovering. Small companies respond better to a pick-up in corporate capital spending than when the economic recovery is geared to consumer spending. So, since corporate spending tends to rise relatively late in the economic cycle, that is the time to consider investing in smaller companies. The reason the small company effect was in abeyance right up to the end of 1995 was that corporate spending was low or negative during this period. Smaller company shares are autumn crocuses not spring flowers.

Of course, the moment commentators started writing obits for the mighty minnows, shares in small companies started beating the broader market again. In early 1996 they did well. So the jury remains out on whether the small company effect has indeed turned negative. But even true believers should note that the performance of individual small companies varies enormously. Earlier London Business School research had shown both that the strong average performance of small companies stems largely from the very good performance of a minority of companies, and that the smallest companies do best of all. This suggests two possible strategies for small company investors. If you believe that the effect will turn positive again, hold a wide enough spread of very small company shares to participate in their overall strong performance. If you are sceptical about the effect in general, just select a handful of the right ones! Easy.

Dividends are dynamic

Dividend yield is sometimes seen as a very crude investment yardstick: suitable only for the novice used to building society deposit rates. What matters is the total return produced by dividends and capital growth. True enough. But unfortunately for the sophisticates dividend income is important. It makes a major contribution to the strong long term performance of equities compared with gilts and building societies. And shares with high yields often do better than ones with low yields over the medium term.

Studies in both the UK and the US have shown that reinvested dividend income accounts for a significant proportion of the total return on equities. This is partly because company dividends are steadily increased over time. So even if the initial yield on a share is comparatively low, it will rapidly catch up with the income on a fixed deposit and keep growing. Meanwhile the reinvested income generates both capital growth and income of its own. Mathematicians have long argued that compound interest is the eighth wonder of the world.

A more sophisticated way than yield to value shares, also based on the dividend, factors in the expected growth in dividends. It divides the dividend by the return the investor requires minus the expected growth in dividends.* A seemingly small increase or reduction in the expected

* Assume the company pays a gross dividend of 4p a share, dividends are expected to grow at 10 per cent a year and the investor needs a gross return of 12 per cent. The sum is:

4 divided by (0.12 − 0.10) = 200p.

But if growth expectations drop to only 7 per cent, the value of the shares drops to only 80p.

The sum now is 4 divided by (0.12 − 0.07) = 80p.

dividend growth rate can produce a large valuation change, particularly if the shares had originally derived most of their value from the expected growth in dividends.* That is why growth shares often fall very sharply after what looks like a minor set-back to prospects.

Investing in high yielders

Portfolios of high yielding shares often do better than portfolios of growth shares on a total return basis. High yielding shares are usually those of companies out of favour with the market, and the market always overdoes things. So portfolios of high yielding shares will normally include several poised to perform better than the market expects, which prompts a substantial recovery in the share price. These include cyclicals and turnarounds.

Several stockpicking theories are based on the superior performance of high yielders. (See Chapter 13 pages 310–14.) Benjamin Graham made dividend yield one of his latter day criteria for cheap shares. Fund manager M&G's best known fund concentrates on buying recovery shares. American weekly newspaper *Barron's* annual 'Dogs of the Dow' feature is based on portfolios of the ten highest yielders in the 30 share Dow Jones index. Michael O'Higgins has several stock selection methods based on high yield (see Chapter 13 page 312). The *Investors Chronicle* successfully ran portfolios based on its High Yield system for years.

But the High Yield theory raises several questions. Does it work equally well in all markets? How many shares does the investor need to have in a high yield portfolio? Does the investor need to apply any other screens apart from yield?

Common sense suggests that the best time to find high

---

* Repeat the earlier calculation for a sluggish company whose dividends were originally expected to grow at 4 per cent, with a subsequent revision to 2 per cent. The value attributed to the shares would move down from 50p to 40p, a far smaller percentage fall than in the earlier example, even though the percentage reduction in growth rate was higher.

yielding shares is when a recession is bottoming out but before the market has recognised this; the worst is when the market is so optimistic that the only shares with very high yields are undeniable basket cases. Prolonged bull markets can make it hard to find new shares which qualify.

In the early 1990s the *Investors Chronicle's* High Yield portfolios ceased to produce good results. Many income-oriented funds provided disappointing total returns. And several split-level investment trusts, which had relied on producing some capital growth out of portfolios designed to give an above average yield came unstuck. Most cut the dividends to their income shareholders, because they were afraid they would be unable to meet their capital obligations.

Most high yield investment systems involve a wide spread of shares. The *Investors Chronicle* system has 30. The argument for a spread is that although individual high yielding shares are usually riskier than the market average, the risk of a portfolio of such shares is reduced to near the market average. But the O'Higgins system offers different selection methods for investors with different risk tolerances. The riskiest involves buying a single share.

Such systems usually use one or more additional screens. The *Investors Chronicle* system rules out shares which are standing lower than they were a year ago, a test designed to filter out companies whose fortunes are still deteriorating. A similar screen might be achieved by saying that only companies whose charts show relative strength can be chosen.

Other statistical screens which complement yield are **dividend cover, cash flow per share, gearing** and **interest cover.**

Dividend cover is obvious. Most companies are only prepared to pay a short-earned dividend if they have plentiful reserves and are convinced that their problems are temporary. If cover is thin, the chances of a cut to come are higher – unless trading performance is patently on the mend.*

---

* Most calculations of dividend cover are done on a historic

But companies need cash to pay dividends. If the cash flow statement is weaker than the p&l, the company's dividend paying capacity may be less than dividend cover suggests. The first step is to check both the absolute level and the trend in **cash flow per share** against that of earnings. Then to see how the cash flow figure relates to the dividend and other future liabilities. If, for example, capital expenditure is running at a high level or is forecast to increase, it may absorb a high proportion of the cash flow. **Free cash flow** or Buffett's **owner earnings** (see page 204) provide a better check than simple cash flow.

Gearing, which tests the strength of the balance sheet, and **interest cover**, which shows how much of trading profit is absorbed by interest on borrowings are other ways to check the safety of the dividend behind a high yield.

Earnings need to grow

Earnings per share are the innocent victims of their own popularity. Intrinsically a perfectly sensible measure of company performance, they have been reviled on several counts:–

- Too much attention is paid to them by investors and investment analysts.
- This has meant that many companies manipulate their accounts to produce a smooth earnings record.
- The new FRS3 earnings figure, introduced to counter such creative accounting, is too volatile to be useful to analysts.
- The new IIMR earnings figure (see page 114), introduced to counter the last objection, is too rigid.
- The new normalised earnings figures, introduced as a compromise between FRS3 and IIMR earnings figures,

basis, even though forward projections are common for yield and earnings calculations. This caution is sensible enough. But anyone wanting to invest in a high yielder with thin cover could usefully calculate what the cover would be on his earnings projection.

which allow analysts to use their judgement, means that
there are altogether too many earnings figures around.

- Earnings figures are a very inefficient predictor of prices.
- The basic concept behind the PE ratio, the main investment yardstick which is based on earnings per share, is
  flawed. Why should there be any connection between a
  historic figure and a future price movement?

As this list shows, the argument has moved on in the last
few years. There are now two rival schools of analysts
championing different yardsticks in place of the PE ratio.
One says that provided the PE ratio is used in conjunction
with earnings growth, through the price earnings growth
factor (PEG), earnings remain a useful tool. The other insists
that discounted cash flow estimates are the only sensible
way to value companies. Meanwhile the PE ratio continues
to reign supreme in newspapers and statistical services.

The **PE ratio** itself gives a broad brush idea of what the
market is expecting from a share. A high one means it is
expecting above average earnings growth, a low one means
it is expecting below average growth. It does not guarantee
that the market is right in its expectations. It does not
explain the basis of those expectations: recovery or continuing growth, for instance. It does not even say how far out the
market is looking: one year, five years, ten years?

Nor does it give any indication of the market's assessment
of the outlook for the sector to which the share belongs. PE
ratios are best used in comparing shares within the same
sector. (See Fig 7.2 on page 174.) If a whole sector is
expected to do relatively badly over the next few years – for
example, housebuilders when interest rates are on the rise –
all PE ratios in that sector are likely to be low compared
with those of shares in other sectors.

A low PE ratio does not mean a share is cheap. What
matters is whether the rating is appropriate to the prospects.
Investors are looking for a company whose PE ratio is lower
than is justified by its prospects: an anomaly.

Even newspapers recognise that statistics based on historic performance are of limited value. The *Financial Times*
uses IIMR figures in its share price pages and ensures that

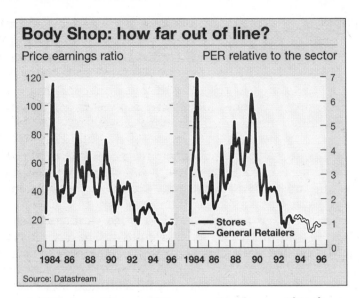

Fig 7.2 PE ratios are best used in comparing shares within the same sector. PE relative charts are a quick way of checking how a share's rating compares with that of its peers over a period.

the PE ratios incorporate interim figures into the calculations as soon as possible: they are a matter of record. But PE ratios mentioned in the comment will be based on stockbrokers' forecasts where possible.

One of the best solutions to the choice between the multiplicity of earnings figures available comes in a useful handbook called *Company Refs* (see page 355–56). It bases its prospective PE ratio on the rolling consensus estimate of normalised earnings for the next 12 months. The fact that it is a rolling estimate increases the validity of inter-company comparisons.

The **price earnings growth factor** (PEG) is former financier Jim Slater's contribution to analysis. (See Chapter 9 page 226.) It is calculated by dividing the prospective PE ratio by the estimated future growth rate in earnings per share. Both the earnings and the earnings growth figures usually relate to brokers' estimates for the next 12 months. Slater argues that PEGs, unlike PEs, are comparing like with like. A low PEG suggests that investors are paying relatively little for future growth; a high one suggests that they are paying a lot. The calculation takes account both of investors' expectations and of how the market is valuing those expectations. So it should highlight anomalies.

As a rule of thumb shares with PEGs of one or less are superficially attractive. This could mean a company with a PE ratio of 10 and growth of 13 or one with a PE ratio of 13 and growth of 16. What matters is that the rate of growth is high relative to the price investors are paying for it.

Slater, who designed the *Company Refs* system, has a number of caveats designed to protect PEGs against misuse.

- The PEG yardstick is only suitable for growth companies, preferably sustainable growth rather than a one-off spurt. To qualify a company must have at least four years of consecutive growth in earnings per share. This can be either a combination of historic and forecast growth or all historic if no forecast is available.
- A low PEG factor is not a sufficient reason to buy a share. Ideally the company should also have competitive advantage, strong cash flow, insignificant debt and a positive news flow.
- Share selections using PEGs based on very high PE ratios are risky, because even a modestly disappointing bit of news could prompt a sharp downwards reassessment of the shares. His favoured area is companies with PEs of 12–20.
- Growth is based on consensus forecasts from brokers. The larger the number of brokers and the closer the consensus, the more reliable the estimate.
- Beware of growth estimates assuming a subnormal tax charge will continue. It may not.

Cash is king

Cash flow yardsticks vary in sophistication. The simpler tool uses cash flow as a substitute for earnings, and calculates a Price Cash Flow (PCF) multiple in place of a Price Earnings ratio.

The more complicated one uses computer models to forecast cash flows for several years ahead, and then discounts them back to calculate a present value for the shares. It is also used as a management tool in deciding whether particular projects appear to be worthwhile.

The **Price Cash Flow ratio** is calculated either by dividing the share price by the cash flow per share or by dividing the market cap by the total cash flow, which is another way of looking at the same thing. It provides a handy check on the PE ratio: if the PE ratio is relatively low but the PCF is relatively high, it could be a sign that creative accountants have been at work, or that the company has been overtrading and will need to raise fresh capital.

Cash flow itself can be used to test whether the company looks able to meet its future liabilities. Compare it with the cost of dividends, planned capital expenditure, and the short term loan repayments. It is also the basis of forecasts of future cash flows. Many commentators argue that it would be useful if companies had to divide their capital expenditure into maintenance and expansion. The latter can be expected to produce additional revenue, and so increase future cash flow estimates, the former cannot. So outside analysts are always at a disadvantage to the company itself when estimating future flows, the start of **shareholder value analysis**.

Shareholder value is defined as the total return to the shareholder, including both income and capital growth. **Shareholder value analysis** or **discounted cash flow analysis** discounts future cash flows back at a rate appropriate to the risk inherent in the business and any expansion projects planned. Forecast revenues from a high risk business will be discounted back at a higher rate than those from stable businesses. This kind of analysis has both the advantages and the disadvantages of using forecasts rather than past performance as a starting point. It is forward-looking, but it may not see the future clearly.

Commonplace in the US, shareholder value analysis is still treated gingerly by many conventional UK analysts. It is probably unfortunate that when it has had publicity on the financial pages it has usually been in connection with some greenfield project with a long payback: Eurotunnel, Euro Disney and the cable companies. Some of these have caused shareholders much grief.

Some special yardsticks

Most of these ratios are only appropriate in particular types of industry or for companies in particular situations.

The **price to sales ratio** is a good way of spotting potential recovery shares. But the shares are only worth considering if there is a realistic prospect of profit margins improving soon. Some gearing will mean that even a small improvement in trading profits translates into a large increase in earnings. But excessive gearing could be the prelude to refinancing and dilution of earnings. An American fund manager called Jim O'Shaughnessy has used this ratio to pick bargain portfolios. His refined version picks stocks which have done outstandingly well recently as well.

The **price to research and development ratio** is only relevant in businesses such as drugs where expensive research is a necessity. It provides a comparative measure of how much different companies are spending, but cannot predict whether their expenditure will prove worthwhile.

Price to book value is one of the oldest yardsticks. And many cautious investors still like the idea of it, but it is getting increasingly hard in Western markets to find companies which perform well and also have good price to book ratios. Slater describes it as a primitive measure. Interestingly, it is one of the yardsticks that Jim Rogers, an American emerging markets pioneer, uses when deciding whether to buy shares in very new emerging markets. The right tool depends on the job.

How to work out the ratios*

- **Dividend yield:** gross dividend as a percentage of the share price.
- **Dividend cover:** at its simplest earnings per share divided by the net dividend per share – but the calculation is sometimes complicated by tax.
- **Price earnings ratio:** the share price divided by the

* Explanations of the main operating and financial ratios are given in Chapter 5 (pages 100 to 110.)

earnings per share, or projected earnings per share. (*Caveat*: some analysts use the term P/PER to denote PE ratios based on projected earnings; some, however, would take this term to refer to PE relatives based on projected earnings. Tricky thing, jargon.)

● **Price earnings growth factor:** the PE ratio divided by either the actual or the projected growth in earnings.

● **Price cash flow ratio:** share price divided by cash flow per share.

● **Net asset value (or book value) per share:** ordinary shareholders' funds (excluding intangible assets) divided by the number of shares in issue.

● **Price to sales ratio.** Share price divided by sales per share or market cap divided by total sales.

● **Price to R&D ratio.** Market cap divided by R&D expenditure.

● **Price to book value.** Share price divided by asset value or market cap divided by total net assets.

Enterprise Value for Beginners

Many investors may feel that is quite enough tools to be going on with. But investment analysts are great exponents of the art of selling the customer tools he didn't know he needed until he discovered he'd bought them.

Their latest gadget for sophisticates is **Enterprise Value** (EV). EV is the equity market capitalisation plus the market value of the net debt. (If the company has net cash instead of net debt, that cash is *subtracted* from the market cap.) It can be calculated either for the whole company or per share – just as the market cap is simply the collective version of the share price. Like the share price, EV is not itself a yardstick; it is the basis for a series of yardsticks. How much cash flow or sales can you buy for £1 of EV?

The justification given for introducing EV multiples is that share price-based yardsticks are not good at coping with companies with either net debt or net cash. The market tends to put companies with net cash on relatively high PE ratios, those with net debt on relatively low ones. Would it not be useful to have a yardstick which allowed investors to compare the trading operations of different companies without being influenced by their financial superstructures?

The EV evangelists aim to strip away distortions caused by the different ways companies finance their business. They argue that their multiples do measure the trading operations of a company, without regard to its capital structure. EV is what you would have to pay to buy the company in its entirety. Fans of EV tend to have little time for earnings. And EV-based ratios use various cash flow numbers or sales instead. (See Chapter 5 page 124 for a brief explanation of how to work out the Enterprise Value version of some common cash flow numbers.)

- **EV/EBITDA.** This compares EV with EBITDA – operating profit plus depreciation. The ratio will usually be very much lower than a PE ratio: a company with a PE ratio of 20 might well have an EV/EBITDA of only 10. It can be used in conjunction with growth forecasts. Broadly a company with a low EV/EBITDA number and high expectations for growth offers good value. But unfortunately most companies with low EV/EBITDA ratios have correspondingly low growth prospects. The introduction of new ratios does not necessarily mean the discovery of new investment bargains.
- **EV/Operating cash flow.** This one is similar but adjusts cash flow for increases (or decreases) in working capital and any spending against provisions.
- **EV/Post-tax earnings** (or cash earnings). This knocks all necessary expenditure off cash flow but leaves in discretionary ones including capital expenditure. Said to be a good tool for judging MBOs and acquisitions.
- **EV/Post Capex cash flow.** More cautious, but probably realistic given that most capital expenditure is undertaken simply to maintain the existing business.
- **EV/Sales.** A good yardstick for measuring companies in similar businesses even in different countries. Also a good way to highlight recovery stocks. And it has the great advantage that even non-accountants can work it out.

It is too early yet to say whether EV will catch on with British investors at large. Like most yardsticks it has its weaknesses. In particular, it makes perhaps too little of both cash and borrowings. High cash holdings can be a very comforting characteristic in a company, particularly when the economic cycle is mature. High borrowings have their appeal when the cycle is turning up. As its fans themselves point out, EV yardsticks are an addition to the toolshed, not a substitute for familiar favourites.

Portfolio yardsticks

Portfolio theorists apply other yardsticks to shares to measure whether they move in line with the overall stockmarket or any other chosen group of shares. The most common is the **beta**. Broadly, shares with a beta of more than one tend to exaggerate moves in the overall market; those with a beta of less than one are relatively inert.

Even beta theorists admit a couple of problems with their tool. First, do past betas foretell future betas? Tests have shown that they are not perfect predictors, but do give a rough idea of how stocks are likely to behave. Second, how long a period of price data provides the most valid beta calculation? Companies change. So although statisticians would prefer a longer series of data, most betas are based on a five year price history.

Betas are used to adjust the risk profile of portfolios. They are of limited relevance to the private investor, since he does not normally have enough shares in his portfolio to attempt to fine tune its risks. But the factors which create risk, high gearing, heavy fixed overheads and cyclical revenues are part and parcel of investment analysis.

Another yardstick professionals use is **standard deviation**, which measures the share's own volatility: how much it deviates from its own average. They also work out how different shares' movements correlate with each other – to find out whether they go up and down at the same time. By using these two statistics in conjunction they can produce a portfolio with a much lower overall risk than that of its constituents. (See Chapter 13 page 296 to 305)

Again, private investors are unlikely to use standard deviation as such. But when constructing a portfolio, it is worth considering whether you want all your shares to act in the same way at the same time. Where investors may well meet standard deviations is in the context of unit and investment trusts. Most fund measurement services now provide volatility ratings as an adjunct to total return figures, or in some cases provide risk-adjusted figures. For example, *Weekend Money* in the Saturday FT includes volatility figures for the funds included in its unit and investment trust statistics.

How accessible are these yardsticks to the amateur?

Some of these investment tools are readily available in most newspapers. Others are difficult to calculate. Some of the best sources are:–

- The *Financial Times* share price pages. Price, market cap, historic dividend yield and PE ratio for most companies Tuesday to Saturday.
- The *Investors Chronicle*'s company tables. A wider variety of statistics, including the normal market size, the number of market makers, the touch and earnings growth for a small number of companies each week rotating round the year.
- *Interpreting Company Reports and Accounts* by Holmes and Sugden will help you work the figures out from a set of accounts.
- *Company REFS* provides all the figures mentioned here (except Enterprise Value-based yardsticks) and more on a company by company basis and also screens companies by yardstick.

Appendix A on Information Sources gives more details.

Stockmarket Tools

IN A NUTSHELL

1. No single measure sums up the performance of a company. No single investment yardstick tells the investor whether its shares are worth buying. And whether a share is worth buying depends on investment objectives and strategy.

2. Investors use standard yardsticks, such as the PE ratio, dividend yield or gearing, to screen large numbers of shares looking for ones which fit their requirements needs. They can approach these screens from two directions. Start with the company, and then see whether it gets past the screens. Or start with the screens and use them to produce a short-list for further consideration.

3. Investors use sector ratings as a rough benchmark for ratings of individual shares within the sector. The separate FT table of FT-SE Actuaries All-Share indices lists the dividend yield, net cover, PE ratio and the total return in the year to date for every sector.

4. Size makes many practical differences to investors. Small companies are harder to buy and sell and normally have much wider dealing spreads than large companies. Most professional investors stick to the largest companies.

5. The small company effect – the theory that small companies do better than large ones – made them popular with investors in the 1980s. But the theory has not worked for most of the 1990s. The jury remains out.

6. Shares with above average dividend yields have often provided better total returns than growth

shares. But this depends on the markets. More sophisticated calculations use yield adjusted for expected growth to calculate the value of a share.

7. The PE ratio tells you what the market is expecting from a share, but does not tell you why or whether the market is right. The PEG factor takes account of expected growth.

8. The price/cash flow ratio can be a more reliable yardstick if the company is tampering with its earnings or has heavy capital expenditure.

9. Discounted cash flow is used in shareholder value analysis to work out what a share is worth. It is popular in the US, but has yet to gain widespread acceptance in the UK.

10. Measures used to assess companies in special circumstances or with particular business characteristics include price to sales, price to research and development and price to book value.

11. Yardsticks based on Enterprise Value are a new contender. It is too early to say whether the fashion will last.

12. Professional investors use yardsticks such as betas and standard deviation to determine the risk of their portfolios. They are not of much use to the private investor, because he does not have a big enough portfolio. But he should consider most of the factors that make shares risky as part of his normal research.

Section Three:
Investment Techniques

Chapter 8
Great Value Investors

Like most good investment ideas, Value Investment was
born in the US. It is normally contrasted with Growth
Investment. Value is worthy, growth is fun. Value looks for
shares which are underpriced, and often finds them
attached to rather boring businesses. Growth jumps upon
some amazing new trend, and swears that this one will hit
the sky. Growth is the hare; value the tortoise.

Unsurprisingly, many laymen find value investing dull.
They think of stockmarket investment as a dare-devil
activity akin to bungee jumping. Value investment is totally
lacking in swagger. It believes in having both belt and
braces. Its objective is to remove all risk from investment, so
that it becomes a simple business proposition, which either
adds up or does not. It is akin to what banking ought to be –
but so often is not.

Value investors find value investing fascinating. They
enjoy the mathematics underlying their stockpicking criteria, and are happy to continue testing hypotheses until they
find one which works. They like the fact that the successful
value investor has to banish emotion. And, like a true
scientist, if a cherished theory ceases to work, the value
investor discards it without a tear, and starts looking for one
that will work. Value investors believe in disciplines and
processes, not flair. They look on the frenetic follies of other
investors with mild amazement. How odd that the world at
large should be blind to the self-evident truths of value
investment.

The nub of their religion is that the stockmarket is not
perfectly efficient. Pockets of inefficiency do exist, and
these anomalies are the value investor's opportunity. He
buys shares selling for below their real value, and waits for
them to rise – as they inevitably will. Part of the value
investor's job is to find mathematical criteria which will

infallibly pinpoint these cheap shares. The equally important part is to say 'no' to all other investments.*

There are several snags with value investment. First, the greater the number of true believers, the fewer the anomalies which remain. This has been particularly true since cheap computing power made it comparatively easy to apply mathematical screens to large numbers of stocks. Second, value investment works best when the stockmarket as a whole is low or in a bear market: there are few guaranteed bargains when the whole market is highly priced. Third, if the market as a whole is rising strongly, frivolous growth shares often rise much faster than value shares. Uncommitted investors sometimes switch their money between value and growth funds, according to the state of the stockmarket.

The disciplines of value investment are still evolving. Benjamin Graham, its founder, changed his stockpicking criteria several times during his lifetime. Warren Buffett, his most eminent disciple, has even harnessed growth to the service of value investment. Indeed, his ecumenical tendencies have led purists to accuse Buffett of apostasy, while acknowledging his outstanding success.

Strict value investors insist that the value they are measuring must already exist and can be identified in the balance sheet, and that the merits of the company are irrelevant. Latter day value investors argue that value can also embrace future cash flows, in which case the merits of the company are of central importance.

---

* Most value investors are interested in individual companies, not the market as a whole. But some market analysts question whether the market itself is even broadly efficient in discounting the future. Research shows that there are often big gaps between the actual level of the market and what it would have been if it had enjoyed perfect foreknowledge. So either its forecasting or its discounting mechanism – or both – are imperfect. But this is hardly surprising. First, what the market is actually discounting is not the future but a patchwork of guesses about the future. Second, ideas of what the future is worth change significantly over time. The market is actually shooting at a moving target in a fog. Value investors, by contrast, wait until they fall over a sitting duck.

Benjamin Graham: the past master

If the investment industry went in for the title Grand Master, Benjamin Graham would have earned it. Before his death in 1976, he wrote both a seminal textbook, *Security Analysis*, still revered by professionals, and a popular classic, *The Intelligent Investor*. Warren Buffett, the best known and most successful investor of modern times, describes *The Intelligent Investor* as 'the best book on investing ever written'.

Author, lecturer and investment manager, Graham is the gurus' guru for American money managers dedicated to value investment. Buffett worked for him for a couple of years, and acknowledges his intellectual debt, though his own approach differs from Graham's in several respects.

Graham and Dodd's *Security Analysis*, published in 1944, explains the essential financial characteristics of every industry, what the standard operating and financial ratios are for each, how to tell which companies in a sector are performing well and are financially sound, and how to sort out the cheap shares from the expensive ones. As Chapter 5 shows, most of these measures are still in use by analysts today.

However, 30 years later Graham argued that these elaborate techniques no longer worked. Bargains were rarer than they used to be. Too many professional analysts were doing too good a job for the expense of extensive detailed research to be cost effective. The market had become too efficient for the analysts' good.

But what was bad news for the professional analyst was good news for the amateur. In *The Intelligent Investor* Graham explained some far simpler litmus tests for picking out cheap shares. Still bruised, perhaps, by the 1929 Wall Street Crash, Graham's list of warnings for novice investors is as memorable as his suggested strategies. As he himself pointed out, successful strategies are often the victims of their own popularity. And today it is often hard to find any stocks which fit his simple criteria. But most of his caveats look as fresh as the day they were written.

Graham's general principles

He had lots. Here are some of the most useful:

• Do not confuse investment with speculation. Graham defines an investment as something which 'upon thorough analysis promises safety of principal and an adequate return'; anything not meeting this test is speculation. Only a strictly systematic approach to share selection is likely to produce consistently satisfactory results. Systems should be based on mathematical rather than qualitative criteria.

• Investors should normally divide their portfolios between good quality bonds and good quality stocks. A reasonable norm is 50:50, with variations of between 25 and 75 per cent depending on the investor's view of markets. They should consider **pound-cost averaging**.

• Private individuals should only invest actively them-selves if they understand enough about investment analysis to be able to regard their investment activities as a business. Such people can adopt an **aggressive** or **enterprising** role.

• Investors who rely on others to invest for them should restrict themselves to conservative strategies, unless they have 'unusually intimate and favourable' knowledge of their adviser. They should only be receptive to unconventional suggestions if they have learnt so much that they can pass independent judgement on the suggestions. Such investors should adopt a **defensive** or **passive** role.

• A little knowledge is a dangerous thing. As an investor you cannot sensibly become 'half a businessman', and expect to get half the returns of a fully-fledged pro. So most investors should adopt a defensive role.

• Following stockmarket fashion is usually a way to lose money. Investors should ignore the market, except to take advantage of its folly to sell high and buy low. Technical analysis, which favours shares because they have gone up, and new issues, timed to benefit the seller, are both likely to damage your wealth.

• How to be right. 'The fact that other people agree or disagree with you makes you neither right nor wrong. You will be right if your facts and reasoning are correct.'

• Growth shares do exist but reliable ways of selecting

them do not; so avoid them. Investing in expanding industries can be dangerous. 'Obvious prospects for physical
growth in a business do not translate into obvious profits for
investors.' And even if an investor does pick a growth share,
he will be unlikely to have enough of it to make a significant
difference to the overall performance of his portfolio. 'The
experts do not have dependable ways of selecting and
concentrating on the most promising companies in the most
promising industries.' And why should a private investor
expect to be able to do better than the pros?
● Buy shares when they are cheap and sell them when they
become expensive. 'For 99 issues out of 100 we could say
that at some price they are cheap enough to buy and at some
other price they would be so dear that they should be sold.'
● Watch out for creative accounting – particularly when it
comes to companies manipulating their earnings figures.
One reliable measure of real earnings is dividends plus the
increase in net assets per share.
● Investment analysis is a tricky business. Analysts place
most emphasis on mathematical calculations in precisely
those areas where their calculations are most likely to be
wrong, that is in respect of the future. Most intelligent
analysts eventually confine themselves to groups where the
future appears reasonably predictable, or where the existing
value provides so wide a safety margin that it does not
matter if their forecasts are wrong.
● The central concept of investment is the margin of safety.
This is complemented by the principle of diversification –
just in case the safety margin for a particular share fails.
● Investment theories often cease to work as they become
popular. And even good theories (including Graham's own)
do not work in all market conditions.

Graham's stock selection methods

If the **defensive** investor sticks to the following criteria
when picking blue chips, there should be no need for
frequent changes to his portfolio.

● The portfolio should contain between 10 and 30 stocks.

- Each company should be large, prominent and conservatively financed.
- Each company should have a long record of continuous dividend payments.
- Stocks should only be bought below a certain PE ratio (perhaps 25 times average earnings for the past seven years and 20 times latest earnings*).

The **aggressive** investor should stick to companies which offer good value but are out of favour with the stockmarket. And this is where Graham introduces his concept of **bargain issues**. His definition of a bargain is a security worth 50 per cent more than the current price. But he distrusts valuations of growth shares.

- **Bargain Issues.** Graham's central ratio is share price as a percentage of net current assets, defined as current assets minus current liabilities minus all prior claims.

His criterion for selecting shares is that the current share price is less than the net current asset value, in other words making no allowance for any fixed assets. The investor buys shares when they are selling at two thirds or less of their net current asset value and sells them when they have fulfilled their potential, by rising to their net current asset value. That one third under-valuation is the investor's safety margin – which means that the share is unlikely to go down even if the news is bad. The investor sells the shares once they have reached their price target, because he has no reason to continue holding. He was never enthusiastic about the company's prospects; he merely thought the shares undervalued. So once they have become fully valued, they cease to be attractive.

Towards the end of his life Graham added additional criteria for pinpointing stock bargains.

- **Limited debt/low PE ratio.** A company needs to pass

---

* Those are quite demanding multiples, even when markets are high. Graham did emphasise that he was talking only about companies which are leaders in their fields not stodgy has-beens. And if a PE ratio of 20 was his upper limit, it would surely have been substantially lower when markets were low.

two tests. First the debt to equity shareholders' funds ratio should be less than one: ie borrowings of less than 100 per cent of shareholders' funds. This is quite hefty gearing. But Graham's definition of shareholders' funds was strict: it excluded intangible assets from the calculation and treated even preference shares as debt.

Second, the earnings yield (the reciprocal of the PE ratio) should be twice the prevailing AAA bond yield. If, for example, the yield on gilts is 9 per cent, the acceptable earnings yield on the share is 18 per cent or more: ie its PE ratio must be 5.6 or less.

This criterion is the grandfather of stockpicking systems based on low PE ratios.

• **Limited debt/High yield.** First, the familiar stipulation that the debt/equity ratio should be less than one. Then, the dividend yield should be at least two thirds of the AAA bond yield. So if the yield on gilts is 9 per cent, the minimum acceptable yield on the share is 6 per cent.

This criterion is the grandfather of stockpicking systems based on high yield. And in Graham's day the high yield criterion may not have looked that taxing. But the major re-rating of equities compared with gilts, which began in the 1960s, has made it highly demanding in modern markets.*

For the last 20 years the gilt/equity yield ratio (the long gilt yield divided by the yield on equities) has normally been between 2 and 3. So if the gilt yield is 9 per cent, equities as a whole normally yield between 3 and 4.5 per cent. On Graham's criterion a high yielder would normally have to yield between 1.3 and two times the equity market average.

Graham conducted tests which showed that portfolios of stocks which combined either his basic bargain criterion with his low PE criterion, or his low PE and his high yield criteria did better than the market. But he stipulated that the

---

* The BZW Equity Gilt Study which goes back to 1919 shows that the long term average for the UK gilt/equity yield ratio is 1.4, and equities actually yielded more than gilts until the 1960s. Between 1919 and 1959 the range was 0.5 to 1.0.

investor could not be selective. He had to buy every stock on the market which passed his screens.

● **When to sell.** Selling is as much a part of Graham's discipline as buying. The rules are:–

(a) Sell when the stock has risen 50 per cent, or after two years, whichever comes first.

(b) Sell if the company passes its dividend.

(c) Sell if earnings fall so far that the market price is 50 per cent higher than the new target buying price.

In all cases Graham recommends selling once a stock has exhausted its safety margin, either because the share has fulfilled its potential or because that potential has evaporated.

How to apply Graham's strategies

Benjamin Graham invented investment analysis and pays far more attention to company accounts than many of his disciples. He limits his ambitions to searching for value that already exists rather than value which depends on the analyst's growth forecasts.

The big snag with his theories is that it is often impossible to find any shares on the stockmarket which meet Graham's criteria, particularly if the stockmarket as a whole is high. Anyone wanting to use Graham's systems today will probably need to adapt his criteria to take account of the relative re-rating of equities – though tampering with patent systems is notoriously tricky.

Some investors turn this defect into a stockmarket criterion of its own. They say that any market in which it is impossible to pick a portfolio of bargain issues is overvalued. The increasing efficiency of the stockmarket resulting from the widespread availability of computers may simply mean that bargain issues are a thing of the past. But in the right market they can still work with a bit of tweaking.

In early October 1992 the *Investors Chronicle* published a portfolio of shares selected on Graham's basic bargain criterion. This was shortly after the UK government's decision to take sterling out of the Exchange Rate Mechanism (ERM), which sent the stockmarket soaring. But even though the stockmarket was still relatively low, the *Investors Chronicle* had to relax Graham's criterion in order to secure enough candidates. The selection process subtracted only long term debt from current assets and included all shares selling at up to 130 per cent of net current assets calculated on this basis. It then chose the best known 'and most widely researched' companies. A year later the portfolio had risen by over 80 per cent, compared with 40 per cent for the market.

Graham himself would probably be slightly scornful of any investor unimaginative enough to stick to the letter of his systems. After all, he was one of the first to point out that investors have to change along with the markets they study.

Warren Buffet: the modern legend

Warren Buffett of Omaha, Nebraska, has the best long term growth record of any modern fund manager. One of America's richest men, all his wealth has come from his own successful investment in the stockmarket, mainly shares. His first investment vehicle was a partnership, which he dissolved in 1969. His current one is Berkshire Hathaway, an investment company with chunky long term holdings in a relatively small number of companies. Berkshire's asset value has risen by 23 per cent compounded annually for 30 years. And at the end of September 1995 it was Number 44 in the FT 500 worldwide corporate league table, with a market capitalisation of $35.2bn, larger than General Motors.

Buffett himself once said that his investment philosophy was 85 per cent Benjamin Graham. And the debt is obvious in many ways. He pays little attention to the economy or the stockmarket. He believes in following his own judgement, ignoring the views of other investors and avoiding frequent portfolio turnover. He fully embraces Graham's beliefs in quantitative analysis, only buying shares when they are demonstrably good value, and leaving a comfortable safety margin.

But there are important differences between the two men. Graham argues for a purely mathematical approach to

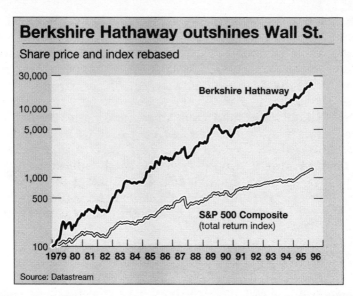

Berkshire Hathaway outshines Wall St.

Share price and index rebased

Fig 8.1 Berkshire's asset value has risen by 23 per cent compound for 30 years, and it is one of the world's largest quoted companies. Chairman Warren Buffett argued in 1996 that its shares had become overvalued.

stockpicking. It is not the investor's job to worry about the quality of the business, the management, the competition, the outlook or anything except the numbers.

Buffett accepts Graham's basic principle that it is only worth buying companies where the numbers are attractive. But he transforms the implementation of this principle by adding the rider that he will only buy good businesses with good management and good long term prospects. Unlike his mentor, he does not buy with a set profit ceiling in mind. He continues to hold shares for as long as the business continues to look good.

Graham's static world of certainties has been modified to a dynamic one which also entertains probabilities. Growth shares have crept in through the back door, but only those rare growth shares which also carry a 'value' hallmark.

There should be little risk of losing money on a Buffett company; what cannot be predicted with total accuracy is the long term scope for above average profits growth. But by restricting himself to only buying shares in companies that he is totally comfortable with, Buffett stacks the odds in his own favour. It takes a lot to make Warren Buffett feel totally comfortable. Understandably, even he finds that there is a very limited supply of 'Buffett companies', particularly when the stockmarket is high.

Buffett's general prejudices

Buffett's chairman's statements in Berkshire Hathaway's annual reports are collectors' items. Here is a digest of some of his more stringent comments:

- **On the stockmarket.** Short term forecasts of stock or bond prices are useless. 'The forecasts may tell you a great deal about the forecaster; they tell you nothing about the future.'
- **On inflation.** It 'acts like a giant corporate tapeworm.'
- **On risk.** 'Academics compute with precision the "beta" of a stock – its relative volatility in the past – and then build arcane investment and capital allocation theories round this calculation. In their hunger for a single statistic to measure risk, however, they forget a fundamental principle. It is better to be approximately right than precisely wrong.'
- **On lumpy portfolio allocation.** 'When prices are appropriate, we are willing to take very large positions in selected companies.'
  'We believe that a policy of portfolio concentration may well decrease risk if it raises, as it should do, both the intensity with which an investor thinks about a business and the comfort-level he must feel with its economic characteristics before buying into it.'
  'If you have a harem of forty women, you never get to know any of them very well.'
- **On portfolio churnover.** 'What is good for the croupier is not good for the customer. A hyperactive stockmarket is the pickpocket of enterprise ... Investors' penchant for financial flip-flopping also lands them with investment management charges for chair changing advice.'
- **On other investment managers.** 'Investment managers are ... hyperkinetic: their behaviour during trading hours makes whirling dervishes appear sedated by comparison.

Indeed, the term "institutional investors" is becoming one of those self-contradictions called an oxymoron.'

'Most managers have little incentive to make intelligent-but-with-some-chance-of-looking-like-an-idiot decisions. Their personal gain/loss ratio is all too obvious. If an unconventional decision works out well, they get a pat on the back and, if it works out poorly, they get a pink slip. Failing conventionally is the route to go; as a group lemmings may have a rotten image, but no individual lemming ever got a bad press.'

● **On efficient market theory.** 'Observing correctly that the market was frequently efficient, they went on to conclude incorrectly that it was always efficient. The difference between these two propositions is night and day.'

The disservice done to students and gullible investment professionals who have swallowed EMT has been an extraordinary service to us and other followers of Graham. 'In any sort of contest, financial, mental or physical it is an enormous advantage to have opponents who have been taught that it is useless even to try'.

● **On the disadvantages of size.** Over the first 19 years of Buffet's hegemony Berkshire Hathaway's book value grew at 22.6 per cent per annum compound. 'Considering our present size, nothing close to this rate can be maintained. Those who believe otherwise should pursue a career in sales, but avoid one in mathematics.'*

● **On change.** Most bad ideas are born good . . . Tragedy can only be averted by reversing course when danger flags start flying as the cherished ideas of the past are faithfully followed. 'Unfortunately the mind tends to reject the message from a danger signal . . . we started coping better with reality when it stopped waving danger flags at us and started using them to poke us in the head and stomach.'

● **On trends.** If something can't go on forever, it will end.

● **On investment.** 'An investor cannot earn superior profits from stocks simply by committing to a specific category or

---

* From BH's 1983 report. As it turned out Buffett's prediction was wrong, though few of his shareholders are likely to hold it against him.

style. He can earn them only by carefully evaluating facts and continuously exercising discipline.'

Buffett's stock selection methods

Buffett is famous for his businessman's eye. He buys shares as if he were considering buying the whole business. His own explanation of his investment process, like so much about Buffett, is deceptively homespun:-

'We select our marketable equity securities in much the same way we would evaluate a business for acquisition in its entirety. We want the business to be (1) one we can understand, (2) with favourable long term prospects, (3) operated by honest and competent people, and (4) available at a very attractive price.'

● **A business we can understand.** What each investor can understand will depend on his own interests and background. One of the businesses Buffett refers to most fondly in his annual reports is his local furniture store. Quoted companies in which he has long term equity interests are involved in insurance, newspapers, television radio and magazines, and soft drinks. Holdings in convertibles* (fixed interest with an equity kicker) have taken him into investment banking, airlines, and credit cards. Equity stakes of a less permanent nature involve razors, defence, mortgages, and brewing and distilling.

Buffett generally steers clear of high tech companies and most foreign companies. The one foreign company in which he did take a stake, Guinness, was a large international drinks business, not dissimilar to his long-standing favourite Coca-Cola.

Some of his other dislikes stem not from failure to understand the business, but from the fact that he understands it too well. A business such as agricultural supplies has endemic problems of slow stockturn and potential bad

---

* Graham was wary of convertibles, but only as new issues. He argued that, like other new issues, they were normally issued in circumstances more favourable to the seller than the buyer.

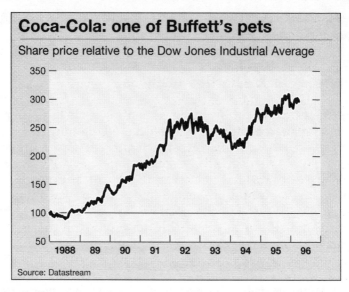

Coca-Cola: one of Buffett's pets

Share price relative to the Dow Jones Industrial Average

Source: Datastream

Fig 8.2 Buffett is not afraid of lumpy holdings – in the right company. He first bought into Coca-Cola in 1988 when new management started to grapple successfully with the company's problems.

debts. Textiles (an area he struggled with for years) are a commodity business, condemned to earn 'inadequate returns except under conditions of tight supply or real shortage'. Understanding the business is a necessary but not a sufficient reason for investment.

● **A business with favourable long term prospects** 'One of the lessons your management has learned, and unfortunately sometimes relearned, is the importance of being in businesses where tailwinds prevail rather than headwinds.' What are the yardsticks for favourable long term performance and what kind of business can deliver it? Buffett's prime yardstick is **return on capital employed**, rather than earnings. By this he means **return on equity capital employed** rather than total capital employed. He is suspicious of returns that depend on excessive borrowing or accounting gimmickry.

He has slightly different yardsticks for short and long term performance measurement. He argues that over the long term it is appropriate to include realised capital gains and extraordinary profits in the total return, and to include investments at their market value rather than cost in financial statements. For capital gains and losses are just as important to shareholders as routine operating profits. But because such profits and losses are one-offs it is not appropriate to include them in assessments of a single year's performance.

But profits are only worth having if they translate into cash. What matters is **cash flow**, not the profits or earnings shown on the p&l. Buffett distinguishes between **unrestricted earnings** and **restricted (ersatz) earnings**. When calculating cash flow, he deducts capital spending requirements so that he looks at **free cash flow**. This leads him naturally to **avoid businesses which involve high capital investment**.

Some businesses sop up capital all their lives, not just in their early years. It is hard for such a company to produce a return high enough to both meet capital spending needs and produce a good return to shareholders. Capital intensive industries are subject to an inflationary 'tax': the higher the capital requirements, the higher the tax. But the problem is not solved by the managers refusing to pay this tax. 'A company which consistently distributes restricted earnings is destined for oblivion unless equity capital is otherwise infused'.

What investors should be looking for are businesses whose **revenues are inflation-linked but whose capital spending is not**. They need to be able to preserve their **profit margins** regardless of conditions: this means they can increase prices easily regardless of supply and demand without loss of market share or unit volume. And they need to be able to increase turnover substantially with only a small increase in capital investment.

Buffett's name for such business sex appeal is **economic goodwill** (not to be confused with accounting goodwill). Economic goodwill exists when a business produces earnings on assets considerably in excess of market rates of return. The prime source of economic goodwill is a **consumer franchise**, which 'allows the value of the product to the consumer, rather than its production cost, to be the major determinant of selling price'. Coca-Cola, Gillette,

Amex cards, and the *Washington Post* newspaper are examples from Buffett's own portfolio. Such businesses are not vulnerable to the long term competitive pressure on profit margins which blights many initially successful companies in growth industries.* The other two sources of economic goodwill that he identifies are **governmental franchises not subject to profit regulation** such as television stations (for example, his holding in Capital Cities now merged with Disney) and **an enduring position as the low cost producer in an industry** (for example, GEICO, the direct insurance company he 'inherited' from Ben Graham).

Many of these businesses are what is described as **royalty businesses**. A business such as insurance broking enjoys what is effectively an ad valorem tax on the sales of the insurance company. A local newspaper thrives on the back of the local business community, without needing to invest itself. He does not favour companies with large research and development commitments. This rules out both drugs groups and high-tech companies. Future cash flows are hard to predict, particularly for high-tech companies. Both sometimes involve 'bet the company decisions' which might not come off. For Buffett dullness is a virtue.

● **A business operated by honest and competent people.** Buffett cares a lot about the people he does business with. His definition of a good manager is one who is owner-oriented: manages the company in order to produce the best possible returns for shareholders.

This seemingly uncontentious objective affects both the manager's strategy and his distribution of the company's earnings. Buffett condemns managers who pursue size for its own sake as likely to be more interested in getting themselves into the *Fortune* '500' list of large companies than watching the return on capital. Expensive takeovers are a sign of managerial machismo which are seldom of long term benefit to shareholders.

---

* When the changing requirements of UK retailers first made distribution a significant sector, it was an excellent business: the market was expanding and contract prices were fixed at levels ensuring comfortable profits. By the time it had been rechristened logistics, margins were under great pressure and profits plunged.

Indeed, good managers should often shrink their company rather than seek to expand it. How the managers distribute their unrestricted earnings is of vital importance to their shareholders. They have three choices: plough it back into the business, distribute it to shareholders or use it to buy back the company's own shares. Buffett has a simple test:-

'Unrestricted earnings should be retained only when there is a reasonable prospect backed preferably by historical evidence or, where appropriate, by a thoughtful analysis of the future that for every dollar retained by the corporation, at least one dollar of market value will be created for owners. This will happen only if the capital retained produces incremental earnings equal to, or above, those generally available to investors.'

If the managers cannot produce above average returns, Buffett favours **share buy-backs**, when the share price is below the intrinsic business value of the shares. In less than 20 years the *Washington Post*, one of his key holdings, bought in over 40 per cent of its own capital. Buy-backs give a double boost to the remaining shares. First the simple arithmetic impact: provided the buy-back price is right, intrinsic value per share rises. Second, the improvement in status: the market raises its estimate of future returns, and re-rates the shares upwards, so the price moves more into line with intrinsic value.*

Buffett likes investing in companies in which the managers have a worthwhile share stake. It is like a restaurant sign saying 'We eat our own cooking'. But even good managers need to be in a good business in order to produce good returns. Managers who can rightly trust to their magic to turn round bad companies are rare: – 'with a few exceptions, when a management with a reputation for brilliance tackles a business with a reputation for poor fundamental economics, it is the reputation of the business that remains intact.'

• **A business which is available at the right price.** There

---

* Intrinsic value, though central to Buffet's approach, remains an irritatingly slippery concept. Buffet himself says that he can value only a minority of businesses. (See next page for some valuation sums and page 206 for a definition.)

are two steps to implementing this rule. First, valuing the business. Second, deciding how much to pay for it.

Essentially Buffett's valuation method is a version of shareholder value analysis. It takes his own definition of **free cash flow**, which he calls **owner earnings**; estimates future cash flows by applying a given growth rate to these owner earnings; and then discounts those flows back to arrive at a present value: the intrinsic worth of the company.

He defines **owner earnings** as '(a) reported earnings, plus (b) depreciation, depletion, amortization, and certain other non-cash charges such as special inventory costs, less (c) the average annual amount of capitalized expenditures for plant, equipment and so on that the business requires to fully maintain its long term competitive position and unit volume.'

Robert Hagstrom's contribution to the Buffett book industry* contains detailed examples of discounted cash flow projections used to value Buffett's existing long term investments. He assumes a certain growth rate (or even a couple of growth rates for different periods) to forecast what the future cash flows will be. For example, he might assume 15 per cent growth for the first ten years and 5 per cent growth thereafter. Then he discounts those cash flows back to calculate a present value.†

So far most exponents of shareholder value analysis would agree with him. But equity analysts usually choose a discount rate which is higher than the risk-free rate of return (the yield on US government long bonds or UK gilts), because the return on equities is less certain. Thus if gilts are yielding 9 per cent, they might use a discount rate of 11 or 12 per cent. The higher the discount rate used, the lower the present value of those future income streams.‡

---

* *The Warren Buffett Way*. This book is good on sums. But John Train's chapters on Buffett in *The Money Masters* and *The Midas Touch*, give a more thoughtful and enjoyable analysis of Buffett's investment approach.

† The present value of cash flows in the first ten years is usually less than the residual value of the business (what it will earn thereafter), but the precise relationships depend both on the assumed growth rates and on the discount rate chosen.

‡ £100 falling due in ten years time is worth only £38.60 today,

Buffett uses the actual risk-free rate of return, because he argues that he has removed that additional equity risk by choosing only companies whose future cash flows can be predicted accurately. No matter how attractive the company, he will not attempt to value it unless he can predict its cash flows with confidence.

Making no allowance for the additional risk of equities in valuations sounds surprisingly rash. But Buffett is cautious about what he pays for his shares. Like Graham, he will only buy if he can get them cheap: he demands a safety margin. If he buys shares below his estimate of their value, he is protected against the downside, and he has the potential for above average returns if his valuations prove correct.

Hagstrom also quotes Buffett's description of the traditional growth/value debate as nonsensical. Buffett nowadays argues that growth is simply the calculation used to determine value.

Buffett versus Hanson

Corporate predators, such as Hanson, have tended to receive a less favourable press than gurus like Graham and Buffett. Yet the criteria they use, when looking for companies to take over and asset-strip, are often remarkably similar to those of many portfolio investors.

The late Lord White, who masterminded Hanson's acquisitions strategy, could have been Benjamin Graham's brother when it came to demanding a safety margin. No matter how tempting the deal, he was never prepared to bet the company. He always looked at the downside, and drew back if there was one. And, again like Graham, he concentrated on the bargain, not what the company did.

And while Buffett avoids companies which need heavy capital investment, Hanson notoriously abhors the thought of almost any capital investment. 'Money frightens us to

using a discount rate of 10 per cent. It is worth £61.40 using a discount rate of 5 per cent, but only £24.70 using a discount rate of 15 per cent.

death,' Lord Hanson once said, when explaining the company rule that any capital expenditure of more than £500
had to be vetted, and must pay for itself within four years.

But Hanson eventually ran out of road. In the 1990s its
share price drooped, and in February 1996 the company
announced a four-way demerger. Andrew Arends, who was
Hanson's acquisitions manager between 1989 and 1992,
wrote an interesting analysis of why Buffett had continued
to thrive, while Hanson's star had waned. He argued that
Buffett's acquisition strategy had evolved to suit changing
markets, while Hanson's had not.

His thesis was that both were dedicated to pursuing
shareholder value. And in the vintage years, with acquisitions such as Berec and Imperial, Hanson's tight targets for
return on capital employed duly produced the goods in
terms of large cash returns. But Hanson remained too fixed
on the yardstick of rising earnings per share as the primary
indicator of shareholder value. The snag, which became
apparent in later deals such as Peabody and Beazer, was that
deals which might indeed boost short-term earnings per
share, did not necessarily increase intrinsic value.

Buffett's use of cash flow analysis allows him to consider
deals which Hanson would have ruled out, and rule out
deals that Hanson would have considered. To Buffett
intrinsic value is 'the discounted value of the cash that can
be taken out of a business during its remaining life'. But this
means acquisitive companies have to practise enlightened
foresight: 'Go to where the puck is going to be, not to where
it is'.

As Arends explains, cash flow analysis shows two ways of
creating shareholder value. The first, largely applicable to
mature or declining businesses, involves generating higher
cash flow returns from existing investments. The second,
more appropriate in expanding industries, is to increase the
value of the business by making investments whose cash-
flow exceeds the cost of capital. Hanson relied on the
former; Buffett increasingly embraced the latter, in the form
of companies such as Coca-Cola and Gillette.

Hanson's conservatism meant that, like the sabre-toothed
tiger, it was fated to become extinct. The supply of easy
meat at bargain prices simply ran out. Buffett's capacity to

adapt, and his awareness of Berkshire's mortality, ensured its survival.

The need for a flexible approach to investment, pointed out by Graham and practised by Buffett, is unfortunately hard to encapsulate in tidy lists of investment maxims.

How to apply Buffett's strategies

Buffett aficionados, like Grahamites, need a thorough grounding in company accounts. They must to be able to calculate **return on equity capital**, **free cash flow**, and **gearing**; they need to be able to spot creative accountants at work, and to handle a **discounted cash flow** spreadsheet.

American investors have the alternative of investing in Berkshire itself or in funds which invest on similar principles or duplicate Buffett's holdings. The best known used to be Sequoia fund – though that has long been closed to the public. More recently, the threat of a clutch of new unit trusts designed purely to create an affordable way into Berkshire itself prompted Buffett's decision to split some of the stock and issue mini-shares priced at one thirtieth of the cost of the existing shares. Demand was heavy even though Buffett told the Securities and Exchange Commission (SEC) in April 1996 that he did not consider the shares good value at their current level, and would not recommend his family or friends to buy them.

British investors determined to acquire the real McCoy have to be prepared to ignore Buffett's formal warning in his SEC filing that the share price will encounter 'periods of underperformance, perhaps substantial'. And since Guinness was Buffett's only known UK holding, buying stakes in the companies he invests in is hardly an option for UK funds or individual investors.

But there are some Buffett edicts that will improve the performance of most active private investors:–

● Stick to businesses you thoroughly understand. If, for example, you work in television, you have a real advantage in assessing television companies, provided you look at them from a business point of view.

- Avoid risk. Guesswork has no place in investment. The key to value investment is that it aims to deal only in certainties. Remember that Buffett will only value companies if he can be certain of their future cash flows.
- Only buy businesses which you expect to produce above average returns. Otherwise you are far better off with all your money in a tracker fund.
- Only buy if you can get the shares for less than they are worth. That gives you the safety margin that both Graham and Buffett insist on. If you buy a business producing above average returns for more than it is worth, the best you can expect is average returns; if it does worse than expected or its share rating slips, you will get subnormal returns.
- Do not churn your portfolio. First, dealing represents a voluntary tax on your returns. Second, you need to give compound interest a chance.
- Keep an open mind. Remember, Graham's book was called *The Intelligent Investor*. Buffett was not afraid to improve on Graham's formulas. Markets change. And only dinosaurs stick to yesterday's rules.

Value Investment

IN A NUTSHELL

1. Value investment uses mathematical criteria to find
   cheap shares. It relies on the belief that, even if
   stockmarkets are efficient overall, pockets of inefficiency exist. But it concedes that, since conditions
   change, the criteria needed to find cheap shares also
   periodically need to change. Value investment works
   best when the stockmarket as a whole is low.

2. The father of value investment is Benjamin Graham,
   who invented investment analysis with his treatise
   Security Analysis, and also wrote the classic *The
   Intelligent Investor* for laymen.

3. Graham divided investors into those who thoroughly
   understood investment, and could sensibly become
   active investors, and those who did not, who should
   confine themselves to defensive investment. There is
   no middle ground. Most people's knowledge is inadequate for them to invest actively.

4. Growth shares exist, admitted Graham, but reliable
   methods for identifying them do not. So even active
   investors should stick to value investing, which relies
   solely on quantitative criteria.

5. Graham argued that most shares are worth buying at
   some price and worth selling at another price. His
   systems establishes rigid buy/sell criteria. Best known
   is his system for selecting bargain stocks. He relied on
   a safety margin and diversification to ensure a good
   result.

6. Warren Buffett, the sage of Omaha, is Graham's best
   known disciple, and is commonly described as the
   world's most successful investor. He has become one

of America's richest men by practising his own version of value investment.

7. Buffett shares Graham's beliefs in quantitative analysis, only buying shares when they offer good value, and the importance of having a safety margin. But he differs from his mentor in believing that it is important to invest in good businesses, and that potential value can be identified as well as actual value. He is also a long term investor.

8. Buffett buys shares as if he were considering buying the whole business. His criteria for a good business are that it should be one he can understand; with favourable long term prospects; run by honest and competent people; available at an attractive price.

Chapter 9
Great Growth Investors

Growth Investment is a slippery term, for it has come to mean very different things to different people. The original concept of a growth stock was clear enough: it was an outstanding company whose profits and share price would beat the market over a long period. But the term was rapidly diluted to include any share likely to produce short term capital gains – even if those stocks belonged to rotten companies.

In the UK investing for growth can nowadays mean almost any style of investment whose primary aim is to produce capital growth rather than income. Some unit and investment trusts classified as growth funds specialise in recovery shares, some in special situations, some in emerging markets, some in blue chips, some in second-hand life assurance policies – as well as the more predictable smaller companies and technology companies. The distinction between growth and capital gain has remained clearer in the US, where old-style growth funds based on old-fashioned growth stocks still exist.

Old-fashioned **growth stocks** are what novice investors' dreams are made of. The investor buys shares in a wonderful little company that promptly turns into IBM, Glaxo or Reuters. The company's earnings rise at a phenomenal rate, and so does its share price. The inspired investor gets pleasantly rich because of his acumen in spotting that this particular acorn was indeed destined to grow into a mighty oak.

Whereas value investment is based entirely or mainly on quantitative criteria (sums), growth investment is based mainly on qualitative criteria (value judgements). The successful growth investor is the one with a truffle-hound's nose for the right kind of acorn. It can happen. Growth stocks can be found in two areas. Sometimes new industries

Rentokil beats the market

Share price relative to the FT-SE-A All-Share Index

Fig 9.1 Rentokil was a growth company operating in unfashionable areas such as pest control. But its 1996 bid for BET caused some worries that it might be running out of steam.

develop. Railroads were the growth industry of the nineteenth century. Today, many growth industries are technology-based, notably the US computer industry. But some are comparatively humdrum: waste management, for example.

Alternatively, some companies find a particular niche in which they thrive without much real competition. Xerox was virtually unchallenged in the photocopier industry for years. Rentokil managed several years of above average profits growth in the unglamorous areas of pest control and damp-proofing and office plants (See Fig 9.1.). Many growth investors emphasise that they prefer growth companies which have found a lucrative niche in unglamorous industries. There is less risk of competition developing.

The additional attraction of investing in growth stocks is that it is a game almost anyone can play. Peter Lynch, who built up America's largest mutual fund, Magellan, tells encouraging stories about picking up growth share ideas in the local shopping centre or high school.

Alas, it is not quite that easy. Some growth industries never produce any growth stocks. The industry grows, but competition is so fierce that none of the companies involved make any money. US airlines were a classic example of profitless expansion cited by Benjamin Graham.

Few industries keep growing for ever, and even when they do continue expanding they often change. IBM dominated the computer industry, when what mattered was slugging it out with a handful of less powerful international rivals in the mainframe industry. But when personal computers (PCs) took over from mainframes, Big Blue was caught off balance. The second phase of computer market growth has been dominated by firms selling cheap user-friendly PCs and software. It is the equivalent of railways being overtaken by the rise of the motor car in the transport industry.

Knowing when to sell an erstwhile growth stock can be as important as the original decision to buy. And the timing will depend on what kind of growth stock it is. Most growth investors distinguish between different types: the best growth stocks are relatively stable long term holdings, others may have a limited life and some may be merely passing through a growth phase.

Top of the list come the franchise stocks beloved of value investor Warren Buffett. These are lifetime purchases, which happily ride out business cycles soaring from share price peak to share price peak. Then come what Lynch calls tenbaggers – companies with a very good idea which will return your original investment ten times over: they can be kept for a long time but may eventually run out of puff. Much further down the pecking order come cyclicals and recovery shares: companies not capable of long term growth but caught at the right stage of the business cycle. Such shares are strictly for buying and selling.

Growth stocks come into their own when the stockmarket is rising strongly. But even their fans agree that they can be dangerous if the stockmarket as a whole is high. The favourite yardstick of the growth stock investor is the PE ratio, and latterly the PEG factor. PE ratios on growth stocks are normally above the market average. As the market rises so does the average, but the PE ratio on fashionable growth stocks tends to rise even further. When the market as a whole falls, growth stocks usually fall further and faster than others. Some never rise again. In late 1972 some of the companies included in Wall Street's favourite Nifty Fifty were selling on PE ratios of nearly a hundred. By the bottom of the 1973–74 bear market more than half of them had lost over 80 per cent of their value.

This chapter first sets out the rules for classic growth stock investing as explained by T. Rowe Price, who invented it. Then it looks at how Peter Lynch happily mixes growth shares with others in his pursuit of overall capital gains. Next come some modern criteria for picking growth shares, devised by Jim Slater, the only British fund manager with any pretensions to guru status. And finally, as a footnote for investors tempted to blur the borders between growth and speculation, some cautionary lessons from George Soros, the master speculator.

T. Rowe Price: growth guru

Growth investment is not identified with any single investor as closely as Value is with Benjamin Graham. But it was T. Rowe Price, yet another American fund manager, who first set out the *Principles of Growth Stock Valuation*. When he started buying growth stocks in the 1930s his approach was unconventional; in the 1950s he launched a very popular growth fund; and by the 1960s investing in growth shares was the new orthodoxy.

As much of a purist in his way as Graham, Price allows only stable long term growth stocks into his flock.* A growth company is one with long term growth of earnings 'reaching a new high level per share at the peak of each succeeding major business cycle' and which gives indications of reaching new high earnings at the peak of future business cycles. Translation: it has a good long term record and good prospects.

But he warns that the most profitable time to own such a share is in the early stages of growth. The more mature the

* Initially he had included cyclicals as a sub-category of growth stocks, because they often provided more bang for the buck when a market was on the turn. Later he excluded them.

company, the less the opportunity and the higher the risk. By the time everybody else has read the growth label round its neck, the price is sky high and growth probably tapering off.

● **Growth stock characteristics.** Price is clear about the attributes the investor is looking for. They include:

An industry where both unit sales and earnings are rising.

A company which either manages to improve unit sales and earnings even during economic downturns, or at least rises higher in each cycle. Good margins and above average earnings growth.

Good management. Strong research. Valuable patents. Sound finances. A good location.

Some of these overlap with Buffett's criteria. But Price's inclusion of research highlights a difference between the value and growth schools. It is not possible accurately to quantify the future profits which will result from even the strongest research in areas such as drugs, for example. Buffett is only prepared to value a company if he can project its future cash flows with confidence.

The objection would not bother Price, who argues 'No one can see ahead three years, let alone five or ten.' Rather than constructing discounted cash flow models, he believes in riding the wave as long as it lasts.

● **How to buy growth stocks.** Price eschews mathematical rules but gives plenty of suggestions.

One of his basic measures is the total return (including dividends) the investor expects to make or would have made on the money he actually invested.* First, how does it compare with the return on other types of investment, notably bonds, as well as other shares? Second, is it increasing or declining?

Other suggestions include:–

Look at the record, but be wary of extrapolating past growth too far ahead.

Buy when growth stocks as a whole are out of fashion and PE ratios not much above the market average.

Pay more for blue chips than smaller companies and more

---

* He suggests 10 per cent, but inflation must alter the appropriate target.

for stable growth companies than cyclicals and recovery stocks.

Consider the general level of interest rates. When they are high, investors should not buy growth stocks on such high PE ratios as when interest rates are low.

As a rule of thumb Price suggests that a reasonable PE ratio on which to buy a stock is around a third higher than the lowest level its PE ratio has touched in the last few market cycles. He warns against being too greedy when buying. Buy when the stock comes within the buying range, rather than trying to catch it on the turn.

● **When to sell.** An investor who has chosen correctly should hardly ever need to sell. But if the return on his own investment in the share starts falling, it is time to consider quitting. For the growth company may have matured. The correct selling strategy depends on the market.

If the market as a whole is rising, the investor should wait until the share has risen 30 per cent above the target level for buying and sell 10 per cent of the holding. He then sells a further 10 per cent for every additional 10 per cent rise in the share price. If either the market or the share has started falling, or company announcements are ominous, he should sell the lot.

Like Graham, Price was more flexible than some of his disciples. When the stockmarket reached dangerous levels in the late 1960s, Price was one of the few to say publicly that the growth concept had outlived its usefulness.

Price switched to natural resource shares towards the end of his career in the late-1960s, because he reckoned the bull market in growth stocks was over. His successors in the firm bearing his name still kept right on pursuing growth investments until the 1974 collapse.

Peter Lynch: master of all trades

Peter Lynch is not a traditional growth stock investor. He is a trader who loves growth shares. He argues that being eclectic is an enormous advantage in that you are not bound to follow a particular discipline when the market is no longer suitable.

'As the manager of a capital appreciation fund . . . I was not constrained the way a manager of a growth fund was. When the entire growth sector was overvalued, which happened every few years, the growth-fund manager was forced into buying overpriced inventory, otherwise he didn't have a growth fund. I was free to wander off . . .' Most value and growth investors would agree with Lynch that there are times when their systems cease to work. But many would argue that changing style to suit the market is easier said than done.

Lynch's prescriptions for successful investment are deceptively simple. His practice is rather more complicated. Hardly surprising, given that almost single-handedly he built up America's largest and best known mutual fund. When Lynch started to manage the Magellan fund for Fidelity in 1977 it was worth $20mn; when he retired in 1990 it had grown to $14bn. Part of the increase was due to his own pulling power as a fund manager: his proven investment success attracted new money from new investors. But that success was very real. Anyone investing in Magellan when Lynch first took over the fund would have been nearly 30 times richer by the time Lynch retired.

He attributes his success as a fund manager to 'continuing to think like an amateur as frequently as possible'. When looking for retailing stocks, he heads for the local shops. And he argues that 'an amateur who devotes a small amount of study to companies in an industry he or she knows something about can outperform 95 per cent of the paid experts . . . plus have fun . . .'

What he does not emphasise is that he spent eight years quarrying away in Fidelity's research department before graduating to managing money at Magellan. And his capacity for sheer hard work is daunting: two proper holidays in 20 years; a 13 hour day in which he read all the way to the office and all the way back; a daily schedule so packed that telephone callers were limited to 90 seconds with a kitchen timer ticking away in the background. He is fanatical about actually visiting and monitoring all the companies he invests in himself. If genius is an infinite capacity for taking pains, Peter Lynch is well on the way to being an investment genius. But there is more to it than a quick trip to the shops.

Lynch is a stockpicker by inclination and conviction. He does not attempt to predict the market, and his biggest concession to a weak market is to increase his holdings of defensive shares. He never holds cash. Lynch invests in a far wider range of securities, both by number and by type, than the other investors we are looking at, but he has no time for conventional portfolio management theory or asset allocation. Unlike Graham, Buffett and Rowe Price he is not a thinker or theorist; he is a practical man and a born opportunist.

How Lynch runs a portfolio

What he does himself and what he tells his readers to do are very different things.* Lynch is a trader who ran a $14bn fund containing 1,500 to 2,000 stocks at a time, including several foreign ones. He turned the whole portfolio over once a year on average. He loves growth stocks – and these are what he recommends to his readers – but they formed only one part of his own portfolio. As a fund manager he bought virtually any share that both looked cheap and looked as if its fortunes were on the turn. A talent spotter with a gift for timing, he auditions several types of share for different roles in his portfolio.

Lynch classifies shares into six broad categories: slow growers, stalwarts, fast growers, cyclicals, asset plays and turnarounds. He is not interested in slow growers. But all the others find a place in his affections, and his portfolio.

● **Stalwarts.** These are what many people wrongly assume all 'blue chips' to be: reliable earners (10–12 per cent a year on average) which chug along in all weathers, usually large and often in humdrum but necessary businesses such as food. (Coca-Cola, one of Buffett's core holdings, counts as a stalwart.) Lynch has two uses for stalwarts. If he sees one

* Lynch has written two popular books, *One up on Wall Street* and *Beating the Street* together with John Rothchild.

that looks undervalued, he will buy, but he'll turf it out ruthlessly once the share price has reached his target: a profit of 30 to 50 per cent. And he is looking for such gains over a relatively short period of time. He also uses stalwarts as a protection in bad times.

The key concern here is the price, and the PE ratio the main yardstick. Potential worries are ill-judged diversification plans, and any sign that the company is moving from the stalwart category down to the sluggards.

- **Cyclicals.** Cyclicals are companies whose profits expand and contract in time with some exterior cycle. Many, such as building and construction companies, are tuned into the economy. Some, such as insurance companies, dance to a specific cycle of their own. Timing is everything. Their shares are only worth buying when they are depressed ahead of a strong upwards movement. But if the investor gets it right, there are big profits to be made out of cyclicals. Lynch is particularly keen on local knowledge as an aid to timing here. And he warns that predicting a downturn in cyclicals is much harder than predicting an upturn.

- **Turnarounds.** The share price behaves a bit like a cyclical, but the background is different and the chances of getting it wrong higher. These are companies that might well be basket cases, but are actually saved. **Recovery shares** is another name for them. Some of the biggest profits come from turnarounds. And, unlike cyclicals, their share prices are relatively insensitive to overall market movements.

Balance sheets are crucial here. Can the company survive a raid by its creditors. How much cash does it have? How much debt? How is that debt structured and what is the company likely to have to do to get out of its hole. No point in buying shares if a corporate restructuring gives everything of value to the banks. What is the company actually doing to turn its business round? Will asset sales still leave it with worthwhile businesses? What about the cost structure?

- **Asset plays.** Essentially companies sitting on something valuable – usually cash or property – whose worth is not reflected in their trading results. Manchester Ship Canal was for years traded mainly on brokers' estimates of the value of its property holdings, not its traffic revenue. But sometimes the assets are less obvious. For example, sleepy publishing companies sometimes have back lists of titles worth more than their market capitalisation; the same can be true of record companies.

Again these are all about balance sheets. Ideally you need a company whose assets (including those not adequately reflected in the balance sheet) are well above the market price, even after you have knocked off all the debt. And you need to check it is not about to ruin those assets by taking on fresh debt. A raider in the wings to help shareholders reap the benefits of those assets could also come in handy.

● **Fast growers.** Lynch's name for **growth stocks**, which he defines as small, aggressive new enterprises that grow at 20–25 per cent a year. This is where he looks for what he calls 'tenbaggers' companies which give a tenfold return, and where he dreams of '200-baggers.' Such companies do not need to be in a growth industry, but they do need a winning repeatable formula. He likes to catch the companies young. But since any super-growth company can expand itself into financial trouble, he tends to pick ones

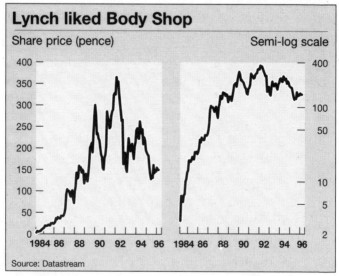

Fig 9.2 When Lynch put Body Shop on his buy list in early 1992 he considered it a wonderful company but overpriced. He bought more in the summer after the price fall. But his original judgement looks sound.

with good balance sheets which are already making substantial profits. Bodyshop is a British example he quotes. (See Fig 9.2 opposite.)*

Points to check are whether the company's key business franchise is a major part of its overall business, and what the recent earnings growth has been. Lynch is as wary of companies which grow too fast as he is of 'hot' industries. He likes to know that a company has both proved that its formula will work in more than one site and that it still has room to grow. He likes a PE ratio at or near the growth rate, which ought still to be accelerating. He also wants to be one of the first investors aboard. So the fact that other investors and analysts have not heard of a potential star is a good sign – provided everything else stacks up.

Lynch has a penchant for simple businesses which anyone can run. Not because he thinks management unimportant, but because he considers himself incapable of identifying the good managements.

He is more charitable to growth companies than others, in the sense that he will not necessarily sell them if their shares look a bit on the high side. But he watches them fiercely for the first hint that their growth days are over. And that may just be a question of size. If even a good company gets too big, it cannot keep up its former pace, and the stockmarket downgrades it savagely. Lynch tries to be first out of the exit, just as he was first in.

How Lynch picks shares

His method of looking for winners is to check out an enormous range of different stocks, searching for ones that satisfy his criteria. Those that look promising he buys, but that is not the end of the winnowing process. Lynch's portfolio is in a constant state of flux. His ultimate quarry may be the 'tenbagger', but he accepts that the majority of his holdings will be more mundane. He is an unsentimental investor. Some of his holdings will be sold because they

---

* But that is in a book published in 1993. Bodyshop is an excellent example of a growth company whose magic faded.

disappoint his hopes; others will go because they have fulfilled them. He argues that the investor's ultimate objective is to avoid a big loss, but that the occasional winner will offset lots of small losses.

In his own eyes Lynch has an edge because he is looking for reasons to buy a share; many other investors are looking for reasons not to. So Lynch is trying harder to spot that aspect of a company which gives it its appeal. As a talent spotter he demands that all applicants pass three tests:–

- The basic business has to be attractive – though its attraction can be anything from a niche market to recovery prospects.
- The shares need to be cheap in relation to the company's real prospects, and again there are many types of cheap share – unknown companies in unfashionable businesses such as funerals, troubled businesses which are capable of being turned round, overseas companies which are modestly priced compared to their American equivalents.
- The company must have a reasonably clean balance sheet: a good balance sheet would never be a sufficient reason for buying, but a bad one would be a sufficient reason for avoiding a share.

Unfortunately for lazy-minded investors, companies are dynamic entities, which tend to move from one stockmarket category to another at different points in their history. Yesterday's growth company is today's stalwart and tomorrow's slow-grower. Sniffing out the change in a company's status earlier than other investors is one of the key tasks of an active investor.

This need to stay ahead of the pack is another reason why Lynch is so keen on simple businesses and so insistent on doing his own research. He dips into enormous quantities of research material but talks to and visits every company himself. Every share recommendation is judged on its own merits not on the previous record of the man making the recommendation.

He cares enormously about the provenance of a share

recommendation, and has no time for what most laymen would consider tips. The people who will be aware of a significant change in a company's prospects first are those closest to it: employees, competitors, customers. If a middle manager of a company's rival tells Lynch that company is improving, it probably is, and it is unlikely that other fund managers will as yet have any inklings of its metamorphosis. The early bird can gobble the worm unchallenged. But if the same middle manager recommends a stock in an alien field, his recommendation is totally lacking in authority.

Lynch's interest in 'insider dealings' (the US term for legitimate share purchases and sales by directors and employees of the company concerned) is consistent with this approach. So is his scorn for takeover specs and other 'whisper stocks'.

Lynch's tips for buying shares

Magellan's record shows that Peter Lynch is an extremely successful stockpicker. Bookshop sales suggest he is also a successful author. What is not clear is whether ordinary people who read his books are automatically transformed into successful stockpickers.

His first book was subtitled *How to use what you already know to make money in the market*. His thesis is that everybody has an area in which he is an expert, and that each person's stockpicking universe should be confined to this area of knowledge. His wife unwittingly gave him one of his best tips, when she commended a brand of tights called L'eggs on sale conveniently near the grocery checkout. Lynch discovered they were made by a company called Hanes, bought it and found himself with a sixbagger. His daughters led him to Bodyshop and Apple Computer. Children from the local school picked a company making marker pens, Disney, two companies making trainer shoes, Pepsico and outstanding US retailer Wal-Mart.

As a fund manager, Lynch kicks himself for failing to buy the shares of other quoted fund managers during the financial services boom. What about a rural hermit? Lynch suggests that all that peace is bound to give him an ulcer, which should lead the anguished hermit to ulcer drug

Tagamet, and so to what is now SmithKline Beecham. Of course, the initial idea is only part of it. The inspired amateur then has to check the company out.

Lynch's golden rules

Lynch happily admits 'I never had an overall strategy. My stockpicking was entirely empirical, and I went sniffing from one case to another like a bloodhound that's trained to follow a scent.' His 20 Golden Rules smack more of the enthusiasm of a cheerleader than the careful science of a quantitative investor such as Graham.

- You can outperform the experts if you use your edge by investing in companies or industries you already understand.
- You can beat the market by ignoring the herd.
- Be patient and own successful companies.
- Know what you own and why you own it.
- Long shots almost always miss the mark.
- Don't get involved with more companies than you can handle. There don't have to be more than 5 companies in a portfolio.
- If you can't find any attractive companies, stick your money in the bank.
- Never invest in a company without understanding its finances.
- Avoid hot stocks in hot industries.
- Wait for a small company to start making a profit before investing.
- You need only find a few good stocks to make a lifetime's investing worthwhile.
- In every industry and region the observant amateur can find great growth companies before the pros discover them.
- Stockmarket falls provide an opportunity for bargain-hunting.
- Everybody has the brain for stockpicking; not everybody has the stomach to invest on the stockmarket. If you can't stand the heat, keep out of the kitchen.

- Don't listen to the pundits. Sell a stock only because its fundamentals are deteriorating.
- Nobody can predict interest rates, the future direction of the economy or the stockmarket. Dismiss all such forecasts and concentrate on what's actually happening in the companies in which you've invested.
- There's always a pleasant surprise to be found in the stockmarket – companies whose achievements are being overlooked by Wall Street.
- Buying stocks without studying companies is like betting without looking at your cards.
- Time is on your side when you own shares in superior companies; it is against you when you own options.
- In the long run a portfolio of well-chosen stocks will always outperform a portfolio of bonds or a high interest account; a portfolio of poorly-chosen stocks will do worse than money left under the mattress.

Slater: the codifier

Jim Slater's Slater Walker Securities* was a founder member of the UK conglomerates boom in the 1960s and the most notorious casualty of the secondary banking crisis of the early 1970s. A spider's web of cross holdings rapidly unravelled. Slater himself subsequently admitted: 'A number of moves that were right and expedient in the short term went wrong in the long term'. The large number of private investors who backed him to the end lost everything they had made on the way up. He is unusual amongst the investment gurus in having once stood under the double shadow of a Department of Trade and Industry (DTI) enquiry at home and the threat of extradition to Singapore.

Now that the dust has settled, he has started a second

---

* John Train, whose books *The Money Masters* and *The New Money Masters* provide by far the best explanation of great investors' theories and strategies, collected data on Slater when he was a promising young tycoon. Alas, Slater's empire collapsed before Train had started to write the first book.

career as the author of several investment books. Hemmington Scott publishes a useful investment service, *Company Refs*, devised by Slater.* Investors who find Lynch's intuitive knack for sniffing out cheap stocks hard to pin down and imitate may find Slater's systematic approach to picking growth shares helpful. He is an accountant by training.

Slater's selection process for **small dynamic growth companies** is a refined version of the theory he first worked out for himself over 30 years ago. It puts every company through an extensive screening process: eleven separate health checks. Some of these are mandatory; if the company doesn't pass, reject it. Some of the criteria are described as important: you might put up with one of them being weak or unfulfilled if the company scored highly on the others. And some criteria are merely desirable. Slater gives each of the non-mandatory tests a weighting, but warns against taking these too literally.

● **Mandatory criteria**
(1) A positive growth rate in earnings per share in at least four of the last five years. Steady growth of around 15 per cent is the acceptable norm. A shorter record might be acceptable if growth is accelerating.

(2) A low PEG factor. The PEG factor is Slater's patent name for the relation of the company's price earnings ratio (PE ratio) to its growth rate. If a company's earnings are growing at 15 per cent a year, and its PE ratio is 15, it is on a PEG of 1. If that company has a PE ratio of 30, its PEG is 2. Very crudely the thesis is that a PEG of 1 is fair value, a PEG of substantially over 1 is expensive, whilst a PEG of well below 1 points to a cheap share. PE ratios alone are a misleading way of measuring relative value, since corporate growth rates vary. The PEG provides a useful ready reckoner of value.

(3) The chairman's statement must be optimistic. If even the company is expecting a setback, the historic earnings growth is not worth much.

(4) A strong financial position. This is defined as strong

* *The Zulu Principle* is also strong on investment yardsticks.

liquidity, low borrowings and a high cash flow. Look for self-financing companies that generate cash, and avoid those that are capital intensive and constantly sopping up more capital.

(5) A competitive advantage. This advantage can range from a strong brand name to a niche business, where entry costs for competitors are high. Basically Slater is trying to check that there is no obvious exterior threat to the chosen company's profit margins and hence its earnings growth.

● **Important criteria**

(6) Something new. Share prices tend to rise most rapidly when the stockmarket has just latched onto a new company 'story', and the company's status is being upgraded. A new chief executive or a new drug are obvious examples of such stories. *Rating 8.*

(7) A small market capitalisation. Small companies more often show big price movements than large ones. *Rating 7.*

(8) Relative strength. You want to catch your share when it is already on the move and one way of checking this is to measure its relative strength against the market. A high relative strength helps you get your timing right. You don't want to wait for ever for other investors to wake up to the share's charms. *Rating 6.*

● **Desirable criteria**

(9) Dividend Yield. Most institutional investors need income from their investments, and steadily increasing dividends add weight to the management's growth forecasts. Any threat of a dividend cut is usually a sell signal. But a really good company may use its earnings better than you can. So don't worry if the yield is small, provided cover is strong. *Rating 5.*

(10) Reasonable asset position. No one is bothered about asset backing per se in a growth company. But they do want to know that it has enough working capital to be able to carry on growing at an above average rate. *Rating 5.*

(11) Management shareholdings. What's desirable is a management with enough of a personal stake to think of the company with an 'owner's eye', but not enough to control it or block a bid. Significant share sales are a danger sign, purchases a good one. *Rating 5.*

Soros: the master of timing

Can the world's most notorious currency speculator really have any messages for private investors in shares? George Soros is the man who bet £10bn against the pound staying in the EC Exchange Rate Mechanism in September 1992 – and won. He is also the man who correctly predicted the 1987 stockmarket crash, but wrongly thought it would start in Tokyo rather than Wall Street, and lost a fortune. Soros's Curaçao-based Quantum fund, which uses gearing extensively both by borrowing money and by using futures, has a remarkable record. But it's had some sickening short term lurches.*

Any private investor who decides not to stick with classic long term value or growth investment needs to understand markets. Trading markets successfully involves understanding market psychology, risk and timing. Soros has theories on all three. And his theories have been thoroughly road-tested. He describes financial markets as a laboratory for testing hypotheses; the more accurate your hypotheses the more money you make. It's a rather rarefied way of describing successful speculation.

Soros is not much interested in individual stocks. He is a trader who bets on big issues: changes in currencies, markets, sectors. But when he first started his Quantum fund, in partnership with Jim Rogers, a pioneer investor in emerging markets, the pair did successfully short some major institutional stocks: they caught companies such as Avon at major turning points in their fortunes.

The way Soros thinks about markets is surprisingly similar to that of many of the investors discussed earlier. And, like all the others, he stresses the importance of understanding what you are investing in, and of having an 'edge' – some way in which you excel compared with other

---

* This major league gambler is also the Hungarian emigré who is showering millions of dollars on Eastern Europe, mainly to promote an open society. And he is the philosopher manqué whose best known book, *The Alchemy of Finance*, challenges *A Brief History of Time* for obscurity.

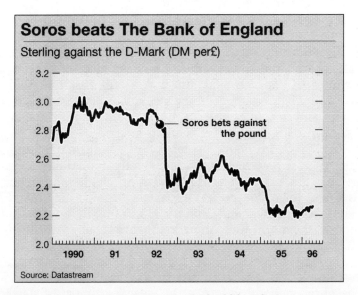

Soros beats The Bank of England

Sterling against the D-Mark (DM per£)

Soros bets against
the pound

Source: Datastream

Fig 9.3 You know the popular simile, 'he lied like a finance minister on the eve of devaluation'. George Soros has it engraved on his heart. He bet £10 billion against the pound staying in the ERM in 1992.

investors. But unlike most of them, he thinks he understands markets and can master them.

The theory of reflexivity

A crude summary of Soros' reflexivity theory is that markets always overdo things, both at the top and at the bottom. A knowledgeable operator with a strong nerve can make a lot of money out of catching them on the turn. Put that way it sounds banal. But Soros's explanation of his theory reflects his philosophical bent.

He agrees with Buffett in rubbishing efficient market theory*, but goes much further. Buffett is content to watch for the odd occasions on which markets are not efficient and take advantage of them. Soros argues not just

---

* The efficient market hypothesis states that the prices of securities fully reflect available information. Soros argues that the reflection is that of a distorting mirror.

that markets are never efficient, but that they never can be efficient. In the stockmarket, for example, investors' views about shares are one of the factors which determine their values. And the actual values of stocks also influence the fortunes of the company by, say, facilitating issues and takeovers. Each element in the stockmarket both acts on the others and is acted upon by them. There are no constants.

Unsurprisingly, then, all markets are in a permanent state of flux. Every investor's perception of what is happening is inherently flawed, because it is logically impossible to form an objective assessment of a market of which you are part. And any idea that stocks can have a true or fundamental value (as Graham and Buffet believe) is equally flawed. Indeed, the more efficient market theory is believed, the less efficient markets become.

The market's instability matters to Soros because his awareness of it is what (in his view) gives him his edge. He has christened the interplay between participants' flawed perceptions and the actual course of events 'reflexivity'. His superior understanding of the interplay makes it easier for him to understand what is happening when a stock is going through a typical boom/bust cycle. And if his understanding is correct he can make money from trading.

Take a practical example: the US conglomerates boom of the 1960s. Investors' perceptions were flawed: they failed to distinguish between normal earnings growth and acquisition-generated earnings growth. They bought conglomerate shares, whose prices rose higher than they would have done without this misconception. The rise in the share prices had two consequences. First, it fuelled investor enthusiasm and expectations. Second, the conglomerates were enabled to make more acquisitions with their highly-rated shares.

And so the self-fuelling boom moved further and further out of touch with fundamentals: the total pot of earnings produced by the operating subsidiaries. The wider the gap between investor expectations and share prices on the one hand and fundamentals on the other, the more vulnerable those expectations and prices. Eventually then, the whole conglomerates boom came crashing down.*

* But it does not always end that way. Sometimes a company

Soros made money out of the conglomerates boom both on the way up and on the way down. He attributes his success to his understanding of what was going on: both the basic misconception and the interplay of the various market factors thereafter. But what is equally significant is that he took the risk of acting on his hypothesis.

What he is always looking for is a gap between expectations and shares prices on the one hand and fundamentals on the other which widens far enough to leave the connecting string taut. Then some development in the real world of fundamentals snaps the string. For example, Britain's ejection from the ERM in 1992 or the central banks' intervention to support the dollar in 1995.

Sometimes, as with his sterling bet in 1992, Soros's speculative activities actually nudge events forward in the direction he wants. And in 1993 just letting the markets know that he was buying gold and property prompted an imitative stampede which condensed a normal boom into a period of a few weeks.

Soros would agree with Buffett that 'wild swings in market prices . . . cause the gains to be inequitably distributed among various investors.' But his rider would be that he wants an unfair share, thinks he knows how to get it, and is prepared to pay for his mistakes. Getting that unfair share is painful, because it involves risk and the danger of being wrong and losing money.

The speculator's first job is to stay as clear-minded and as open-minded as possible. There is no point in speculating unless you have a relatively sound grasp of the fundamen-

can take advantage of an inflated share price to buy something which will justify that share price. For example, when Sir James Goldsmith's Cavenham began its acquisition spree in the early 1970s, it was a hollow company behind the inflated paper. But once it had used that paper to buy the asset rich Bovril in August 1971, the sham was well on the way to becoming a reality. A neat example of Soros's point that investor perceptions and share prices can actively influence a company's fortunes. It helps if, like Goldsmith, the company's management has a good understanding of what is going on. He too made money by testing his hypothesis in the laboratory of the stockmarket.

tals. But there is also no point in speculating unless the fundamentals are changing. Since the target is moving, the speculator's hypothesis must also be flexible: he is constantly testing it against reality and adjusting or sometimes abandoning it. 'I make as many mistakes as the next guy,' says Soros, 'Where I excel is in recognising my mistakes.'

The speculator's other job is deciding how much risk to take on when. Soros tends to start small and increase his exposure as a trend intensifies and approaches its climax. 'One of the hardest things to judge is what level of risk is safe. There are no universally valid yardsticks; each situation has to be judged on its own merit. In the final analysis you must rely on your instincts for survival.'

Lessons from Soros

There are several morals the amateur investor can draw from Soros' explanation of how he conducts his financial experiments.

- Know your limitations. Do not speculate unless you understand what is going on better than anybody else in the market. For the amateur this is effectively saying don't speculate. You are never going to understand what is happening in the market as well as the pros.
- Be flexible. Markets are constantly changing. So investors need to be flexible if their strategy involves taking a view of markets. A theory that looked plausible yesterday, may look quite wrong today.
- Markets always overheat. Stay as objective as possible when assessing them. But remember that they can keep getting further out of touch with reality for a long time before the string snaps.
- Weigh up the risks. Be realistic both in assessing the risks involved in a particular strategy and in assessing what level of risk you are happy to take on. Timing is a key part of intelligent risk-taking.
- Stay humble. If you discover you are mistaken, the sooner you admit it, the less it will cost you.

Postscript: over to you

One of the best recent examples of an outstandingly successful private investor was a New York woman, called Anne Scheiber, who died in 1994 aged 101 and worth $22mn. She started by putting $5,000 into the stockmarket in 1944 when she retired. She researched very thoroughly (in the public library), before she bought and her portfolio had some overlap with Buffett's. She stuck to blue chips, and picked several franchise companies, such as Coca-Cola and Schering-Plough. She never sold unless she needed the money. Her success has been attributed to three things: picking the right blue chips, patience and the benevolent laws of compound interest.

Was she a value investor or a growth investor? Both schools could claim her. But the label doesn't really matter. There is more to successful investment than writing down a formula. What Scheiber had was method, diligence and passion.

This book has deliberately avoided providing a summary of 'Twelve rules which can turn you into a great investor'. The purpose of these two chapters is to provide some examples of how different successful investors go to work. It is up to the reader to use them in whatever way suits his own personality and aims.

Growth Investment

IN A NUTSHELL

1. Whereas value investment is based entirely or mainly on quantitative criteria (sums), growth investment is based mainly on qualitative criteria (value judgements).

2. Most growth investors distinguish between different types of growth stock: the best are relatively stable, others may have a limited life or merely be passing through a growth phase.

3. T. Rowe Price defined a classic growth company as one with long term growth of earnings 'reaching a new high level per share at the peak of each succeeding major business cycle' and which gives indications of reaching new high earnings at the peak of future business cycles.

4. When the stockmarket reached dangerous levels in the late 1960s, Price was one of the few to say publicly that the growth concept had outlived its usefulness.

5. Peter Lynch reckons it is easier to achieve capital growth if growth stocks are not the only constituents of a portfolio. He insists that any growth stock must be an attractive business, whose shares are good value, with a clean balance sheet. He argues that most people can find promising growth stocks in their own backyard.

6. Jim Slater has publicised the Price Earnings Growth factor (PEG) as a more reliable yardstick for growth shares than the traditional PE ratio. He suggests ten other criteria for growth shares.

7. George Soros's theory of reflexivity explains how the

well-informed and intelligent speculator can make money out of the stockmarket's excesses at both top and bottom. He regards the market as a laboratory for testing hypotheses.

Chapter 10
Stockbrokers' Analysts

Analysts are the research arm of the stockbroking trade. They spend their time devilling around in the details of company finances, market prospects and profits projections with the aim of adding some science to predictions about where a market, a sector or a particular company's shares are headed next.

All of the large institutional stockbroking firms and investment banks employ analysts, and some brokers who cater for retail investors are also starting to provide a rudimentary analysis service. At the large City brokers, most analysts are employed looking at individual companies, under stockmarket sector headings. Depending on the number of companies in the sector, and the size of the brokerage house, anything up to half a dozen analysts will work on each individual sector such as banking, engineering, oils and utilities, with a similar number of dedicated sales staff advising on these stocks. That can add up to a research staff of over a hundred in the large City brokers.

The general sales force, and the broker's own market makers, will come to these analysts for advice on where they think a particular stock or sector is heading, or for an interpretation of a particular piece of news. If, for example, airline traffic figures drop or retail sales bounce unexpectedly, analysts will offer views on which airlines or stores are likely to suffer or benefit most.

As well as those specialising in detailed UK stockmarket sectors, brokers employ analysts to look at overall equity market trends and switches from one sector to another. Many will have teams looking at gilt and other bond markets too, plus some who look at which direction Wall Street and Tokyo are heading for. The largest will also have some sector specialists in New York or Tokyo looking at individual American and Japanese companies, though British forays into this field are declining. More recently there has been a spate of foreign purchases of British brokers to add a global dimension to the largest US and European firms: the acquisition of UK broker Smith New Court by Merrill Lynch is a case in point.

Some brokers which are integrated with banks also employ professional economists and currency analysts, and a good few have chartists on the books to provide technical analysis. The economists usually work with the equity market strategists on developing an overall view of market trends, while the chartists plough a more lonely furrow.

Each year overall market views and individual stockmarket sectors are judged in the *Extel* analysts' survey (publicly available for £300), in which institutional investors vote for the analysts they feel have been the most impressive over the previous year. These rankings are hotly contested. There is a great deal of kudos associated with becoming an '*Extel* rated' analyst, and success more or less guarantees increased business and higher bonuses.

The two main weapons in the analyst's armoury to score in the Extel survey, and to attract business day-to-day, are telephone advice and published reports. Analysts, who often have many years of experience looking at particular industries, periodically produce detailed assessments of what is happening to their individual business sectors and the prospects for each of the companies in their sector. These are often backed up with individual company notes if there has been a factory visit or the company had produced annual profits figures, and shorter 'flash' notes overnight in response to some unexpected event.

All of these reports will include specific stock recommendations of varying complexity. Some will have a basic, 'buy', 'hold' or 'sell' view of a particular company, others a one-to-five score which ranges from strong buy to strong sell, others again a short and long term view of the stock with a risk weighting attached. There will normally be a phone call blitz to clients following publication of a big report, with the aim of getting business before other broking firms catch up.

Analysts are also on the phone to institutional investors every day to flesh out or update views, explain a point which has not come across or just to stay in touch.

Institutional investors who are minded to could drown in the volume of detailed and apparently high-quality information which is available, and certainly would never have time to do anything else if they read it all.

By now, many private investors who yearn for that kind of service may be feeling more than a touch jealous. But the level of service is only supported by the millions every large fund manager pays each year in commission. There is also a wide spread in the quality of analysis and the usefulness of the research. Star analysts' output is eagerly read and their opinions are frequently sought, but there is a long tail of me-too work which adds very little to the sum of stockmarket knowledge.

The tendency to bias

In judging analysts' output, it is also important to remember where they came from: analysts were originally conceived as a marketing service provided by brokers to justify those huge sums in commission which institutional investors pay for dealing in stocks and shares. Nowadays that defensive rationale as been put to work as part of the stockbroker's sales push: the analysts' objective is to persuade clients to deal, because turnover generates commission, and commission is what keeps stockbrokers in their Ferraris.

Inevitably, analysts' recommendations are coloured by this. They will, for example, constantly come up with ideas for why an investor should switch one share for another. When an analyst takes a view on a market or company, he recommends purchases more often than sales. This is partly because markets have a tendency to rise and institutions have a continual flow of money from pension contributions and investments to put into markets; but also because investors tend to be optimistic and like to hear good news stories. More cynically, a 'buy' recommendation can be touted to any client, but a 'sell' note is usually of interest only to the much smaller proportion of investors who happen to own a particular share or bond.

'Break-up valuations' are a classic tactic which show just how much analysts are driven by the need to generate

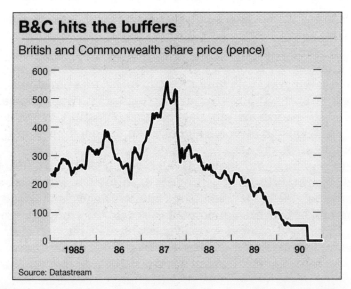

B&C hits the buffers

British and Commonwealth share price (pence)

Source: Datastream

Fig 10.1 Even analysts don't get all their sums right. One 'break-up valuation' calculated that British and Commonwealth was worth over £2 a share, just six months before it collapsed.

turnover. In a quiet market trading desks and sales people will press analysts for some recommendation or other. An easy response is to take a conglomerate, perhaps seen as a little sleepy, and work out how much its constituent parts would fetch from ideal buyers. The result normally adds up to much more than the current market valuation of the conglomerate's stock. So the broker issues a buy note on the basis that either someone will bid for these undervalued assets, or parts of the business will be sold, or that the current management will be forced to stimulate the business.

Business may be generated, and if the stock price moves it may make the market reports of the newspapers, but the number of such valuations which lead to real corporate raids and takeover bids is tiny. Such valuations can also be hopelessly wrong. One break up valuation calculated that the financial conglomerate British & Commonwealth was worth well over £2 a share, just six months before the company collapsed worthless.

Besides the incessant need to deal, there are other

pressures which skew analysts' views. Companies hate sell recommendations and do all they can indirectly to discourage them. Analysts, who are only human, depend on companies for a lot of their information and spend much time talking to their senior executives. No-one much cares for the frosty atmosphere at meetings which follow a sell note, so analysts will try to avoid them, possibly by the use of euphemisms in published notes and a quiet chat on the telephone to clients.

In one infamous incident, the blue-blooded broker Cazenove was accused of telling its institutional investors to 'bargepole' – that is, avoid – the retailer Kingfisher, just after the broker had been appointed to act for the company. The truth of the allegation was never established, but despite the sharp and sustained fall in Kingfisher's price over the next 18 months, the incident left a bad taste in everyone's mouth. Companies are extremely sensitive about criticism.

Some companies adopt an aggressive approach and 'forget' to tell wayward analysts some juicy titbits of information about the current market scene. Strong buyers of a stock, by contrast, are greeted like favoured sons and daughters, and are privy to dark secrets. While all analysts would protest strongly that they resist such influences, it remains true that it takes more courage to issue a sell note than a buy report.

This is particularly so if the broking firm acts as a company's stockmarket adviser, the house broker, or if the merchant banking arm of the broking house does business for the company. Worst of all is when the company in question actually owns the broker. The BZW banking analyst who issued a sell recommendation on Barclays just after the clearer had taken over the broking business a decade ago was widely seen as having taken his career, if not his life, in his hands.

The upshot of all this is that investors have to look well beyond the pure analyst's recommendation before taking his advice. First it is important to establish whether a broking house has a business relationship with a company which may, however unconsciously, affect its view. Then investors have to be on the look out for ideas likely to produce excessive churning, where holders are encouraged to buy and sell too often.

Take a case where a company is viewed as a long term growth stock with the potential to double in value over a couple of years. Analysts may well be tempted to advise strong buying at certain times, and profit taking at others, arguing that the share is about to spurt higher or that its rise is temporarily overdone. Yet from the investor's perspective, given that it is not always possible to be so agile or so accurate, the best strategy for such a good long term prospect may well be to buy and lock away the holding in the bottom drawer until it has fulfilled its promise. Doing that, however, means turning a deaf ear to many an analyst's siren phone calls.

To avoid some of these problems, many of the larger institutional investors have set up their own analysis teams. Some fund management groups now use the fact that they have their own research department as a competitive marketing tool. Another reason for the trend is that institutional investors are becoming increasingly aware of their responsibilities for keeping company managers up to scratch, rather than just voting with their feet. It is hard to have your finger on the corporate pulse if all your information comes second hand. If this trend continues, it could prompt stockbrokers and investment banks to re-think the objectives of their own research departments.

But analysts employed by fund managers also depend on companies for detailed information, and they also feel under pressure to come up with a continuous stream of ideas to justify their existence. A media analyst who announced one January that she thought little or nothing was likely to happen in her sector that year may have been honest, but she was also effectively inviting her employers to dispense with her services. The problems of churning stocks, and of a systematic positive bias, are hard to eliminate.

Both broking and institutional analysts also have something of a herd mentality. Their sources of information are often similar, and they watch each other's forecasts carefully. But it is rare for one analyst to spot a real opportunity

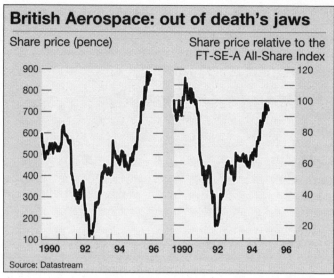

Fig 10.2 Leading analysts failed to spot the cash haemorrhage that
nearly killed BAe in 1991–92. They reckoned the company had misled
them and were slow to forgive it.

or impending catastrophe that has not been seen by others
too.

In the classic case of the near-collapse of British Aerospace in 1991–92, for example, none of the mainstream
analysts had spotted the cash drain from the business which
necessitated a huge rights issue and which almost brought
the company to its knees. Embarrassingly the leading
analysts were mostly forecasting 1991 profits almost equal
to those in 1990 – partly because the company had led them
to expect that result – just a month before the company
launched its rescue rights issue and the share price collapsed. It took many analysts a long time to forgive BAe, but
the damage to their reputation had been done, and few
investors avoided the crash courtesy of timely warnings
from analysts.

For all that, analysts do provide a great deal of useful
information on companies and can act as a helpful sounding
board. Investors simply have to recognise the systematic
bias in their recommendations and adjust accordingly. They
also have to acknowledge analysts' limitations.

How they do it

Sector and individual stock analysts will tend to start with a 'bottom up' approach to their work. This involves them in assembling a detailed picture of each company's finances and projections for its future profitability, which are then aggregated to produce an overall view of prospects for a sector. Normally, these views produce a picture of a company's trading and stockmarket prospects over the next 18 months.

This, say analysts, is the time-frame most investors look at, but it is important to note that such an approach can ignore longer term factors which could have a substantial impact on the company's business. This can at times be extremely important. It is not that analysts are stupid, or have failed to appreciate long term factors; rather they form the pragmatic view that investors will ignore falling pianos which are unlikely to hit them in the next couple of years. In the case of some very long term industries such as aerospace, this can be a severe limitation.

The basic building block for a bottom-up approach is a computer spread-sheet model for each company. Normally, this produces a model for the company's profit and loss account, in the current year and the year following, with the details based on the previous year's published accounts, plus any statements the company may have made about trading conditions in the meanwhile, adjusted for any more general information about conditions in the markets where the company operates.

To take a relatively straightforward example, Sir Richard Greenbury, Marks & Spencer's (M&S) chairman, might say at an annual meeting in July that trading was a 'lot better than last year', or 'a little ahead of last year,' 'broadly in line with last year' or even 'difficult'. Since M&S has a March 31 year-end, this gives analysts a view of trading four months into the new period. Many retailers also give specific trading statements in the New Year about Christmas trading, since this is such an important element of their business.

The retailing analyst will take such trading statements, along with government figures on retail sales, into account in guessing how much more M&S will sell this year than last. He will also adjust sales for how much retail inflation is likely to put up sale prices, and how much new store space the company opens during the year.

Even in a reasonably simple business like M&S this adds up to a fair number of variables, and the analyst will have to try to conduct the exercise for both the food and clothing sides of the business separately, as they may well be affected by different factors. Depending on the sophistication of his model, any or all of these factors may be explicitly included, but one way or another he will end up with a guesstimate of the current year's turnover for M&S and a more speculative view of prospects for the following year.

The analyst then moves down the profit and loss account and makes similar adjustments to the other figures. Whole-sale price inflation may give a guide to changes in M&S's raw material costs. The pay settlement with the workforce will also have been published and the analyst can assess the total pay bill by working out how staff numbers have changed as a result of new store openings increasing numbers, and efficiency savings cutting staff. Interest costs or income can also be estimated from last year's numbers and a view of what is happening to the company's cash flow. If there has been a change in depreciation policy, the analyst can adjust accordingly.

Once the analyst has determined his guess of M&S's turnover and deducted its expenses, he ends up with a prediction of pre-tax profits. Deducting tax – easy for M&S but tricky in some other cases – he can calculate post tax earnings and earnings per share, and then come to a view about how much the company might be able to increase its dividend.

He can then compare M&S's earnings and dividend growth prospects with, say Boots and Kingfisher, to see how the company is doing relative to its competitors. If the analyst then thought that M&S's earnings growth prospects were better than other retailers', but the company's price-earnings ratio was lower than the average for the sector, he might rate the company as a buy.

Other examples are more complicated, but the same principle applies. Engineering group GKN, for example, has a motor components business, a defence equipment arm and a wooden pallets operation, all of which need to be individually modelled. Within that, the motor components operation produces drives for front-wheel vehicles in most of the world's markets, so currency and local car market conditions need to be factored in. The defence operation is made up of Westland Helicopters and an armoured vehicles business, which have different order books and profit profiles.

Sophisticated analysts will also produce models of a company's balance sheets and cash flows, to give a more complete picture. However, before any of them publish their figures, they will normally send their calculations to the companies concerned, to make sure they have not dropped any particularly large bricks. Companies then nudge the analyst if a particular figure is wildly out of line with reality, a service which saves analysts embarrassment, but does tend to lead to a uniformity of view.

Some figures, such as the tax rates which apply to complex multinationals, may not be calculable by an analyst, and in these instances, companies will tend to give advice on an appropriate rate to use when they publish their annual figures. A finance director might say, for example, 'that as a result of the acquisition of the loss-making Widgets plc during the year, the group's effective tax rate will drop from a standard 33 per cent to 25 per cent for the next three years.'

Once again, however, analysts are dependent on the companies for much information, and those who have become persona non grata may also not find any but the most basic help forthcoming.

A focus on results

Because the publication of a company's annual and half-year profits figures is the time at which most new financial information becomes available, analysts pay particular attention to these figures and normally make the most significant changes to their forecasts then.

Typically, a company will publish its figures on the Stock Exchange's information system at 7.30am, and follow this up with a senior management presentation to analysts somewhere in the City at around 9am the same morning. Analysts will question the finance director in detail about the line-by-line financial issues to update their models, and the company's chief executive about market conditions and trading prospects.

Once the meeting has ended, the analysts will phone their trading desks with any new information which has emerged and any changed recommendation. It is not particularly unusual to see a share swing one way in response to a quick glance at the profit figures first thing in the morning, and then swing another after issues have been clarified at the meeting. Companies put a lot of effort into these results presentations, as they are the only opportunity to influence City opinion about a company en masse.

Despite their confident air, many directors are nervous of the baying analytical pack, especially if there is something about the company's performance to be nervous about. Back at their offices later, analysts will follow up their early calls to investors with chats to the financial press in the afternoon. Many then produce a short reaction note to investors overnight, and a more considered piece on the figures a few days later.

And a focus on business

As well as the detailed financial information, many analysts will keep an eye on the trade press for their particular markets and, stay in touch with new product developments which could have a significant impact on a company's future profits. Companies also organise visits to factories which produce a spate of brokers' notes at otherwise quiet times of the year.

Such detailed research tends to be restricted to the top 350 or so companies in the stockmarket in which there is a substantial share trade. Many below that go largely unregarded, although there a few small-cap stock specialists, and some of the regional brokers will follow smaller local companies in Birmingham, Manchester, Newcastle or Edinburgh.

However, since the big 350 account for over 90 per cent of the overall UK stockmarket's value, the mainstream City stockbroking firms can aggregate these 'bottom-up' views into assessments of the overall sector and stockmarket's earnings prospects, and compare them with the outlook for gilts or overseas stockmarkets.

The view from the bridge

Most brokerage firms will also have a much smaller team of grandly-named strategists, who take large scale economic forecasts to produce figures for the likely earnings prospects of the stockmarket over the forthcoming two years. Working with the firm's economists, they will take into account overall growth in the economy, likely productivity gains, the impact of any interest rate changes on company finances, and exchange rate movements on export prospects to produce forecasts of 'top-down' earnings. Interestingly, these often differ by a couple of percentage points from the aggregate 'bottom-up' view of the sector analysts.

Frequently the sector analysts' views are more optimistic than the strategists. Cynics argue that, since not all analysts are born Pollyannas, once again their bias in favour of the companies they study is showing. But it is probably slightly more complicated than that. Sector analysts do tend to be influenced by the companies they talk to, and these companies are likely themselves to have a more parochial view of the broader economic influences than sector strategists. So gaps between top-down and bottom-up forecasts may in practice reflect a gap between what economists expect and what companies expect. If this gap is wide, it can be an advance warning sign, and is certainly worth pondering.

In Spring 1996, for example, BZW remarked that its sector analysts were less optimistic than its strategists in their earnings forecasts, but less pessimistic in their cash flow forecasts. If so, was it the sector analysts or the companies that failed to recognise the size of future capital spending needs? Or were the strategists wrong?

The market strategists produce monthly or quarterly advice notes on which bond or stock markets look the most attractive and how assets should be divided between them, as well as giving day-to-day views to institutions on the phone. They will also dissect the UK stockmarket to produce specific sector recommendations, often in concert with their bottom-up teams.

Such themed analysis might take as its starting point an expected sharp rise in consumer spending as a way of recommending which retailers might do well, or a fall in company investment to identify capital goods companies likely to suffer. Again the themes are all about generating ideas for turnover.

Applying the research

Both the bottom-up and top-down analysts will use some of the more sophisticated investment yardsticks to manipulate their data once they have assembled their basic models. Private investors cannot mimic the detailed modelling of analysts without great effort, but they can make use of their conclusions if they can get hold of the publications, and they can use many of the same tools in analysing investment prospects.

Individual stock analysts, for example, will look at the price-earnings ratio of a company, relative to its sector or the market. Such price-earnings relatives (PER) are normally expressed as a percentage, so for example, if a company has a PE ratio of 16.5 and that of its sector is 14.5 its PE Relative would be 114:

$$16.5/14.5 \times 100 = 114$$

In a more extreme case, another company which had a PE ratio of 9.5 while that of its sector was 18, it would have a PER of 53:

$$9.5/18 \times 100 = 53$$

More normally, PERs are between 80 and 120, and if a company has a PER of 80 while an analyst thinks the market has underestimated its growth prospects, he may put out a buy note. Similarly for a company with a PER of 120 which the analyst thinks has been over-rated he might publish a sell note.

For income stocks, which are mostly rated on their dividend-paying capacity, analysts will also look at the yield of a particular stock, divided by the yield of its sector or the market. So if a share has a yield of 4.5 per cent, while its sector is yielding 3.5 per cent, its yield relative will be:

$$4.5/3.5 \times 100 = 129$$

These yield relatives can be a useful guide, because if in the view of the analyst the company with a 4.5 per cent yield has as good dividend growth prospects as the rest of its sector, it may well be a cheap yield stock.

Such PER and yield relatives are usually included in the data on brokers' notes. One important point for the unwary to note here is that analysts are always dealing in prospective PE ratios and yields, which means that for the current year, not the year which has just been completed. On the other hand the prices pages of newspapers publish historic PE and yield figures, because they are the only certain data. The prospective figures used by analysts are a spread of forecasts.

Sector analysts will also use their profits forecasts two and three years out to assess the worth of recovery stocks. In the midst of the last recession, for example, many engineering companies were making small profits or even losses, and some were not even paying a dividend from which to calculate a yield, yet the shares were not worthless. Analysts would look forward two or three years to assess what the earnings for the company might be at the peak of the next cycle. They would also form a view of the earnings of the market as a whole for the same period.

The analyst might then somewhat arbitrarily calculate that at the peak of the cycle the company's stock should be at a PER of 80 to the market as a whole, that is to say be valued at a 20 per cent discount to the market, to take into account the uncertainty of the forecast and the cyclical nature of the company's earnings. He can then back-track to give a valuation for the shares today, which could be higher or lower than their actual level in the market.

While such mathematical tools are used every day by analysts, it is the comparison of these figures with the broker's view of business prospects which gives rise to the meaningful recommendations. The text in a broker's note of why he thinks some trend or valuation tool is significant is thus at least as important as the figures themselves. It may be that something as apparently far removed from the stockmarket as that the fashion success of the Ultrabra is the important element driving the profits of Courtaulds Textiles, and so making it an attractive stock. The fact that the company's PER then looks cheap is an effect, not a cause, of the stock's attractiveness.

Hands on the cash

The more forward-looking UK firms admit that US brokers and analysts are more sophisticated than they are in the tools and techniques that they use. Just as UK markets were very slow to come to grips with derivatives, UK analysts tend to be slow to adopt new analytical methods. Some argue that the problem lies not with them but with their clients, who are reluctant to move away from conventional valuation techniques. But the fact remains that many sound slightly apologetic when publishing a circular based on something as 'novel' as price-to-cash flow ratios.

Many US analysts prefer to use price-to-cash flow ratios (see Chapter 7 pages 175–76 and 179) rather than PE ratios in assessing companies. This is because cash is a much harder figure for companies to disguise than profits, and because it often gives a much better sense of the underlying health of the business.

In 1992–93, for example, US investors were buying BP stock after its dividend had been halved and the profits had collapsed. US analysts were recommending the stock heavily as its price to cash flow ratio was much lower than the other oil majors. UK analysts were looking at the company's profits and capacity to pay dividends and were much more pessimistic. In fact the US analysts were right. BP's cash was being used to repay huge amounts of debt, cost cutting was improving cash flow further, and the company's ability to pay dividends was rapidly being restored. Such cash flow analysis is beginning to catch on in the UK, but still lags behind the US.

Other US cash flow models are also used by some analysts to calculate the value of start-up businesses which are growing fast. Mobile telecoms companies have been valued in this way, since in their early years they have to spend heavily on establishing networks and advertising to attract subscribers, but once that five years investment phase is passed, they earn good profits from the subscriber base. Analysts try to model how cash will flow in the business over the next decade to establish a view of what financial shape the mobile phone company will be in. They will then produce a notional profit and loss account for the company, and apply a suitable PE ratio to give a value for the company at that long range.

Having formed a view of what the company will be worth in ten years time, the analyst has to relate that to what it is worth today. He will discount the value in ten years time for the fact that investing in a company today which does not yet pay dividends means foregoing dividends or interest elsewhere. These 'forfeited' returns are replaced by a discount for every year until the company reaches its 'normal' state, in this case a decade away. The rate of discount for every year is compounded over the decade to produce a much lower valuation for the company now than it will be worth, but the numbers can still be substantial. Orange, the mobile phone company, was valued in exactly this way and had a value of £2.8bn when it was floated on the stockmarket in March 1996, just two years after the network had opened.

These 'discounted cash flow' models are of course beloved of those with mobile phone businesses to sell, but many other investors have become a little wary of them, as they were used to inglorious effect in producing valuations for Eurotunnel and EuroDisney prior to flotation. Investors who had their fingers burned in the subsequent slump in both companies' shares may think the method is invalid. In truth the tool carries the same warning as other analytical methods: the model is only as good as the data and assumptions which go into it.

Taking the wider view

As well as making use of the bottom-up analysts' techniques, individual investors can latch on to the views of the top-down strategists. They will normally produce views on the direction of global markets and stockmarket sectors, which are aimed at institutions. The institutions still stick closely to the average, and only occasionally venture a ha'penny on an unconventional view. So if, for example, the banks account for 10 per cent of the UK market by value, institutions will tend to have 10 per cent of their UK equity funds in banks.

Brokers will tend to say either that they like banks and so would recommend clients to increase their weighting in banks to 15 per cent, or think their prospects are lousy, and so would cut their holding to 5 per cent of the total. A similar process applies for weightings held in UK gilts and property, and in dividing up assets between countries.

It is impractical, and may be unwise, for individuals to attempt to follow such models slavishly. It makes sense for British private investors to have a core holding in UK equities, possibly via a low-cost tracking unit trust, as well as some money on deposit and perhaps some bond holdings. And it may in some circumstances be useful for some types of investor to put a proportion of their funds overseas, though not more than 25 per cent of the total invested: again mostly in US or Japanese tracking funds. (See Chapter 13 for more on asset allocation and Chapter 14 pages 323 and 327 for some model portfolios.)

But investors can use the asset allocation recommendations of professionals to weight the more discretionary part of their funds. If strategists are pushing emerging markets or the US, investors who buy the argument can up their holding in these markets, either through direct holdings of stocks or funds. Similarly, they can follow recommendations to avoid stagnant markets or stockmarket sectors by cutting their holdings of these stocks. However, it is not sensible to be too mathematically precise about this. And it is never worth incurring high dealing costs by churning your portfolio in order to keep abreast of market fashions.

Always remember analysts are producing these views because they want people to deal. Bear in mind too that the view of those who would shift your assets around is only a view. Just because it is dressed up in fancy arithmetic does not make a strategist's judgement any more right.

Getting your hands on the product

For all the limitations of analysts' publications, they are something most private investors would love to have, but often find it very difficult to get hold of. Small investors can, however, get some reading of analysts' views from the press. The *Investors Chronicle* and *The Daily Telegraph* regularly publish details of analysts' views, which normally omit most figures, but do give a flavour of the outlook.

Most stock comment columns in the newspapers are also heavily influenced by brokers' views, and in most cases the conclusions reached in newspaper comment notes the day after a company's results do not stray far from the analytical consensus on prospects. (See Chapter 11.)

Unfortunately, most investors will have little hope of getting more direct access to brokers' research. The majority of broking firms will not allow their analysts to send their detailed research to personal investors in any circumstances. An FT telephone poll in early 1996 showed that 12 of the 19 broker firms which came top in the Extel poll would not provide research to the general public. Some left it up to the individual analyst to decide. And some of those prepared in principle to be helpful, said that they would charge for the research.

Some firms use the Financial Services Act as a reason for not sending research to people they do not know. With others it depends who you are. If you work for the company concerned or are a student you may stand a better chance with some firms. Others will send it to their own private clients, but not to unconnected people. Charges are usually high enough to be a deterrent. A few sheets of paper could cost up to £100.

The larger private client stockbrokers do themselves get research from the top broking houses, but most of them would be very reluctant to pass it on to individual investors. How much institutional research a private client broker gets depends broadly on how much business the firm gives to the market-making arm of the bigger firm. A large private client firm might rate high enough to get a phone call from a salesman, be able to pick up the recommendations off the 'closed user' group on Topic, an electronic stockmarket information service, and get the written back-up.

But most brokers who deal with the public argue that research intended for an institutional market needs substantial processing before it can be useful for the retail market. Private client brokers often have their own research teams. And they will incorporate some of the facts and forecasts from the professional research into their own research reports, but sometimes come up with different conclusions. This is partly because private investors normally have a longer time horizon and always have higher dealing costs. So, for example, an analyst's recommendation to institutional clients to sell might be translated into a hold for private clients.

Private client brokers' own research teams tend to number between five and 20. Their emphasis varies. Some concentrate on the larger UK companies, some reckon they can add more value by looking at the comparatively neglected smaller companies and searching for special situations. Provincial brokers may be strong in local companies. These firms are often willing to send out their own research, even to people who are not clients – yet.

Electronic information is in its infancy but expanding very fast. Barclays, for example, has been experimenting with touch-screen video terminals in some of its branches, which will give an opinion on popular questions, such as whether an imminent new issue is a buy. One website provider, ESI, plans to put leading brokers' forecasts published by the *Estimates Directory* (See Appendix A) on the Internet.

But the most interesting part of professional brokers'

research is usually the background information. That is what the professional investor relies on to make his investment decisions, and that is what the private investor needs to make his investment decisions. But his chances of obtaining it are slim.

Who wins out?

With all of the weight of resources behind them, analysts do have a big edge over small investors in the information game. But the way in which they use it is not always the same, since their primary concern is turnover rather than market direction. They also live in a hot-house environment where people tend to stick close together in their views for fear of looking silly, and where companies are constantly pouring honey into their ears. As a result, they do not hold all of the cards.

Private investors can form a pretty good view of business prospects from reading the financial press, and can often get more information on any particular business which catches their eye from the companies involved or the trade press. They can often get hold of earnings and dividend forecasts from the *Earnings Guide*, the *Estimates Directory*, or the *Company REFs* guide (see Appendix A). They can then apply the same tools as the analysts without the hard sweat of producing the models themselves.

Those who are able to get their hands on brokers' analysis as well can enjoy the luxury of the detailed analysts' views without the necessity to follow the crowd. But the vital thing to bear in mind, as with most investment, is that you will probably have the brokers' views after the professionals have had time to read, learn, inwardly digest, and act on it. There will be no quick killing to be made by following a broker's advice, and you may be the last in on a quick hit. But if you are looking for long term gains and want to plan strategically, brokers' analysts and their techniques can be a useful aide.

Stockbrokers' Analysts

IN A NUTSHELL

1. Stockbrokers, investment banks and some large fund management firms all employ large numbers of stock-market analysts. Most brokers' analysts specialise in companies in specific sectors. But some look at UK and global market trends, usually in conjunction with the firms' economists and currency analysts. Some of the larger firms also have sector specialists for overseas markets, notably America and Japan. The annual Extel analysts survey, which gives the analysts rankings, affects their pay and prospects.

2. Be aware of two inherent biases in analysts' work. First, analysts exist to generate business for their firm. So they have a predisposition to look for tactical switches, rather than encourage clients to sit tight. Second, a company's house broker may find it hard to be overtly rude about its client. And all analysts who want to continue to have good access to the companies they cover, need to be circumspect in what they say about them.

3. Sector specialists normally use company statements, industry figures and information in the trade press to produce spreadsheet forecasts for each company's p&l, balance sheet and cash flow statement. Much of their activity focuses on the announcements of annual and interim results. Market strategists work from the broader economic picture downwards. Forecasts from sector specialists and top-down strategists often vary slightly.

4. Different analysts favour slightly different tools in their comparative analysis. But all are looking for a mis-match between the current rating and their view of the prospects for the company.

5. It is extremely difficult for private investors to get hold of any of this research directly, though some private client brokers use it as the basis for their own newsletters. If you do get it or read about it remember that the market will already have adjusted for the recommendations.

Chapter 11
Newspaper Comment

Newspapers are many people's most immediate and closest approach to the buzz and hum of the City. Business developments, company results, market predictions, corporate takeovers and flotations are all given in the financial pages of the press. For the individual investor, the question is, how much reliance can he place on what he reads there?

In the case of routine reporting of financial events, newspapers will get their information from much the same sources as brokers' analysts, albeit normally in less detail. In the case of annual results, for example, journalists from City desks will collect a copy of the annual results announcement published on the Stock Exchange system, and go along to a presentation by the company's executives in the City, which often follows on immediately from the analysts' meeting, typically at around 11am.

They will hear a simplified version of the same message given to the analysts by the finance director and chief executive. Then they either shoot back to their offices to compare notes with analysts, or stay on to have their ears bent further over a good lunch.

First the news

Much of the straight reporting of news which follows this provides some useful raw material for individual investors, though many small companies go unreported by newspapers. In any well-written account of a company's annual figures, a reporter will include figures for the company's turnover, pre-tax profits, earnings per share and dividends, with comparative figures for the previous year. There will also normally be some discussion of salient developments in the company's business, and a mention of how the company's share price has reacted to the day's news.

This is sufficient to give investors enough raw information to calculate PE ratios and yields and, along with the large *Financial Times* table of sector and market PEs and yields (see Fig 11.1 on page 260), the dedicated investor can work out PE and yield relatives for the year which has just ended. Some reports will also contain analysts' projections for the year which has just started, which may allow investors to work out prospective figures for all of these yardsticks. If the investor has current forecasts for the prospective yield and PE of the market, he can even calculate his own prospective relative PEs and yields.

Statements about trading conditions may also be useful in interpreting the investment prospects for a share. If a retailer insists that trade is brisk, despite a string of reports in economic news stories that retail sales are slack and the 'feel-good' factor is missing, is it time to ask more questions? Perhaps the particular store chain has some edge which will allow it to escape the rigours that others on the high street are going through. Equally, the company may have a semi-permanent sale going on which is keeping sales volumes up, but at practically no profit.

Remember, while chief executives ought to be as honest as possible with shareholders, most are as scared of losing their jobs or appearing foolish as anyone else. The chances of any corporate baron standing up and saying, 'to be honest, things are pretty lousy at the moment and we have no idea what to do about it,' are slim. Companies will tend to put the best gloss available on their public statements. Any good news is likely to trumpeted; investors have to work harder to find the bad news buried in a euphemism.

Then the interpretation

Having digested the financial data and business message in the initial newspaper report, the investor can then decide whether this changes his investment view of the company. If this is a share which he owns already, do the annual figures contain anything to confirm his view that the company is a good bet? If so, it might be worth putting more money in. Or does it contain some nasty surprise that could

FT-SE Actuaries Share Indices

		Jun 3	Day's change,%	Year ago	Div yield,%	P/E ratio	Total return
	FT-SE 100	3739.2	-0.2	3376.6	4.04	14.37	1528.31
	FT-SE Mid 250	4505.5	-0.1	3690.1	3.35	21.29	1807.28
	FT-SE SmallCap	2229.39	....	1867.32	2.94	24.10	1827.55
10	MINERAL EXTRACTION(24)	3459.77	-0.1	2875.35	3.87	17.62	1490.58
12	Extractive Industries(6)	4436.37	-0.3	3839.33	3.62	13.83	1314.31
15	Oil, Integrated(3)	3474.58	-0.1	2871.45	4.12	17.60	1535.39
16	Oil Exploration & Prod(15)	2499.29	-0.2	2063.29	2.09	36.93	1504.14
20	GEN INDUSTRIALS(275)	2092.22	-0.1	1980.26	4.06	16.21	1144.86
21	Building & Construction(34)	1209.80	-0.1	1005.37	3.41	20.42	1014.75
22	Building Matls & Merchs(29)	1905.13	+0.4	1815.03	3.99	17.97	964.68
23	Chemicals(25)	2516.41	-0.4	2437.46	3.94	16.23	1197.77
24	Diversified Industrials(19)	1679.86	-0.6	1894.75	6.19	11.91	947.29
25	Electronic & Electrical Eq(37)	2480.07	+0.7	2075.14	2.96	25.31	1280.04
26	Engineering(71)	2424.80	-0.3	1992.72	3.15	16.02	1470.10
27	Engineering, Vehicles(13)	3065.35	-0.8	2338.53	3.48	18.36	1591.69
28	Paper, Pckg & Printing(28)	2726.61	+0.3	2996.99	3.74	16.50	1135.92
29	Textiles & Apparel(19)	1417.40	-0.3	1693.77	4.98	16.33	873.38
30	CONSUMER GOODS(80)	3505.16	-0.3	3137.24	4.00	16.67	1300.93
32	Alcoholic Beverages(9)	2775.76	0.7	2783.71	4.51	17.14	1007.52
33	Food Producers(23)	2429.84	-0.3	2503.64	4.26	15.93	1102.82
34	Household Goods(15)	2690.80	+0.2	2608.92	3.69	14.05	1032.29
36	Health Care(20)	2080.76	+0.3	1767.56	2.58	26.26	1267.01
37	Pharmaceuticals(12)	4984.90	-0.3	3888.42	3.41	19.51	1696.46
38	Tobacco(1)	4370.97	-0.6	4239.92	5.81	10.14	1097.96
40	SERVICES(253)	2535.97	-0.2	2060.41	2.82	21.74	1324.37
41	Distributors(32)	2978.44	+0.4	2609.49	2.83	25.01	1099.30
42	Leisure & Hotels(23)	3188.56	+0.2	2343.43	2.77	23.16	1717.22
43	Media(46)	4213.50	-0.1	3035.70	2.15	30.32	1526.58
44	Retailers, Food(15)	2050.36	-0.4	2066.92	3.70	14.61	1315.68
45	Retailers, General(43)	2086.36	-0.1	1688.31	2.97	19.29	1198.39
47	Breweries, Pubs & Rest(24)	3156.47	-0.7	2415.04	3.21	18.11	1518.80
48	Support Services(49)	2434.43	-0.1	1637.85	1.89	27.05	1548.57
49	Transport(21)	2384.01	-0.9	2288.89	3.70	22.56	996.56
60	UTILITIES(33)	2426.39	+0.3	2392.79	5.39	11.33	1032.80
62	Electricity(12)	2644.59	-0.5	2262.41	5.90	8.84	1279.32
64	Gas Distribution(2)	1257.69	-2.0	2045.74	9.53	9.68	659.66
66	Telecommunications(7)	2065.95	+1.0	2068.40	4.23	15.50	939.26
68	Water(12)	2270.82	+0.5	1956.42	5.59	9.22	1231.45
69	NON-FINANCIAL(665)	2005.28	-0.2	1773.40	3.82	16.84	1525.88
70	FINANCIALS(105)	2888.58	-0.3	2480.89	4.13	11.38	1252.31
71	Banks, Retail(8)	3924.48	-0.2	3355.06	3.97	10.88	1292.40
72	Banks, Merchant(6)	3669.13	+0.2	3322.75	2.69	19.55	1162.31
73	Insurance(23)	1505.42	-0.1	1376.92	5.24	7.14	1141.23
74	Life Assurance(6)	3505.57	-0.2	2724.31	4.26	13.09	1469.56
77	Other Financial(21)	2707.54	-0.9	2039,20	3.83	18.99	1547.08
79	Property(41)	1538.51	-0.5	1483.03	4.12	23.32	949.88
80	INVESTMENT TRUSTS(125)	3201.04	-0.6	2825.66	2.18	53.42	1119.35
89	FT-SE-A ALL-SHARE(895)	1882.29	-0.2	1656.47	3.81	15.96	1596.68
	FT-SE-A Fledgling	1273.46	+0.1	1013.24	2.70	21.26	1331.85

Fig 11.1 This table is based on one published each day in the *Financial Times*. (The actual table includes more market indices and more information on each index.) The dedicated investor can use it to work out his own PE and yield relatives.

spell the beginning of a slide – or explain the existing one? Is it a signal to sell?

If it is a company that he has been monitoring as a potential investment, is there anything there to suggest that now is time to buy a stake? Alternatively, perhaps the original idea which interested him in the company is no longer valid and he should cross it off his list. If the news report brings a company to his attention for the first time, is there anything about the company's figures or prospects which merits further investigation? Or perhaps the report on one company prompts doubts or hopes about an entirely different company in which he has an interest.

Heavy topspin

Contested takeovers are one area where companies try particularly hard to manipulate news reporting. Tendentious hints about one company will be slipped quietly to journalists by the other side in the hope that they will find their way into print as 'exclusive' stories. Slanging matches, with the ring held by the Takeover Panel, make good copy.

Meanwhile the executives of the companies involved will be working full tilt to influence journalists by telling them how wonderful they are, and how astute to see the merits of one argument or another. If the carrot does not work and a journalist persists in taking a dim view of a company, then journalists can find themselves cold-shouldered in much the same way as analysts.

Takeovers are the most obvious area for the exercise of these kind of tactics. But they are there all of the time and do tend to produce a positive bias in the press. While not all of these attempts to influence will work, enough do to make it worth the effort.

Editors are not immune from such pressures either. Newspapers, ever hungry for copy and an edge over their rivals, will jump at the offer of interviews with the chief executives. The company bosses will be only too happy to wax lyrical about why the way they run their company is fantastic, with the implicit suggestion that the way in which the other side is run leaves a lot to be desired. To get some feel for the way in which bid contenders try to manipulate the agenda, take a look at who turns up in the weekly profile or interview slots in the financial pages the next time a big takeover breaks. At least half such features will be about one side or the other.

This attempt to control the news agenda is marshalled by a huge City public relations (PR) industry. Most large companies will have an internal department which handles press enquires and write press releases about new products or developments in the company's business. These departments will also normally work with the senior executives to produce the annual results presentations for analysts and journalists, with the gloss often coming from the PR professionals.

For big set piece events such as bids or annual results, companies frequently also bring in City PR consultants, who profess to have an expertise in what the City wants, and particular influence with journalists. They might, for example, advise a company to see newspapers one-by-one, rather than in a single press conference, if there is some aspect of their business they would rather not call attention to. This means that if one journalist spots the problem in his one-to-one session, the company can work him over to persuade him it is not a real issue, and prevent other papers hearing about it. If the journalist had asked the question in an open forum, everyone would hear about it and latch on.

The Kvaerner/AMEC takeover battle provides a useful illustration of how the financial PR industry works. In December 1995 the Takeover Panel got concerned that AMEC was not sticking to the rules in its battle to ward off an unwanted bid from the Norwegian Kvaerner. The Panel was worried that press speculation about AMEC's 1996 profits might be based directly or indirectly on statements made by directors of AMEC or one of its advisers. The company promptly denied having leaked its 1996 profits forecast. Quite true. It rapidly emerged that it was AMEC's financial PR company that had done the leaking. An embarrassed AMEC found itself a new PR company forthwith.

The Takeover Panel established that during the bid it was routine for the PR company to hold a follow-up meeting with securities firms AMEC had just finished talking to. During at least one of these meetings a director of the PR firm had both given an investment analyst a strong steer on AMEC's 1996 profits and told the analyst that AMEC would not be including a formal profits forecast in its defence circular. In Takeover Code terms it had both given the analyst material new information relevant to the bid, and said that this information was not being officially published. This was in direct contravention of one of the general principles of the Code, which demands equality of information for all shareholders.

The analyst was also given advance knowledge of some of the information which would be in the defence circular several days later – in contravention of a Code rule that information should be made available to all shareholders at the same time. And it was suggested that further information regarding the defence strategy 'might appear in newspapers that weekend, ahead of publication in the defence document.'

As the Panel rather despairingly commented, its concern 'extends beyond simple statements of fact to include any impressions which are given.' The PR firm lost the AMEC account. It was guilty of being found out. But it is hard to imagine that it lost many other accounts because of the incident. AMEC, incidentally, won the Kvaerner battle.

The important point for investors to bear in mind about all of this is that even factual reports have a provenance. While a 500 word report of a company's annual figures might seem like a simple statement of record, what goes into those 500 words – of all the things which have happened to a company over the previous year – is a carefully plotted exercise. Journalists will do their best to decode and probe behind the scenes, but they are only as good as their intelligence and the information they have. And, as with analysts, an awful lot of their information comes from companies or their PR advisers. Investors need to be wary of taking news at face value.

Comment is free

What is true of news stories is true in spades for newspaper comment and analysis. While companies try to influence the mood music of news stories, they bend over backwards to persuade those writing comment of their point of view. That can become almost a full-time job for some company executives and PR people: all of the main daily and Sunday broadsheet national newspapers have their stock and market comment columns.

These columns comment on a range of issues from the overall direction of stockmarkets, to currency moves and individual companies affairs. Annual figures are an obvious time for newspapers to comment on companies, but they are also likely to offer views on takeovers, big news items likely to affect particular companies, management changes or sharp changes in a company's share price.

The quality of comment and analysis varies enormously, as with brokers' research. Unless the journalist is named and familiar, it can also be difficult to know how much insight he brings to the party. Few newspaper writers have the depth of knowledge that an analyst has accumulated. What some will have is very good connections, a sharp mind, and an ability to convey the essence of an argument in few words.

Several columns may be worth reading occasionally, some more frequently. But the investor will have to sift. The journalists writing comment columns in newspapers vary from the newest graduate trainee being given his first break, to someone who is financially astute, has been following a particular company for years, and knows its dealings inside out. Unfortunately, at first blush, it can be difficult to tell the difference. Investors need to keep an open mind about whether they are being told the blindingly obvious under the guise of revelation, fobbed off with complete nonsense masquerading as a radical view, or given a nugget of pure investment gold which no-one else has found. Needless to say, the last is the rarest.

There are some safeguards which help keep even the newest commentator on the straight and narrow. Companies will provide detailed financial information with their results that many newspapers keep in library files. This will give them most of the basic investment information. But journalists are also highly self-referential: they tend to be guided by previous newspaper comment on a subject, which is also normally in their library files, or the on-line news services they subscribe to. If they have not written on a particular company before themselves, they sometimes display touching trust in their fellow journalists. For example, a mistake can sometimes be tracked in several different incarnations as it progresses from one newspaper or magazine to another – a bit like the common cold.

Because most are not financial experts, journalists often focus on the business issues confronting a company, rather than the pure financial ratios. A quick glance at any week's comment will show a greater preponderance of views on whether, say, the rising oil price will be good for BP and Shell's shares, rather than a view of either company's sector relative PE ratios. In a particular instance one journalist might latch on to, say, the imminent revaluation of the car component company Lucas as a recovery stock. But that is the exception, rather than the rule.

In most cases, journalists writing about a company will talk to several of the Extel-rated analysts about their views. Analysts may well discuss the detailed financial as well as business prospects of a company, although the journalist's bias towards the latter will often shape the conversation.

Since analysts usually know that journalists zero-in on business issues, they may well elect to stress those, rather than the more abstruse financial aspects of a company's investment prospects. And the debate about how rapidly mobile phone company Orange will win new subscribers has undeniably wider appeal than arguments about whether the discount rate used in the discounted cash flow sums is appropriate. Editing newspapers, after all, is about selling copies.

An average view, not a hot tip

At a minimum the exchange between analysts and journalists means that some of the worst errors are avoided, though it can turn many comment columns into an amalgam of current analysts' views. Indeed, investors can sensibly regard most run-of-the-mill comment as a cross-section of current City opinion, particularly about the business issues facing companies. Having such a bulletin can be useful in itself, since it will flag up to the private investor current professional talking points and where the balance of attention is directed.

This is perhaps where newspaper analysis is most helpful to individual investors. They can use the comment to inform their thinking about issues which are hot with the City, and to generate medium term strategies. If they then develop trading ideas which follow on from that, or which have not been spotted by the market, or which run counter to the prevailing opinion, they may have a chance to make money.

What this kind of comment patently does not do is give the investor information which has not already been digested by the analyst, his mother, the double-glazing salesman she met in the post office and his golfing partner. This is not to say that there is a huge amount of insider trading going on, merely that by and large newspaper comment will not say anything which has not already been thrashed out in the market and reflected in a company's share price.

Ah, but surely share prices do move on newspaper comment? It is perfectly true that they do, but mostly this is a feedback loop. The fact that a newspaper has picked up an issue circulating in the market and amplified it gives it a new lease of life. When professional dealers arrive at their offices at 7am following a strong buy recommendation for Barclays Bank in the *Daily Bugle* – a recommendation based on analysts' positive reaction to Barclays' annual results – the share price may be marked up. The mark-up will be based on the expectation that hordes of private investors are about to follow the *Bugle*'s advice and buy. The smart money will already be in, however, and the individual investor who phones his broker at 9am risks buying at the top of an artificial bubble. Barclays may well be a good bet for the long haul, but it is next to impossible for individuals to make short term money on the back of newspaper recommendations.

An inside track

What newspaper commentators may also bring to the party is good connections. Newish rules about what information companies can disclose, and when, mean that there are many fewer tip-offs to City editors or analysts than there used to be. (See Chapter 3 page 60.) The prospect of being thrown in jail for leaking price-sensitive information seems to have curbed the tongues of all but the most reckless finance directors and PR spin doctors. Yet some journalists do spend a great deal of their time talking to senior business leaders and are remarkably well informed about the intentions of companies. Sunday newspapers in particular try to make up for their lack of timeliness with inside insights.

At its best, this can provide investors with a good view of how a company sees itself and what new developments may be coming up. At its worst, however, it is information bought at the price of a favourable interpretation of the company's position. Outside observers have to use their skill and judgement to extract the information without necessarily buying the glowing argument which goes with it.

The other point worth bearing in mind about newspaper comment is the restrictions placed on journalists by the libel laws. On top of the PR machine trying to bias journalists and analysts towards positive views, there are the very heavy sticks of libel suits which companies can threaten to use to keep negative comments out of newspapers. Think of the sums handed out to celebrities for apparently trivial slights. Now imagine the potential cost to a newspaper of a successful suit by a company which said that negative newspaper comment had damaged its standing with its banks and creditors to the point where it was forced out of business.

Editors and journalists know these sticks are there and often do not have to be directly threatened with Messrs. Sue, Grabbit and Runne to fight shy of criticism. This is known in journalistic circles as 'self-censorship'. Newspapers may decide to risk libel writs in pursuit of a worthwhile story; they will usually take pains to avoid them over small ones. And, from a purely pragmatic point of view, standing up a contentious story, so that it can pass the newspaper's libel lawyer before publication, takes time.

Because it can be difficult for journalists to say directly that they believe a company is about to go bust, investors have to read between the lines of comment. There is no formal phrasing, as this would have come to mean going bust, and would have been interpreted by the courts as such. But much can be inferred from context. A note of scepticism that a new chief executive will be able to resolve a company's long-standing problems, the thought that a company is persistently troubled, the description of a company as a speculative investment, and the recommendation to avoid what is patently a rescue rights issue, are all hints of big trouble. Equally there is what is not said: if a large company unveils a recovery plan which is greeted by a straightforward write-up of what the executives have claimed, but no comment, this can tell its own story.

Accountants use the delicious phrase that a company's accounts have been prepared 'on the basis that it remains a going concern' – ie that the accountants think it probably will not be. (See page Chapter 5 page 99.) There is no single journalistic equivalent, but the double entendre or the quick written nudge can be equally significant. Investors have to be particularly alert and prepared to admit mistakes. Those affected will usually be existing holders of the stock, and may want to believe good news about a company and ignore anything bad. Without getting paranoid, it will pay to look for the bad news between the lines. It could save you money.

Laying down the Law

The Lex Column in the *Financial Times* is the most highly regarded of the market comment columns. In part that is because of its longevity – Lex recently celebrated its 50th birthday in the FT – but also because of the access to companies, institutions and analysts which its long standing eminence brings. Lex is the best read column among City professionals and so has the most influence, which reinforces its market leadership. Lex also has what many other newspaper financial columns lack: resources.

Lex currently has five full-time journalists working to produce about 1,500 words of pithy comment each day on companies and markets around the world. Most come from within the FT, though some have City experience and others are occasionally drawn from other careers or newspapers. Many are young: the number still in their 20s and 30s might surprise some of those who hang on the column's every word. The journalists often come in from one part of the newspaper, spend two or three years on the column, before moving on to another reporting assignment.

The Lex Column's day normally starts with a morning discussion of the topics most likely to be covered. Some, such as large company results which are known to be coming, recommend themselves; others come up as news items or as a result of ideas generated by the team. The work is provisionally parcelled out, and if there is a press conference or company meeting to attend, the relevant

Fig 11.2 The Lex column is the doyen of market comment columns. This is partly because it is the oldest, partly because it has unrivalled access to companies and analysts.

journalist will tend to go. Those back at base will start to research their subject.

Because Lex and the FT have a particular place in financial reporting, its journalists often get longer sessions with company executives on announcement days, to the irritation of their rivals. Not infrequently this takes the form of lunch with company executives. Once back at the FT in the afternoon, the journalists compare notes with analysts and professional investors on the phone, check background information in library files and manipulate relevant investment information on FT Graphite or Datastream information terminals. Their final conclusions will often then be discussed around the desk before the note, not normally more than 250 words on a subject, is completed for a 7pm deadline.

Each Lex journalist will have his or her own style and interest, and the degree to which they rely on straight investment data, business issues likely to affect a company or market, or analysts' views will vary. What the column is not trying to do is produce a straightforward share tipsheet; its aim is to comment on issues which are of interest to the financial community. Many of its daily newspaper rivals are also moving in the same direction, away from straightforward 'buy, hold or sell' recommendations.

Tips galore

Others, however, take a different view. The *Investors Chronicle* (IC) company coverage (see Appendix A), is still firmly aimed at providing straight investment views on stocks. So are tipsheets. But even a deeply worthy publication, such as the IC, is highly unlikely to come up with half a dozen wonderful tips each week. Its tips are basically the most interesting companies it comes across in each week's company news. You will get the most out of them if you treat them as a source of interesting ideas, not something to follow blindly.

Tipsheet recommendations vary as much in quality as brokers' analysis or newspaper comment. About the only generalisation one can make is that the cost of the tipsheet bears no relation to the likely accuracy of its views. Most are subscription services sent out monthly, or in some cases weekly, with a selection of a few hot stocks to buy or sell.

The analysis is in general much more financially based than most newspaper comment, and greater detail of a company's financial affairs is also given. Since the sheets are mailed out first class to subscribers only, the information in them is not available to all and sundry, so may not have been quite so widely discounted in the market already. This may give investors a chance to deal very early on the first day of publication. But there is no guarantee that the ideas will be any good; they may simply be worn-out suggestions re-cycled from lunch with a broker a month earlier.

Investors who hope to make money from tips are assuming either that they contain inside information or that their analysis is better than that of the market professionals. Investors can reasonably ask themselves, 'if these guys are such great stock analysts, why are they not earning five times as much working for a big stockbroking firm?' A few tipsheet analysts may be brilliant mavericks who prefer sitting on a rock in Cornwall to being embroiled in the machinations of City office politics. But most are not.

Newspaper Comment

IN A NUTSHELL

1. The bare bones of a company news report provide useful information. But remember that most companies aim to put a favourable gloss on the figures. They will also do their best to persuade financial journalists to print the facts they want to see in print.

2. Newspaper comment is more obviously vulnerable to attempts to influence it. Though journalists do their best to remain objective, they are not financial experts, and are often happier dealing with the business story than the financial implications.

3. Journalists also rely heavily on investment analysts. So newspaper comments are often best viewed as a digest of City opinion.

4. Exclusive stories are useful, but journalists tend to be fed stories which favour the informant. Remain alert to possible bias when reading them. And also remember that journalists have to pay attention to the libel implications of what they write.

5. Columns such as 'Lex' are mainly interested in discussing issues of interest to the financial community, not in providing share tips.

6. Tipsheets are just the opposite. But the quality varies considerably. Treat all tips as, at best ideas to be researched, at worst fodder for the bin.

Section Four:
Investment Trading

Chapter 12
Case Study – Sainsbury

Theory is fine. Putting it into practice is harder. In this chapter we apply some of the different tools and techniques explained in previous sections to a familiar UK company. The subject of our case study is supermarket group Sainsbury. It took place in March 1996.

Sainsbury is a good example of a company in transition. During the 1980s it was the leading company in an industry enjoying a once-in-a-lifetime boom. In 1993 the boom ended. Managing change of that order is a challenge for any company. Below we look at the business background, consider a chartist view, pick out the salient points in the accounts, review the investment yardsticks, consider what Warren Buffett might make of the company, and check how the brokers analysts' and the press reported the story.

The business background

Working for a large supermarket chain was nearly as exciting as being a City Yuppie in the late 1980s. Sales, profits and profit margins soared as the space bandits cashed in on the edge of town superstore boom. New systems, such as central distribution and checkout scanning, and new products, such as cook-chill meals and fresh food, produced ever more ingenious ways of honing costs and parting customers from their money. And the purchasing power of the giant food retailers meant they could extract very good deals from their suppliers.

Most imaginative and fastest on its feet was Sainsbury. It remained the UK's premier grocer throughout the boom, though Tesco was challenging powerfully from behind. The big three – Sainsbury, Tesco and Argyll (which owns Safeway) – spent over £10bn building new superstores in the five years up to 1993. But, as Warren Buffett observed, 'If something can't go on for ever, it will end.'

Three things spelled the end of the space race. First, a new breed of foreign-owned limited-range discount grocers, such as Aldi, moved into town – sometimes just a few hundred yards away from an existing edge of town superstore. They put pressure on selling prices for staple goods. Second, the number of good edge of town sites and the potential profitability of new ones dwindled. The rising number of superstores was already squeezing profits all round, but inflated prices were paid for the last few sites. Third, in 1993 the government changed tack on planning, and turned against new food retailing developments away from town centres.

This combination of events meant that all the supermarketeers had to revise both their prices and their expansion plans downwards. The rival supermarket groups employed broadly similar strategies in their defensive campaigns against the discounters. During 1993 they started to cut prices on basic goods, and went on to cut operating costs and improve customer service. Doing all three at the same time was hard, and success patchy. Often it went to those whose planning was most coherent: Tesco, for example, took on more checkout staff to back up its service drive; Sainsbury promoted service at a time it was cutting store staff numbers.

Responses to the end of the space race were more varied. The obvious options were changing the format of their food retailing operations, pursuing a similar format elsewhere, or diversifying into other types of retailing. Sainsbury and Tesco, the two leaders, adopted similar but not identical strategies when they saw the writing on the clocktower. But Sainsbury got off to a bad start. It was initially reluctant to admit that the days of hectic expansion were past. Soon, though, it had to face up to reality: it was losing the vast majority of its planning appeals and the pace of expansion through new stores was tumbling willy nilly.

Tesco was the first to rediscover the town centre and started opening new smaller food stores; Sainsbury made the same U-turn a little later. Both bought their way onto new continents: Tesco headed for Europe, Sainsbury moved

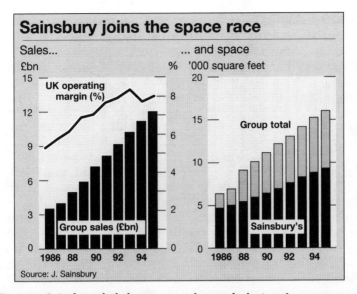

Sainsbury joins the space race

Sales...

... and space

Fig 12.1 Sainsbury led the supermarket pack during the great 1980s space race. But it lost its touch when the market became more competitive, and in 1994 issued its first profits warning.

further into the United States and dug far deeper into its pockets than Tesco. Both cast acquisitive eyes on Scotland, one of the last areas of the UK not overrun by superstores. But Tesco won the battle for Scottish retailer William Low. Both discovered the final frontier, Northern Ireland, at virtually the same moment. Sainsbury, which already had a successful non-food operation, Homebase, bought a DIY chain, Texas Homecare, from Ladbroke.

The jury remains out on Sainsbury's diversifications. US supermarkets are less profitable and more parochial than those in the UK. Sainsbury has the market leader in Washington and one of the biggest chains in New England; but that is a different game from the national leadership it is used to. The Texas Homecare purchase promptly produced a wrangle over whether Sainsbury had paid too much.

Nor was it much better on Sainsbury's home territory. Its 'Essentials' price cutting campaign was handled clumsily. Sainsbury' was slow to accept that loyalty cards, heavily promoted by Tesco and other rivals, were more than a gimmick. Tesco's Clubcard was proving highly successful

in increasing sales, but Sainsbury chairman David Sainsbury still insisted that it was a tactical not a strategic
weapon. And both Tesco and the once-despised Asda
appeared more successful at convincing the public that they
offered value for money and friendly and efficient service.
Tesco made gains in market share.

By late 1995 Sainsbury's sales, profits and margins were
all fraying round the edges. Pre-tax profits, which had risen
at well over 20 per cent a year in the late 1980s, slowed to a
crawl. Its first ever profits warning shocked the market in
January 1994, a trick it repeated a couple of years later.
Chairman David Sainsbury made some changes to the
group's top management which met only half-hearted
applause. The shares, which had always sold on a premium
rating compared with its rivals', lost most of their edge. In
the early 1990s Tesco was the one banished to the doghouse.
But from the start of 1993 until the end of 1995 Sainsbury's
shares were in relative decline compared with Tesco's.

That's the background. What's the business assessment?
For any company as focused as Sainsbury, the assessment
has to be a double one: first the industry, then the company.

The food retailing industry as a whole enjoyed a spectac-
ular boom as it reinvented itself on the edge of town. This
new lease of life allowed it substantially to improve its
profit margins. The space race was one in which everybody
got prizes. The return of competition meant that the companies were back to cutting each others' throats. In early 1996
the UK supermarket industry as a whole appears to have
reverted to steady but unexciting growth, and this is crucial
to prospects for all the companies in the sector. Relative
assessments of the attractions of individual companies have
to be seen in this context.

Sainsbury entered the space race the acknowledged market leader. But by the mid-1990s it seemed to have lost its
touch in its traditional business. Its acquisition policy also
lacks compelling logic. Sainsbury's intrinsic strength
remains enormous. But its management needs to prove that
the company can get its act together again.

Chartist View

And what would a chartist have made of the supermarket

group over the same period? In March 1996 Richard Marshall, technical analyst at Investment Research of Cambridge, gave the following commentary on Sainsbury's share
price during the late 1980s/early 1990s:

• **Late 1980s–early 1990s.** The share price was in a primary uptrend. It was reaching new highs in every major
rally. And this trend in the price itself was 'confirmed' by
the price relative index – which was also reaching new
highs in its rallies. The trend continued until the peak just
above 570p early in 1993.

• **March/April 1993.** A strong correction to the upwards
trend was already evident early in 1993. But at the end of
March the price made a decisive move down through its 200
day moving average. And again there was confirmation from
the relative strength line, which decisively broke its
uptrend.

• **April/June 1993.** The share price made a few attempts to
rally, but the rallies never succeeded in taking it back above
the 200 day moving average around the 490p level. This was
a bad sign.

• **June 1993.** Sure enough, another major downside break
occurred. The price fell far enough to complete a head and
shoulders pattern. The left hand shoulder was in June 1992
at around 480p. The head topped out in January 1993
around 570p. And the right hand shoulder, formed in June
1993 was completed when the price fell below 450p in July.

The earlier chart pattern showed a key resistance level at
around 450p in 1992, when the price was gathering its
forces for its final assault on the peak. An earlier resistance
level normally acts as a support on the way down. So the
fact that the falling price had broken through this 'neckline'
was the signal that the head and shoulders was a legitimate
pattern and that the January peak had been a major turning
point.

The head and shoulders pattern suggested that at some
point the price was likely to fall as low as 350p. Why?
Because on a semi-logarithmic chart, the distance between the
price peak at 570p and the neckline at 450p was matched by
the distance between 450p and 350p. And the rule of thumb

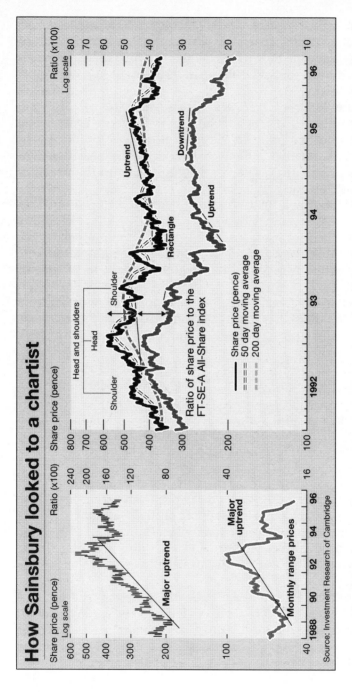

Fig 12.2 The major uptrend which began in the late 1980s had clearly been broken when the price completed a head and shoulders pattern in mid 1993. The technical analyst's next price target was 350p.

is that a price will fall as far below the neckline as the distance between it and the top of the head. So 350p was Marshall's new price target. (Gann fans will note with pleasure that both the peak and the trough are roughly a quarter above and below 450p. Gann noted that 25 per cent was a common distance in both price rises and corrections.)

• **July/August 1993.** Sceptics and Sainsbury shareholders alike rejoiced when the price rallied strongly in the summer, surging triumphantly above the 500p level. But the relative strength chart gave the game away. It notably failed to confirm the trend in the share price. And sure enough, in September the price fell out of bed: it tumbled all the way down to 360p, only a smidgen above the price target of 350p.

• **January 1994.** After another strong rally in late 1993, the share price collapsed back to reach the 350p target.

• **February/July 1994.** The share price began to form a base – dig itself in as it prepared to launch another assault on the heights. In this period it fluctuated between the support floor at 350p and the ceiling of resistance at 400p.

The price itself gave little sign of which way the battle would go. But the smart money was watching the relative strength chart. This had been in a long term downtrend since January 1993. But in April 1994 it reversed direction decisively, and began to trend upwards, with each setback at a higher level than the one before. This was encouraging. And sure enough the share price itself eventually broke upwards through the 400p barrier of resistance in July. This, coupled with the rising relative strength signalled a new bull phase.

• **July 1994–September 1995.** For the next 14 months the share price moved steadily higher with support from the rising 200 day moving average. But again, the first warning signs came from the relative strength. It ceased rising at the turn of the year, and by the second half of 1995 Marshall was sure that it was now trending down. The basic weakness in Sainsbury's price was being concealed by the strength of the market as a whole. Sainsbury might be reaching new highs, but the relative strength was flashing the red light.

• **October 1995.** The share price suddenly broke down,

and the relative strength chart collapsed. This had all the hallmarks of another serious setback, and back came the price to the familiar 350–400p price range.

● **December 1995.** By the end of the year the shares had fallen a long way in a short time and enjoyed a technical rally, which brought the price into contact with the 200 day moving average, which was by now falling. Another squadron of sellers emerged and the price collapsed to its habitual range: 350p–400p. If it went down through 350p, it would be back to levels not seen since 1991. And the relative chart was hitting new lows.

● **March 1996.** Outlook grim.

Accounting aspects

British supermarket finances are unusual. The big chains have a large amount of capital permanently tied up in fixed assets, but their trading stocks are effectively financed by their suppliers. Customers pay cash and suppliers wait for their money.

In most countries food retailers lease most of their premises. In Britain they own 75 per cent of them and paid the earth for new sites during the 1980s. This means both that they are very capital intensive compared with foreign equivalents, and that they need to make their assets sweat.

Sales per square foot are high by international standards. As a result so are profits per square foot and net margins. (The latter can be at least double those in Europe and the US.) However, high profits mean that retail assets do not come cheap in the UK. As a result, return on capital, varying from 13 to 20 per cent, is not outstanding.

Successful supermarkets are wonderful machines for generating cash. During the space race, capital expenditure outstripped cash flow, and the companies ran unusually high borrowings. (Hardly surprising given that between 1986 and 1995 Sainsbury increased the net book value of its fixed assets by 300 per cent and Tesco by 460 per cent.) But once the space race ended, free cash flow surged upwards again.

The big accounting issues for Sainsbury and its rivals in

the mid-1990s concerned capitalised interest and depreciation. But the interest this aroused may have been partly
because there was little else to comment on.

Sainsbury's accounts give an impressive picture of glowing health. On conventional yardsticks, such as sales per
square foot, margins, return on capital employed, and
gearing the company looked rock solid in absolute terms. It
was also still significantly more profitable than its rivals,
even though Tesco had shown a remarkable improvement
during the 1980s. The key concern in early 1996 was that
growth had slowed to a crawl.

- **Sales per square foot.** Sainsbury's food sales per square
foot were £18.50 per week in 1994–95, compared with £17
for Tesco.
- **Sales growth.** This was roaring along at 20 per cent a
year in the late 1980s but slowed to single figures in the
1990s. But the rapid pace was the direct result of expansion.
By 1995 sales growth in the UK supermarkets excluding the
effect of new openings was down to 2 per cent, and would
have been negative if adjusted for inflation. This stands out
as the problem area.
- **Profits and earnings.** Both were also growing at over 20
per cent a year in the late 1980s, but again growth slowed
sharply in the 1990s. The UK supermarket group continued
to provide 90 per cent of total profits.
- **Dividends.** Similar story. Between 1986 and 1995 earnings more than trebled and dividends more than quad-
rupled. Dividend growth also slowed in the early 1990s. But
when it announced its disappointing interim results in the
autumn of 1995, the company promised that in future
dividend increases would be 3 per cent above the rate of
earnings growth. Dividend cover was strong, and would
allow an even more generous distribution policy.
- **Margins.** Sainsbury's operating margins, which rose
strongly in the 1980s, levelled out at around 8 per cent in
the mid-1990s. Pre-tax margins rose from around 4.5 per
cent in the early 1980s to 7 per cent by 1994–95. Over the
same period Tesco's pre-tax margins rose from around 2.5
per cent to 6 per cent, and its overall operating margins were
also below Sainsbury's. On the core supermarket business

Sainsbury's operating margins were over 8 per cent, compared with over 6 per cent for Tesco.

- **Return on capital.** Sainsbury's overall return on capital was 23 per cent, compared around 16 per cent for Tesco. Both Safeway and Asda were around 18 per cent.
- **Gearing.** Nothing to worry about here either. By the mid–1990s the ratio was already down to less than 30 per cent. The only potential cause for concern was that Sainsbury might push gearing up to 70–80 per cent if it bought up the remainder of the US Giant supermarket group.
- **Current ratio.** Broadly current liabilities tend to run at roughly double the level of current assets. This could be worrying in some businesses, but is fairly normal for a supermarket group. All it means is that the suppliers are financing all Sainsbury's stock and quite a lot else. Nice work if you can get it.
- **Cash flow.** This is another deeply reassuring aspect of Sainsbury – and other food retailers. Even in the high spending years, it had a strong gross cash flow, though free cash flow (after deducting capital expenditure and dividends) turned negative. Once spending tailed off, free cash flow was set to turn positive again. The strong cash flow should provide solid backing for a generous dividend policy.
- **Capitalised interest and depreciation.** The favourable financial background explains why the supermarketeers felt it reasonable to employ optimistic accounting policies during the space race. Their evolution into crypto-property companies explains the particular form their optimism took. Instead of charging the interest on development expenditure against their profits, they 'capitalised' it – treating it as part of the cost of the assets – just as property companies have traditionally done.

And until 1994 most of them did not depreciate their properties. These accounting policies meant that they could expand without their profits suffering the normal short term consequences of expansion. They favoured both the absolute profits and also the profits growth, an important consideration for investment analysts.

The main reason the stores cost so much was the rising land prices which resulted from competitive bidding by the supermarket chains themselves. The edge-of-town sites were not worth nearly so much to any other buyer, because no one else would have been able to make such a good return from them.

The properties were carried in the food retailers' balance sheets at what the land and development cost, including capitalised interest on the development finance. The companies argued that those would have been the costs if they had bought the stores from a property developer, so it was reasonable for them to adopt the accounting policies of a property developer in respect of the properties.

They could also justify the lofty valuations by reference to the profits they expected to make out of the superstores in future. But this was always a slightly circular argument. And in 1993 it ceased to have any credibility. For the arrival of the discounters and increased competition among the big groups meant that estimates of future profits were reduced.

Accounting purists may argue that it is not the job of the balance sheet to show the value of a company. But the supermarket groups all took a more pragmatic line. One after another they wrote down the value of the properties in their balance sheets. But interestingly each solved the common problem in a slightly different way. And the impact on their profit and loss accounts varied considerably. The contrast between the two main rivals was sharp.

Sainsbury bit the bullet with what looked like heroism. It made a one-off £342m charge against its 1994 profits, 'representing a permanent diminution in the value of a number of our properties' and said it would be depreciating its buildings in future. But its revaluation policy was in some ways less cautious than those of its rivals. For example, it assumed the land would continue to be used for (still very profitable) supermarkets, rather than some alternative (less profitable) purpose. It decided to write its buildings off over 50 years, and wrote off only part of the capitalised interest.

Tesco elected to handle its write-down through additional depreciation over the next 25 years. Thus, whereas Sainsbury's profits would recover after the one year hit, Tesco's would bear the scars in terms of an additional charge against profits for a quarter of a century. Tesco chose the harsh 'alternative use' basis for its land valuation and decided to write its buildings off over only 40 years.

A note from broker UBS analysing the different methods concluded that if other groups had used the Sainsbury method, their earnings per share would have increased by anything from 1 per cent (Argyll) to 9 per cent (Tesco).

Accounting assessment

Shame about the depreciation hassle. It slightly tarnishes a glowingly healthy series of accounts. However, the row does underline a basic fragility in the market position of all the companies. Do you need to sell food from such expensive space? And healthy accounts are not enough to give the group back its lost growth status. A company showing below average growth in an industry that has just come to the end of a major period of expansion is not overtly attractive. And the dividend promise, though nice enough, seems insufficient on its own to reverse the relative weakness of the share price.

Tools and Yardsticks

Opposite are some of the relevant stockmarket yardsticks in mid-March 1996. We have given figures for Sainsbury, Tesco, the food retailing sector and the FT-SE-A All-Share index. First, what exactly are the comparisons? Tesco is obvious enough. But the sector chosen is actually a sub-sector of the food retailing industry. It consists of the seven true food retailers weighted by their market capitalisations: Sainsbury, Tesco, Argyll, Asda, Kwik Save, Morrison and Iceland. These seven account for roughly 94 per cent of the whole FT-SE Actuaries sector. Quasi food retailers included in the sector, such as Budgens, Geest, Greggs Bakers and Park Food, do not compete in this league.

This is a good reminder of how few companies are of interest to the managers of large mainstream funds. And only four of the seven chosen retailers are really big enough

	Sainsbury	Tesco	Sector	Market
Price (p)	374	276.5	1892	1844
Actual PE ratio	12.9	13.8	14.0	14.9
PE rel. to sector	93	99	100	–
Prospective PE	13.6	12.5	13.2	13.6
P/PE rel. to sector	103	95	100	–
Actual DY (%)	3.9	3.9	3.75	4.0
DY rel. to sector	104	104	100	–
Prospective DY	4.0	4.4	4.1	4.4
P/DY rel. to sector	99	108	100	–
Actual CF (p per share)	40.8	31.5	–	–
Price/CF	9.2	8.8	–	–
Price/Sales	0.6	0.57	0.54	–

Source: UBS Limited (March 1996)

to mop up a large weight of investment funds. This means first, that all are analysed to within an inch of their lives. Second, that sector comparisons have a pretty limited scope. What the analyst is really looking at is Sainsbury against Tesco, Asda and Argyll.

With this caveat, what is interesting about this table is how little the analysts expect from Sainsbury in the future. On the actual PE ratio and yield the shares look fair value compared with their peers. But the comparisons based on the broker's forecasts draw a less appealing picture.

The cash flow figures are taken before capital expenditure and dividends, but after tax and working capital adjustments. They are predictably fine. It might have been useful to do the figures again deducting the capital expenditure. But in this business cash flow problems are within the companies' own control. If they get temporarily embarrassed all they need to do is stop spending.

Analytical assessment. This is a good example of the efficient market at work. The ratings are all so finely tuned that they already take account of everything that the company has said publicly. Only new information is likely substantially to change the relative assessments. What could set the cat among the pigeons is if Sainsbury shows itself in better shape than the analysts expect, or if its rivals disappoint in their turn.

This is a very hard share for a private investor to get special insight into. Where he can score is with common-sense. In 1993 many analysts were reluctant to believe that the space race was over – perhaps because they listened too much to their industry contacts, the outsider only had to look at the bewildering choice of superstores on his door-step to realise that the boom could not continue.

What the gurus might say

What might great investors such as Warren Buffett or Peter Lynch say about Sainsbury? In early 1996 we subjected the food retailer to some of their basic tests. First, how does the UK grocer measure up to the Buffett criteria?

● The business must be understandable. Supermarkets are a business most investors would reckon they understand. But the finer details of logistics and property management are less accessible than the quality of goods and service. Sainsbury's ventures into overseas markets and other types of retailing might not go down too well with Buffett.

● The long term prospects must be favourable. Sainsbury's should be reasonably favourable, provided the company can get its act together again. It has an excellent name, and the business is very efficiently run. But it is not at all obvious that this amounts to enough of a long term competitive advantage to keep Buffett happy – or indeed that it is possible for any company to obtain a lasting competitive advantage in the food retailing industry.

During the glorious 1980s the then chairman John Sains-bury argued that the only way of securing competitive advantage in the food business was to get there first and be onto something else by the time competitors have followed your example.

Sainsbury scores good marks for its endemically strong cash flow, but bad marks for its extremely capital intensive nature. The return on capital employed is healthy. Debt is melting like summer snow.

● Management must be honest and competent. The Sainsbury family certainly qualify as honest people who run the company with an owner's eye. But they seem to have lost their touch in the 1990s. And plans to revitalise the management are in danger of turning into another own goal.

What is more the management seems still to consider that the best use of shareholders' money is to plough most of it back into the business. This may not be true any more. Buffet would surely argue that the Sainsbury management ought to be thinking of using some of its wonderful cash flow to buy back some of its shares, rather than buying into other areas. It could be particularly worrying if the management decided to put a lot more cash into the US supermarkets: a far away business about which British investors know little.

This is undeniably a testing time for management, but it remains unclear whether it can meet this test or who will be running the group in future. Not the ideal time to buy in.

● Available at a very attractive price. The knee-jerk reaction is 'No'. Sainsbury's superficial cheapness vanishes when you start looking at prospects. No sign of a wide safety margin there.

The harder question is whether discounted cash flow sums would make the shares look good value. Maybe. The cash flow is solid enough but the pace of growth is probably too pedestrian. And remember, Buffett never attempts to value a company unless he can predict its cash flows with confidence. Perhaps Sainsbury's management can do this. An outsider would find it difficult. Probably not a Buffett stock, then.

Peter Lynch's fictional assessment is rather shorter. As a master of timing he would probably have unloaded the stock in early 1993, and is unlikely to have given it a serious thought since. Sainsbury is essentially a stalwart, but in the 1980s it turned into a fast grower. By 1996 the worry was that it might be making another category change: into a slow-grower, the only category of shares that Lynch avoids. But if the shares kept falling relative to the sector, and became clearly undervalued, he might buy for the short term.

How the analysts saw it

All the main broking houses have teams of retail food analysts. A cross-section of their reports in early 1996 showed very little disagreement about key facts.

• What matters most to Sainsbury is its UK supermarket chain. Diversification into other types of retailing and into the US are as yet a side-issue. The worry is that they might absorb too much cash and too much management time when that time is needed to pull UK retailing back on track.
• Sainsbury had led the pack in the space race, but made one mistake after another when the climate changed in 1993. Suddenly Tesco was calling the shots.
• The virtual stagnation in like-for-like sales (that is cash sales growth in existing stores) in the mid-1990s is the tell-tale sign that the UK supermarkets have lost their edge.
• Weak marketing, notably in the Essentials campaign and its failure to appreciate the significance of the loyalty cards was a popular worry.
• Top management was not getting it right. The analysts hark nostalgically back to the days when John Sainsbury ran the group, and make comparisons unflattering to current boss David Sainsbury. Some suggest an injection of top retailing talent from outside, without specifying exactly where that talent might go. The local hero was Dino Adriano, boss of the successful Homebase offshoot, and heir apparent to the supermarket chain.
• Sainsbury's earlier success was based on its well-founded reputation for quality. This has allowed it to achieve a far higher 'sales density' than any of its rivals: both sales and profits per square foot are outstanding. But it may find it hard to retain its pre-eminence. One of the gloomier predictions, from Hoare Govett, was that Sainsbury's above average return on capital, due to its better operating returns, is doomed to revert to the mean.
• Cash and dividends were another focus of attention. All the analysts agreed about Sainsbury's outstanding capacity to generate cash. Several were worried that it might play spendthrift in the US. In earlier papers some had argued for a far more generous dividend policy to get the cash back to

shareholders. One firm argued that Sainsbury – and its rivals – should be considering share buy-backs.

● One listed three pre-conditions for the shares to return to favour. First, the food retailing sector as a whole needed to return to favour. Second, Sainsbury needed to provide some evidence that management changes are working and that a trading recovery is in prospect. Third, Sainsbury's rating relative to the sector needed to fall.

The analysts moved from this detailed analysis to some fairly straightforward conclusions. Most agreed that Sainsbury had slipped so far behind in trading terms that it was inappropriate for it to be on a premium rating compared with Tesco. The minority who supported Sainsbury did so with considerable caution: their recommendations were based on its long term strength, not the short term outlook.

It was noteworthy that the harshest comment made was a recommendation to switch into Tesco. The idea of selling right out of the sector was never mentioned.

But as one analyst pointed out, four years earlier the whole pack had been bullish of Sainsbury and highly

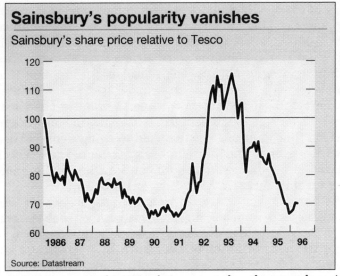

Fig 12.3 Tesco spent the 1980s being re-rated as the up-and-coming alternative to Sainsbury but was banished to the doghouse for a poor performance in 1991–93. Then Sainsbury fell out of favour.

critical of Tesco. 'And what happened next! . . . The odds are beginning to favour a positive surprise, not a negative one.'

How the press saw it

Most press coverage ran on identical lines to the analysts' circulars. The newspapers did not add anything to the brokers' reports. But for private investors who do not get brokers' reports (i.e. virtually all private investors), they provided a summary of what the broking consensus was.

Conclusions

Hindsight is a great blessing in this kind of exercise. One of the interesting aspects of the case study was how much more attention the analysts devoted to the basic business story than to financial details in the accounts.

This supports the contention that number crunching is only of over-riding importance when there are unsuspected problems lurking under the surface. In a healthy company, where it is relatively easy for investors and analysts to find out what is going on, the price action is usually over long before trading problems are reflected in the published numbers.

The technical analyst gave some impressive chart readings. Their signals sometimes lagged behind events, but were in time to be of some use. And warning signs had been plentiful even before the definite signal came. The use of the relative strength chart to test for confirmation or divergence was notably successful.

Ordinary investors relying on newspapers would have obtained a reasonable digest of what the analysts were thinking. But this was one case where Peter Lynch's ordinary housewife might well have trumped the experts because she could have spotted the overcapacity and high prices being charged by the majors before 1993. She might well have sold Sainsbury when she got her first Tesco Clubcard.

And what is the verdict on Sainsbury shares in March 1996? The company still has two basic problems. It is part of an industry wedded to expensive space with strong competition. And Sainsbury continues to be wrong-footed by Tesco at every turn. The business will not look attractive until:-

● Management changes and starts to get things right

● A substantial share buy-back shows that the company has taken to heart Buffet's point that free cash flow belongs to shareholders if the company has no good use for it.

A further bear point would be additional overseas expansions where the market is different.

Conclusion: Avoid until further action is taken. Further underperformance is likely.

Case Study

IN A NUTSHELL

1. All comments relate to assessments made in March 1996. Business background. Sainsbury belongs to an industry which has just come to the end of a period of unusual growth. While the expansion lasted it remained the industry leader, but has lost its way since the climate changed.

2. Chartist view. The long primary uptrend in the share price topped out early in 1993. The basic trend was then downwards. There was another short bullish phase between July 1994 and September 1995. But the downtrend which set in thereafter shows no sign of ending.

3. Accounting aspects. Essentially the accounts are sound despite the questionable treatment of properties. But the company seems to have run out of growth.

4. Investment yardsticks. The shares look overvalued on some forward projections.

5. Great investors. It is hard to see either Buffett or Lynch feeling much enthusiasm for the shares.

6. Stockbrokers' analysts and newspapers. Even former fans have lost patience as the management continues to flounder. Most analysts want the shares to get cheaper relative to the sector before considering recommending them. The newspapers faithfully reflected the analysts' consensus.

Chapter 13
Portfolio Management

There is a difference between owning some shares and having a portfolio. A portfolio uses a team approach to achieve a specific investment objective. Like a unit or investment trust, it is intended to reduce the risk of direct investment in individual shares by spreading your total risk between a number of different shares. Most people suggest at least ten. So even if one of your shares goes bust, you will not be too drastically affected. But any portfolio worthy of the name should be more than just a random bunch of shares. It should have a specific aim: to provide some capital for your retirement in 20 years time, to provide income now that you have retired, or to transform a small legacy into a Porsche.

Most people buying shares are primarily interested in capital growth. But shares can also be useful to people needing an income. We will look first at growth then at income portfolios in this chapter. But some considerations apply to all investors.

Once you have clarified your objectives, try to contain your impatience and hurry slowly. If you are a novice, it is worth doing a dummy run to get some feeling of what your strengths and weaknesses are. When Jim Slater started investing, he bought two years' back copies of the *Investors Chronicle* and refined his theories by seeing what would have happened if he had bought the shares he fancied in the earlier issues.

Another possibility is to park your money in a good deposit account – put some of it in an index-tracking fund if you are optimistic about the market – and run a theoretical portfolio for as long as your patience holds out. Many newcomers get put off investment for life because they jump in at the deep end, without bothering to learn how to swim. One point that emerged strongly in our review of great investors was how much practical experience they all had before they started trying to make money out of the stockmarket, and how hard they continued to work at selecting shares.

Even when you reckon you are ready to start, it is probably a mistake to put all your money into the market at once. A market fall soon afterwards could set you back for a long time. Unless the market as a whole is a screaming buy, or you plan to use one of the patent portfolio selection systems, you are unlikely to find enough attractive shares at one time. And, if you invest because you enjoy it, you might be tempted to churn your own portfolio for kicks.

Portfolio theories

Academic theories about the most efficient way to run a portfolio are aimed at professional portfolio managers. And many are irrelevant to the private investor. But concepts such as the trade-off between risk and reward are central to all investment. And anyone starting up a portfolio may end with a more sensible mixture if he treats himself as a 'client'.

● **The efficient marketeers.** Modern portfolio theory (MPT) argues that it is possible to select portfolios rationally by analysis of risk/return trade-offs and efficient diversification.

Some types of investment are riskier than others. And some investors are willing to accept a higher degree of risk than others. The good portfolio manager starts by finding out how much risk his client is willing to accept and what return he is hoping for. Then his job is to choose the portfolio which offers the best trade-off between the expected return and the risk, bearing in mind his client's requirements. If the client's expectations are unrealistic, the mismatch has to be sorted out at the beginning, and an acceptable compromise negotiated.

Investment offers a hierarchy of risk. Cash is conventionally seen as the safest investment – though it is vulnerable to inflation. Treasury bills and gilts, which are guaranteed by the government and have a set redemption date, are treated as a benchmark for other securities: they offer a risk-free rate of return. The purest risk-free return is the short term Treasury bill rate, but the return on longer term gilts is often used as a yardstick for longer term investments. Any investment which is riskier than gilts needs to offer a higher return to be attractive.

Equities are riskier than gilts, and must offer a risk premium in the form of a higher expected total return. The size of the premium will depend on market conditions and sentiment. If, say, the return on a ten year gilt is 7.5 per cent, equities might have to offer around 5 percentage points more − 12.5 per cent − to attract investors.* But some shares are riskier than others. If a particular share was 30 per cent riskier than the market as a whole, the appropriate risk premium for that share would be 1.3 times that of the equity market as a whole, that is to say 6.5 per cent. So the expected return on that share would need to be 14 per cent to attract investors.

Theorists argue that most major stockmarkets are broadly efficient: securities are priced at a level which balances the expected rewards against the perceived risks.† Pockets of inefficiency do exist, and those offer the greatest opportunities to stockpickers. But any client who wants high returns yet is unwilling to accept commensurately high risks is out of luck.

However, there are accepted ways of blending assets together into a portfolio which slightly improves the odds. A good portfolio is more than the sum of its parts: it offers a better risk/reward trade off. The good portfolio manager's job entails both choosing an appropriate asset allocation (division between broad categories such as cash, bonds and shares), and picking a selection of shares which combine efficiently as a team for the equity portfolio.

Risk spreading is a familiar concept. MPT attempts to go one better. It looks at both the riskiness of individual assets

* The equity risk premium has averaged around 5 percentage points in the UK. But, as explained in Chapter 1, some analysts argue that a premium of 1 to 2 percentage points is adequate.
† Most great investors ridicule the efficient market hypothesis. But there are not many great investors.

and the degree to which they move in the same way at the same time, in order to create theoretically perfect portfolios. An optimal portfolio is the best possible overall combination of risky and safe assets which gives an investor the highest possible return for a given level of risk. An efficient portfolio is the equivalent for a portfolio of risky assets, such as shares.

The academics describe such a portfolio as based on efficient diversification. MPT maintains that any risk averse investor will search for the highest expected return for any given portfolio risk. The efficient frontier is a graph representing a set of portfolios which produce the highest possible return for each level of portfolio risk. (See Fig 13.1.) Pick your risk tolerance, and your portfolio virtually chooses itself.

Actually constructing such portfolios obviously requires that the portfolio manager can form a reasonably accurate expectation of the risk-return attributes of different securities. The Efficient Market Hypothesis (EMH) obligingly argues that the prices of securities fully reflect available

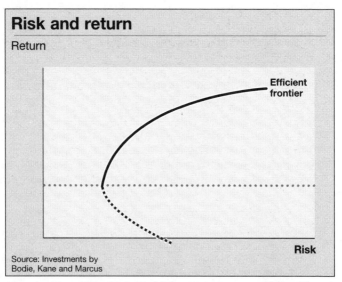

Risk and return

Return

Efficient frontier

Risk

Source: Investments by
Bodie, Kane and Marcus

Fig 13.1 Any investor wants the highest return compatible with a given risk level. The efficient frontier shows the best risk-return trade-offs attainable. It is a yardstick to measure actual portfolios against.

information. (So he cannot be accused of inadequate research.) And the Capital Asset Pricing Model equally obligingly argues that the expected excess return on an unusually risky security will be proportional to that excess risk, which can be measured by its 'beta'.

Deciding which combinations of securities work well together involves looking at covariances: these measure the degree to which the returns on two risky assets move in tandem. A positive covariance means that they move together; a negative one means that they move in opposite directions. The correlation coefficient measures covariance. Minus one is perfect negative correlation – one stock is high when the other is low; plus one is perfect positive correlation – both are high at the same time, but also fall together.

A portfolio whose constituents all had a correlation coefficient of plus one with each other would represent the depths of inefficient diversification: it would be just as risky as holding a single security because all the stocks would rise and fall together. A portfolio with a correlation coefficient of minus one would be the apogee of efficient portfolio management because a rise in one stock would be compensated by a fall in the other.

● **Diversification through asset allocation.** The traditional way of reducing risk is by spreading a portfolio between risky and safe assets: shares and cash (or gilts). The higher the client's risk tolerance the larger the proportion in equities. (The precise effect of particular combinations will also depend on how risky the share portfolio is.) But although this reduces risk, it does not necessarily improve the risk/return trade-off. If, for example, half the portfolio is in shares and the other half in cash, the risk is less than that of an all-share portfolio, but the expected return is reduced commensurately.

If, however, the manager knew that gilts always rose when shares fell and vice versa, this negative correlation would further reduce the risk of a portfolio containing both, and improve the risk-return trade-off. Unfortunately bonds and shares have a high positive correlation, though the real (inflation adjusted) returns on bonds have historically been less than those on shares.

This has led investment bank BZW to the superficially surprising conclusion that gilts have little place in optimal portfolios. Its retrospective calculations show that between 1919 and 1995 most investors in UK securities would have been best served by portfolios consisting of shares and cash, though the proportions depend on the investor's risk tolerance.

Optimal weight (percentages) for UK portfolio (1919–95)

Levels of risk tolerance

Asset	Min. risk	Low risk	Av. risk	High risk	Max risk
Cash	97.4	74.4	49.6	24.8	0.0
Gilts	2.0	0.0	0.0	0.0	0.0
Equities	0.5	25.6	50.4	75.2	100
Total	100	100	100	100	100
Portfolio					
Return	5.5	7.8	10.1	12.3	14.5
Risk	4.3	7.5	13.2	19.2	25.3

Source: The BZW Equity-Gilt Study – January 1996.

However, BZW points out that this does not necessarily mean that there is never a case for holding gilts. Over short periods they have sometimes done better than equities.*

* The same study shows that reducing risk by overseas diversification is more complicated than you might think. Overall international diversification has been beneficial. But the close correlation between the UK and US markets meant that US holdings did not improve the risk/return ratios, whereas holdings of German and Japanese equities and sundry foreign bonds were beneficial. But increasing correlation between the major markets means that overseas diversification is becoming less beneficial. And BZW suggests that investors may need to look to smaller markets (such as those of the emerging economies) to improve their risk/return profiles.

● **Asset allocation for individuals.** Few private investors
are likely to have the kind of portfolio which can benefit
directly from these sophisticated theoretical calculations.
The first decision for an individual is usually how to divide
his total wealth between financial assets, such as shares, and
real assets, such as property. For most of the 1970s and
1980s, a heavy weighting in residential property – usually a
geared investment in your own home – was a profitable
allocation strategy. In the late 1980s and early 1990s it was
poor to disastrous. Investment in other real assets, such as
art, was equally disappointing in financial terms, while
stockmarkets did well.

BZW's research suggests that the expected inflation rate is
the key factor here. Very broadly, when inflation rises above
6 per cent, things go wrong for all financial markets, and real
assets are the better bet. Below 6 per cent and your house
starts to be somewhere to live rather than the cornerstone of
your investment portfolio. The actual split between financial and real assets has to be an individual decision. For
people who rely on their investments for income, the choice
may be more apparent than real. But those who can afford to
should keep a weather eye on inflation when deciding how
much of their wealth to tie down in real assets. Remember
that they are normally relatively illiquid. This means that
they are often difficult to buy and sell, and that if you need
to sell in a hurry you may have to accept a very poor price –
as many homeowners will know only too well.

When it comes to the allocation of their financial assets,
most people will probably content themselves with keeping
a certain proportion of the total in cash or gilts: the lower
their risk tolerance the higher that proportion. Index-linked
gilts, which offer a guaranteed real yield, are an obvious
choice for many private investors. They provided an average
real return of around 3 per cent between 1982 and 1995.
This was substantially lower than those on conventional
gilts and equities – but most analysts agree that these were
exceptionally high. Index-linked gilts offer certainty, which
many retired people rate very highly.

The model portfolios in Chapter 14 suggest how an
investor might alter the risk profile of a unit trust portfolio,

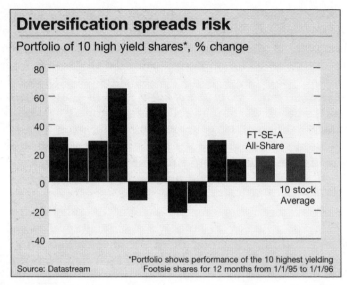

Diversification spreads risk

Portfolio of 10 high yield shares*, % change

Source: Datastream

*Portfolio shows performance of the 10 highest yielding Footsie shares for 12 months from 1/1/95 to 1/1/96

Fig 13.2 Even investors who have never heard of Modern Portfolio Theory can benefit from diversification. It is particularly useful with risky shares, such as high yielders.

as his risk tolerance and need for income alters at different stages in his life.

● **Diversification via a spread of shares.** Even investors who have never heard of MPT can enjoy many of the benefits of efficient diversification in an equity portfolio. An arbitrary selection of ten typical shares will achieve 87 per cent of the potential benefits of diversification; one of 20 such stocks provides 93 per cent of the advantages.* For although the expected return on a portfolio is equivalent to the weighted average return expected from the shares in the portfolio, the risk of the portfolio is usually lower than the weighted average risk of its constituents – because the individual shares in the portfolio do not normally move in unison.

The greater the negative correlation between the constituents of a portfolio, the greater the risk reduction in relation

* See *An Introduction to Risk and Return from Common Stocks* by Richard Brealey, the most accessible introduction to modern investment theory.

to the return, and the more efficient that portfolio. The textbook example is a portfolio combining an ice cream company and an umbrella company, whose shares move in opposite directions depending on the weather. Specialist trusts usually carry above average risk because the shares in them will have a high positive correlation.

Any intelligent private investor can form a rough idea of whether his portfolio is lop-sided, even if he does not know the precise riskiness of each share or how they correlate with the other constituents of the portfolio. A lop-sided portfolio is not necessarily a bad one for an investor with a high risk tolerance – but it needs to offer the reasonable prospect of above average returns to produce an acceptable risk return trade-off.

Just as a risky share has to work harder to earn its place in a portfolio, a risky portfolio has to work harder to satisfy its manager and its client. The lionhearted investor must have justifiably higher expectations than the chickenheart – or he is in danger of being re-classified as a jackass.

● **Market risk and betas.** Even an efficiently diversified equity portfolio will not be risk-free. It will be influenced to a greater or lesser extent by movements in the overall equity market. A beta measures the extent to which a share price mimics the stockmarket's overall movements. The market as a whole is defined as having a beta of 1 (and so does an index fund). A security whose movements exaggerate those of the market in both directions has a beta of more than 1; one which is unusually inert has a beta of under 1. (Cash has a beta of 0.)

A portfolio consisting of shares with high betas is described as aggressive, and is appropriate for investors expecting the market to rise. One consisting of shares with low betas is defensive. High beta risk cannot be reduced by diversification among similarly risky shares. It can only be reduced by switching into assets with lower beta risk: defensive shares or cash, for example.

Market timers (those investors who speculate on broad market moves rather than individual securities) can either increase their portfolio beta or gear up by borrowing to increase their exposure to expected price rises.

One worry for academics – and those who rely on their theories – is that companies' betas change over time as the companies themselves change. So portfolio managers who use betas to implement their market strategies may have unpleasant surprises. High beta shares tend to belong to high growth companies or highly geared companies or both; low beta shares are often slow growers. Most active private investors will naturally gravitate towards high beta companies. There is no quick way for private investors to find out what individual shares' betas are.* And some investors may worry that their chosen shares are excessively risky given their appropriate risk tolerance. What is a conscientious family man doing with a portfolio of racy little growth shares?

One way of calming these guilt pangs is to put some or all of your equity portfolio into an index fund. (See Chapter 14.) These provide a cheap and easy way of tracking the market, and reducing the overall portfolio risk to that of the market. Anyone with enough money can treat the index fund as the family car and indulge himself with a Porsche portfolio of individual shares as a sideline.

● **Active v passive management.** Most professional managers of broadly-based funds nowadays have a large proportion of their overall portfolio in index funds (passive funds) and concentrate their stockpicking skills on the fringe. If they can add sufficient value in their chosen area they will improve the overall return on the portfolio without pushing up transaction costs unnecessarily.

Many keep the proportions constant. Those who are willing to take a view on the market should in theory increase the proportion invested in passive funds when they reckon the market is set to rise strongly. This is perhaps counter-intuitive. But academics argue that the risk/reward trade-off moves against the stockpicker if the outlook for the whole market is good. If you can do well with little risk by 'buying the market', the small additional potential reward

* The London Business School runs a Risk Measurement Service, costing around £350 a year, which provides betas. Or you can get 10 for £80. (0171) 262–5050.

from successful stockpicking does not justify the additional risk.

The choice between active and passive management is one which the private investor can nowadays make as easily as the professional. Index funds are readily available and relatively cheap. (See page 330 for the corrosive impact of big management charges.) The appropriate division of funds depends on the investor's estimate of his ability reliably to beat the market. Roughly 90 per cent in index funds should protect the novice stockpicker from paying too highly for his education.

● **Hedging.** An effective but expensive way of reducing market risk is by hedging a portfolio. If, for example, a portfolio manager believes that a major bear market is imminent, he can buy put options or sell futures as an alternative to selling shares. Investors in overseas markets can also hedge the currency risk.

Many professional fund managers never hedge on principle. They argue that the costs of doing so are certain to reduce portfolio returns, whereas the rewards of doing so are uncertain. A long term portfolio does better by taking market swings in its stride.*

A put option is usually the best choice for a private investor who wants to hedge. But its effectiveness depends on how closely his overall portfolio matches the market.

Investing for growth

Most private investors who enjoy stockpicking are aiming for capital growth. This is partly because buying individual shares is seen as too risky for people who depend on the income from their portfolio.

---

* British savers' recent enthusiasm for guaranteed equity bonds and other artificial equity products implicitly takes the opposite view. Savers are accepting a subnormal equity return in exchange for an expensive capital guarantee. Such investors could reasonably expect to do substantially worse than the market over the long term – but of course most of the bonds only last for around five years.

In practice even retired people should have some equity stake in their portfolios, in order to protect both the capital and the income from inflation, but many will prefer to do so using trusts. The model portfolios reproduced in Chapter 14 on unit and investment trusts suggest appropriate portfolios for income investors. They show how a typical investor's equity exposure gets smaller as he gets older, and how the emphasis switches away from growth shares towards income shares.

Even for the growth investor, a more appropriate target than capital growth as such is the total return on an investment including both capital growth and the reinvested income on the portfolio. Reinvested income – and the capital growth accruing to it – accounts for roughly two thirds of the total real return on UK equities over the long term. Anyone taking his dividends when he does not need them is foregoing a substantial slice of his prospective reward.*

There is no single formula for success in growth investment. A quick flick through the chapters on great investors shows a variety of different approaches, but most of them have some characteristics in common. All rely on their skill to find chinks in the efficient market: shares whose full potential is not adequately recognised

● **What efficient market?** Successful investors have a universal disregard for portfolio theory. But that is because they rate their abilities to beat the market highly. Far from spreading his risks in an efficiently diversified manner, an investor such as Warren Buffett happily puts many of his eggs in the same basket.

But as we said above, even the theorists admit the existence of anomalies. The small firm effect – which says

---

* Personal equity plans, which allow investors to shield £6,000 a year from both income and capital gains tax provide a good opportunity to extract the maximum benefit from reinvested income. Generally speaking it makes sense for the investor to put the higher yielding investments into PEPS, and use his £6,300 annual capital gains tax allowance to reduce the impact of taxation on shares held outside PEPs that produce the bulk of their return in the form of capital gain. (See Appendix C.)

that a portfolio of small companies would regularly beat the market – has long been acknowledged in the textbooks.* (See Chapter 7.) Other companies which are comparatively under-researched may also be under-rated. And so may those whose shares are hard for institutions to buy and sell.

A great investor can be defined as an exception taking advantage of an anomaly. Ordinary investors can learn from them, but should be chary of following their example until they have tested their own stockpicking abilities. Buffett recommends putting regular savings into an index fund to the humble investor who recognises his lack of ability.

● **You need a system.** All agree that the investor needs to work to a system – even though their systems differ. Value investors and growth investors are both aiming at the same target – superior performance – they merely have different views on the best way of getting there. All agree that the investor should find a system which suits him and allows him to make the best use of his particular skills.

● **Avoid losses.** All emphasise how important it is to avoid losing money. Once the investor loses money he has to accept above average risks in order to achieve even average returns. Benjamin Graham argues that the margin of safety is the key investment principle. Others agree that if a stock is cheap enough even a mistake will not cost you money; your capital will merely suffer a brief period of sterility.

Interestingly, the late Lord White followed exactly this principle when picking companies for conglomerate Hanson to buy. He always looked at the downside first; and if the risks were too great, no amount of upside could tempt him.

● **Tightwad tips.** Most warn against excessive turnover and unnecessary costs. Unnecessary transaction costs act as a voluntary 'tax' on a portfolio. This is particularly true if the investor concentrates on small or neglected companies, where spreads are high. Buffett, who argues that liquidity is

---

* Some academics have begun to question whether it should more properly be called the January effect since most of the relative outperformance occurs in early January (a time when American investors frequently indulge in tax loss selling).

a greatly over-rated virtue in a share, is particularly vehe-
ment in his dislike of churnover – and of course expensive
unit trusts.*

Buffett is critical of all unnecessary investment costs.
When unit trusts designed to allow the small investor a way
into Berkshire Hathaway started springing up, he reluc-
tantly proposed splitting Berkshire's shares into more man-
ageable units, because he so disliked the idea of investors
paying unit trust charges in order to get in. Berkshire's
corporate jet was christened *The Indefensible*.

● **Do your homework.** All believe in thorough research
and never investing in a share they do not fully understand.
If they do not know the facts, they stay away. And if they do
not consider themselves competent to evaluate the facts,
they stay away.

One unexpected route to an above average total return,
noticed by Graham, is buying high yielding shares. Equity
income unit trusts have produced better total returns than
growth trusts over most long periods, though their record
faltered in the recent recession. And many patent methods
of selecting shares mechanically use yield as a criterion.
(See pages 310–14.)

Managing a portfolio

The better the investor's original share selection, the easier
the job of managing the portfolio afterwards should be. One
Oxbridge college with a good investment record used to
confine itself to reviewing its portfolio once a year, with the
aim of finishing its business before lunch. It made as few
changes as possible.†

Most people will probably want to keep a closer eye on
their shares, but mainly to check that they are still happy
with their choice. Does it still look as if each share will fulfil

* Peter Lynch is the notable exception here. But this may be
because it is hard to run a large mutual fund without a relatively
high turnover.
† This review appeared for many years under the sobriquet
Academic Investor in the *Investors Chronicle*.

the expectations which won it its place in the portfolio in the first place? The dedicated investor will also be keeping an eye out for new candidates for his affections. Constant monitoring is not to be equated with short-termism or churnover. Buffett is a long term investor. But the paucity of his actions belies the assiduity of his monitoring process.

Some investors always have both a price target and a time limit in mind when they buy a share, particularly if it is one with limited potential, such as a recovery share. Greater licence can be given to growth shares, but even here investors such as Lynch keep them under constant surveillance to check that they are not flagging. Charts, particularly relative strength charts, can be useful for providing early warning that a former star is fading.

• **When to sell.** Knowing when to sell is important. But the answer depends on the basic strategy. The investor who buys only a small number of shares which he hopes to hold for ever will sell only if he has to admit to a fundamental misjudgement. But investors who buy with a specific target in mind, such as Graham with his bargain shares or Lynch with his stalwarts, sell when that target has been achieved or when the basic case for buying has been undermined. In either case there is no longer any reason to hold.

Selling real growth shares is a different proposition entirely. To sell simply because a share has risen strongly and is beginning to dominate a small portfolio is usually a mistake, even in a portfolio with relatively high turnover. Lynch comments that it is a pretty odd gardener who cuts the heads off the flowers and waters the weeds. He argues for running profits on really good growth shares as long as possible. Sometimes a sky high PE ratio is merely a reflection of the company's prospects. The point at which to get nervous is when the basic story – the investor's reason for buying the share – appears to have changed for the worse, but the share price ignores the deterioration. (Sainsbury in early 1993 is a good example.)

Cynics say that the real danger sign is when a great growth company starts getting written up in the press. Jim Slater suggests that the time to sell a growth company is when its PEG rises to 1.2 or the company's growth status is not just recognised but drooled over.

Traders sometimes have a series of stop-losses on their shares: they will automatically sell if the price falls to a certain level or by a certain percentage. But such strategies can be tricky to operate successfully particularly with volatile shares. There is a danger of getting stopped out just before a share recovers. An alternative in many cases is buying a put option, which also allows the investor to lock in a particular selling price. Put options inevitably involve some expense, but avoid the risk of being whip-sawed by a volatile price.

The cost of frequent dealing obviously makes it harder to secure good overall returns. And anyone concentrating on small and illiquid shares will find it prohibitively expensive.

● **Tax.** Growth investors get a reasonably good deal from the taxman nowadays. And they should be careful to take advantage of the £6,300 annual capital gains tax exemption. Capital gains tax rules are very fiddly. But despite our earlier caveats about unnecessary dealing, it is worth bed-and-breakfasting shares in order to ensure that the exemption is not wasted.

Paying gains tax hurts, but can sometimes seem inevitable if, for example, a takeover bid looms. In practice, bids nowadays almost always come with a loan note alternative to the cash offer – which allows the tax to be rolled forward. A competent accountant probably comes in handy here. But one who suggests that the tax should be further deferred by rolling the gain into high risk tax-efficient investments, such as Venture Capital trusts or Enterprise Investment Schemes may be over-zealous in his determination to defeat the revenue. It is always better to pay tax than lose the capital. (See Appendix C.)

Patent portfolios

Apparently foolproof ways of selecting portfolios that beat the market are understandably popular with investors. Benjamin Graham suggested several ways of picking portfolios mechanically. (See Chapter 8.) Here are a couple more.

● **The Investors Chronicle High Yield System.** The *Investors Chronicle* has published and monitored portfolios based on this system for nearly 40 years. Normally they have beaten the market handsomely; occasionally the system blows a fuse: either it is impossible to compile a portfolio which meets the criteria or the portfolios do worse than the market. It is a totally mechanical system that suggests a list of 30 shares to be bought as a package. It is not a recommendation for any particular share in that package. The shares are ones offering an above average yield. Normally most of them turn into so-so performers; a few do brilliantly, a few badly. But overall the winners outweigh the losers and the whole portfolio beats the averages.

The theory behind the system runs as follows. High yielding shares are those which are out of favour with investors, sometimes for good reason, sometimes for bad. What you need is a system which weeds out the real dogs. If the remaining shares are better than investors think, their potential will eventually be demonstrated and recognised. So the share prices will rise. The system selects recovery shares and cyclicals without knowing anything about the underlying business. There are two screening processes: the first filters out bad risks before they get into the portfolio; the second ejects them if they prove disappointing after purchase.

The investor starts by drawing up a list of qualifying shares. To qualify a share needs to satisfy the following criteria:–

(a) The yield on the shares must exceed that on a chosen index, such as the FT Industrials Index. (This one is chosen because it excludes mines and financial shares, since these sometimes behave idiosyncratically.)

(b) Weed out the real tiddlers, because marketability will be a problem. The minimum size tends to rise with time: thus the system began with a minimum market capitalisation of £1.5m and raised it to £3m.

(c) Only shares whose price is higher or at least as high as it was a year ago are considered. That way shares which are on a falling trend can be avoided. And if markets as a whole are falling, the system selects those which are showing relative strength. But if the markets are still falling fast, it may be impossible to find a portfolio.

The investor then simply buys the 30 shares with the highest yields. Once they are bought, there are two conditions which prompt expulsion.

(a) If a company passes or cuts its dividend to such an extent that its yield falls below that on the FT-SE-Actuaries index, and

(b) The share price has slipped below the level of a year previously.

Shares only get the chop if they fail both tests. And of course you do not eject shares whose yield falls simply because the share price has risen. That's what you are hoping for. This system started to produce disappointing results during the recession of the early 1990s, and it is not yet clear whether that disappointment was a one-off.

● **The O'Higgins System.** This American system is like the IC High Yield system in that it is using above average yield as a pointer to underrated shares. But its chosen arena is much smaller: the 30 blue chips that make up the Dow Jones index, and the system's aim is to beat the Dow. It suggests three ways of doing it, all based on the same initial screening process. The two more conservative strategies involve small portfolios, the third is a single stock selection.

The initial screen involves ranking the 30 Dow constituents by dividend yield. The more conservative strategy simply puts the ten highest yielders into the portfolio. An equal amount of money goes into each stock and the portfolio is reviewed and updated annually. Stocks that no longer measure up are sold and replaced by those that do. Dividends are reinvested. Over a ten year period, portfolios chosen on this method rose by an average 16.6 per cent a year, compared with an average 10.4 per cent for the Dow. But there were some years in which the portfolios underperformed.

The second screen involves ranking the ten high yield shares already chosen by their market price. The five shares with the lowest share prices go into the portfolio. (For example, a share with a price of 50p is selected in preference to one with a price of 75p.) Again an equal amount of money is invested in each share and there is an annual review. This is the medium risk strategy. Portfolios chosen on this method showed an average rise of 19.4 per cent a year for a ten year period, compared with 10.4 per cent for the Dow. As with the first method there were some years in which the portfolios did worse than the Dow.

O'Higgins' own explanation for the success of his yield system is that it is cash flow and the dividends based on it, not earnings, that are the driving force in the blue chip market over the medium term; and that American companies (unlike some British ones) are exceedingly reluctant to cut dividends even when earnings fall. So if a share price temporarily follows earnings down, while the dividend remains intact, it is usually a buying opportunity. His interest in low priced stocks reflects the belief that the less expensive a unit of stock, the more prone it is to greater percentage movements.

He has experimented with refining the basic system. For example, he combined it with the Hallowe'en Indicator: stay in the stockmarket from 31 October to 30 April, but keep your money in money funds for the other six months. His portfolios still beat the Dow, though the results were less good than on a fully invested basis. There was less variability in the returns from year to year, and for six months of the year there was nothing to worry about. Another experiment was based on staying out of the stockmarket for the first 18 months of a presidential cycle. O'Higgins' overall conclusion is the gratifying one that the simplest method works best.

But would it work in England? In 1992 the *Financial Times* ran a test on the performance of a five-stock portfolio of high yield/low price shares over a 13 year period. It used the FT 30 Share index as its hunting ground, but measured the portfolio's performance against the broader All-Share index. It also deducted notional dealing costs. Over the whole 13 year period the O'Higgins portfolio did some 60 per cent better than the All-Share. But it was only in the latter years that the gap became significant, and it did worse in five individual years. Interestingly, much of the portfolio's edge came from the dividends themselves. A test based only on capital growth beat the index by a much smaller margin.

But in subsequent tests the FT's O'Higgins portfolio started to produce a rather patchy performance. Interestingly, many of the dud portfolios included Hanson, a company which had earlier prospered through its own successful search for growth in unlikely places. (See also Chapter 8 page 205 for a comparison of Hanson's acquisition techniques with those of successful value investors.)

It is also notable that the system ceased to produce good results soon after it had been adopted by a firm of intermediaries and sold hard to personal equity plan investors. It is not yet clear whether the mid-1990s was just a sticky patch for O'Higgins. But the coincidence does support the argument that by the time any investment theory is adopted commercially, it is past its sell-by date. Anomalies are best exploited in private by consenting adults.

A rather similar American high yield system, published by Barron's – a weekly financial newspaper – is called the Dogs of the Dow. It operates by buying the ten highest yielding shares in the Dow Jones index at the start of each year. Performance has varied. When tried on the UK market in the mid 1990s it did not produce good results, partly because portfolios included some shares, such as Hanson and British Gas, which were in the middle of severe downgradings.

Investing for income

The investors who care most about income tend to be retired people who need it to meet normal living expenses. There are two reasons why shares should play a part in their portfolio planning. The main one is that anyone investing only in fixed interest deposits or securities will find the value of both capital and income steadily eroded by inflation. The second one, particularly relevant in the early 1990s, is that interest rates are sometimes so low that only the rich get a worthwhile return from deposits.

The inflation argument is compelling even when the actual rate is historically low. An average inflation rate of 4 per cent a year, for instance, would halve the value of money in just 17 years. And, assuming the income stays the same, its buying power will also halve over the same period. This double erosion affects both deposits and conventional gilt edged stocks. Increased life expectancy means that many people can expect very lengthy retirements. If they are to have any hope of stemming the fall in their capital and their income, they need to have at least part of their portfolios invested in shares. For, unlike deposits and fixed interest, equities promise both increasing capital value and increasing income – at least over the longer term.

For most people the split between fixed interest deposits and shares will be dictated more by necessity than by textbook calculations. The investments which offer the greatest prospect of capital growth and increasing income in the longer term usually offer the lowest immediate return. But as a general rule your long term interest will be best served by putting as high a proportion of your total portfolio into equities as you can afford, and feel inclined to risk.

Say, for example, you divide your capital equally three ways: one third goes into fixed interest deposits and gilts yielding 7 per cent but with no scope for capital apprecia-tion; one third goes into high income shares and converti-bles with a yield of only 5 per cent, but the hope of producing modest capital growth, say 5 per cent a year; the final third goes into growth shares with a yield of only 3 per cent, but a real prospect of producing capital growth of 10 per cent a year. Average yield is 5 per cent.

What would happen to those investments over a ten year period? First, the capital side: the deposits and gilts would be unchanged, the high income shares and convertibles would have increased their capital value by around half, the growth shares would have increased their capital value by over 130 per cent. Overall the portfolio might even have matched inflation.

What is more over the ten year period the income on the two equity portions would gradually have caught up with that on the deposits. So although the yield on the portfolio's eventual capital value would still be only 5 per cent, it would be over 7 per cent in relation to the starting capital. And the actual income (not adjusted for inflation) would have risen some 45 per cent over the ten years. Such a portfolio would probably be too risky for many retired people, but it demonstrates the principle.

Securities can even have a place in the portfolios of investors who need every scrap of income they can get. If the stockmarket is rising fast, you could theoretically increase your income by selling off chunks of your equity portfolio. This would obviously need to be part of a very carefully monitored financial plan, but it could be sensible when deposit rates are low. Investing in a portfolio of zero coupon preference shares with phased redemption dates is another way of using capital growth to provide a regular income – though again the investor needs to sort out in advance what is spending money and what will need to be ploughed back for the future.

Shares to be wary of are those which promise an exceptionally high return. For often that is a sign that the capital is more than usually at risk. The obvious example is annuity type income shares of split level trusts. They get the lion's share of the income earned on the overall portfolio during the trust's life, but often have only a nominal claim on its assets when it is wound up.

One point to remember is that all investment income will be taxed at whatever the investor's highest tax rate is, provided he has enough income from all sources to get into the tax net. But the first £6,300 (1996 rates) of capital gains in any year are exempt from tax. So turning capital into income can be more worthwhile than comparisons of the gross figures suggest, particularly for investors in the higher tax brackets. Remember too that capital gains on gilts are tax-free. This explains why high taxpayers are encouraged to invest in low coupon gilts, which produce the majority of their return in the form of capital gain. (However, their lower yields reflect this: the advantage is largely arbitraged away.)

Many of the points made in the earlier section on investing for growth are equally applicable to income investors. But the importance of living within your overall risk tolerance means that the income investor should either avoid the riskier strategies altogether or ensure that the vast majority of his portfolio is in relatively safe assets. What the income investor should avoid is landing himself with 'safe' blue chip shares, where safe means dud. Equity income trusts and high yield patent portfolios are a trouble-free alternative for the investor who finds index funds dull.

Bearbull portfolios

The *Investors Chronicle* each week publishes dummy portfolios designed to show the results of a Growth Portfolio, an Income Portfolio, a Speculative Portfolio and an Overseas Portfolio. The last of these demonstrates how to use unit and investment trusts for investing abroad. The portfolios are artificial in the sense that the author does not actually buy the shares that he recommends and that he is expected to take some action every time a portfolio is published. Most genuine investors deal far less frequently. And Bearbull's high transaction costs severely hamper his performance.

But the portfolios are genuine in the sense that they reflect the choices of one individual. Following them can provide some painless lessons in what can go right – and wrong – with different types of portfolio. They are also intended to offer some buying suggestions. But, like all IC tips they are suggestions not categoric recommendations. And it would be impractical for anyone to mimic the portfolios exactly.

Portfolio Management

IN A NUTSHELL

1. A portfolio is more than a motley collection of shares. A portfolio uses a team approach to achieve a specific investment objective.

2. Modern portfolio theory (MPT) aims to produce the best possible portfolios: those which offer the highest prospective rewards for a given degree of risk. The efficient market hypothesis argues that markets are broadly efficient in their pricing of securities, and the capital asset pricing model asserts that the expected excess returns on unusually risky securities will be proportional to that risk.

3. MPT is not directly relevant to private investors planning their own portfolios. But they can ensure that their portfolios are diversified; that the prospective returns justify the risks; and that the portfolio is not lop-sided.

4. Betas are a way of measuring whether particular shares are more or less volatile than the market. Investors unwilling to take on above average market risk should consider using an index-tracking fund as a core portfolio.

5. There are as many ways of running a growth portfolio as there are growth investors. But there are some common characteristics: have a system and stick to it; avoid losing money and look for a margin of safety; don't churn; research thoroughly and avoid shares you do not understand.

6. The better your original share selection, the easier the job of managing it on an ongoing basis. The best way of managing it will depend on what your overall portfolio strategy is.

7. Many investors enjoy trying out patent portfolios. Many systems are based on buying high-yielding shares. The *Investors Chronicle* also publishes dummy Bearbull portfolios designed to achieve different investment objectives.

8. Most investors primarily interested in income should include an equity element in their portfolios as a hedge against inflation.

Chapter 14
Unit and Investment Trusts

Many people prefer to invest through unit and investment trusts rather than picking individual shares themselves. There are several good reasons for doing so. First, it allows even investors of modest means to get a wide spread of different shares without incurring excessive costs. Second, it allows investors who do not have the time or expertise to pick individual shares to 'hire' a specialist fund manager to do it for them. And third, it allows investors who enjoy picking their own shares in familiar markets, such as the UK, to extend their portfolio to include markets with which they are not familiar, notably overseas stockmarkets, but also specialist areas such as venture capital or technology.

Unit and investment trusts are both pooled funds, allowing individual investors to participate in a wide spread of different investments. But since the unit trust business is far bigger and better known, we will concentrate on unit trusts. A note on the pros and cons of using the investment trust route starts on page 338.*

One big City investment firm, Schroders, refuses to assemble portfolios of individual shares for any client with less than £2m. Its argument is that since every client needs a spread of different markets, and a minimum of 25 shares is necessary to get a proper spread of risk in any market, clients with less than £2m do better investing through unit trusts. This definition of 'modest means' is perhaps extreme.

* Nowadays there are roughly as many unit trusts based in offshore financial centres as trusts based in the UK. Many are run by the same UK management groups. Investor protection is generally lower and costs often higher. True, a trust based in a well-regulated offshore centre, such as Dublin, and run by a firm with a solid parent, arguably provides better security than one run by a small independent UK unit trust group. The snag is that the investor has to assess the solidity of the management group and its parent, as well as the investment merits of the fund.

But the point that even millionaires can benefit from the administrative advantages of unit trusts is valid.

The modern investor is faced with a long list of possible homes for his money. The range of 'investable' stockmarkets round the world continues to grow. The increase in the number of quoted securities on each market and the proliferation of different types of security, notably futures and options, means that many individual stockmarkets are really a series of submarkets.

There is little hope of even the assiduous private investor becoming a competent polymath. He can sensibly opt for specialisation: confine his activities to one submarket in which he reckons he has an edge: for example, smaller UK companies. Alternatively he can decide that his job should be limited to selecting the experts to invest for him. That means either going to a firm of investment advisers or managers, or buying trusts. In practice many investors combine the two: pay investment managers to pick trusts for them.

One advantage of investing through trusts is that they can be bought and sold easily. If you are displeased with performance, or simply want to get out of one market into another, you do not have to sack your expert adviser; you just sell your units. And although each fund has administrative costs throughout its existence, you only have to share those costs for the particular period for which you invest in that trust. If you want to stay in a market but do not like the trust you have chosen, it is relatively easy to find a list of suitable alternatives. And if you want to move from one submarket to another, for example, from blue chips to mid caps or smaller companies, as the stockmarket cycle progresses, unit trusts offer an open door in both directions.

What is more, since unit trust performance is a useful shop window for fund management groups, they often put their best investment managers in charge of their unit trusts. Private client discretionary accounts are often run by people good at handling private clients. The two talents do not always co-exist.

The other advantage of investing through trusts is that it allows you – or your advisers – time to concentrate on the other aspects of portfolio management: objective setting, overall asset allocation, and sector allocation. A large part of your total investment returns is governed by your decisions on whether to invest in bonds or shares, which types of company and which world markets to back at which time. Why waste time trying to pick the right shares?

There are of course plenty of disadvantages to investing through trusts. The two most obvious are that picking good trusts is arguably harder than picking good shares and that investing through trusts is expensive. Total unit trust charges have roughly doubled since they were freed from the regulations laid down by the Department of Trade and Industry. Performance inevitably suffers.

Before deregulation in 1979 the most that managers were allowed to charge was 13.25 per cent over 20 years. So if the initial charge was, say 3.25 per cent, the maximum annual charge was 0.5 per cent. If the initial charge was as high as 5 per cent the total was capped at 12.5 per cent, which translated into an annual charge of 0.375 per cent.

Nowadays the norm is 5 per cent initial charge plus 1 per cent to 1.5 per cent a year thereafter. That is the equivalent of 25 to 35 per cent over 20 years, more than double the old rates on average

Building a portfolio of unit trusts

As people get older they want different things from their portfolio and are less able to take risks. In a textbook world the investor's life cycle can be neatly divided into:–

● **The accumulation period:** between 25 and 50 years of age, when the investor is earning money. He can stand some risk, does not need the income from his portfolio and should be reinvesting it to secure the maximum total return. Reinvesting the income substantially increases the total return and also reduces the impact of market fluctuations.
● **The transition period:** this depends on when the investor expects to cease earning but is normally between ages 50 and 60. He should still be accumulating wealth but is becoming more risk averse, and should be gradually

altering the balance of the portfolio towards the more cautious mix appropriate for retirement.

● **The distribution phase:** this may arrive gradually if the investor works part time when he first retires, but normally starts some time after 60. Given that many people can expect to live for another 20 years or more after retirement it is important to keep at least part of the portfolio in investments likely to produce growth in both capital and income. Otherwise both its value and the value of the income it produces are likely to fall in real terms. Equities have historically been by far the most effective inflation hedge.

The model portfolio allocations below are not meant to be followed rigidly.* But investors whose own portfolios are markedly dissimilar may want to check their own strategy.

	Type of Investor			
	Accumulation	Transition	Distribution Early years	Late years
	%	%	%	%
Equity trusts				
Growth	35	15	0	0
General	30	30	25	15
Equity Income	0	15	25	20
Specialist trusts	15	5	0	0
Total equity	*80*	*65*	*50*	*35*
Bond/funds/gilts				
Long term	10	10	20	30
Medium term	10	15	20	25
Short term	0	10	10	10
Total bond	*20*	*35*	*50*	*65*
Total portfolio	**100**	**100**	**100**	**100**

The thinking behind these allocations is that the overall

* Adapted from those suggested in *Bogle on Mutual Funds.* In the US unit trusts are known as mutual funds. In Britain terminology is sloppy. In this chapter the more specific term 'trust' is used, unless the generic 'fund' seems more natural in the context.

equity emphasis gradually shifts away from riskier investments, the growth and specialist trusts. Once the investor
retires, he has no high risk exposure. But he does keep some
equities even after retirement, to provide growth. The
emphasis on income rises the older he gets.

The bond element in the portfolio (trusts investing in gilts
and corporate bonds) is also designed to give different types
of investor different risk/reward exposures. Despite their
reputation for safety, different types of bond carry different
types of risk*. A mixture is advisable for all types of
investor.

But choosing unit trusts investing in bonds with appropriate maturities is hard for the UK investor, because the UK
bond fund market is relatively undeveloped. Few UK
managers of fixed interest unit trusts target specific maturity
dates. Many have the broad aim of producing a high yield
without excessive risk.

Gilt funds have invariably performed less well than gilts
for two reasons: partly because management costs reduce
the overall return, but also because of managers' tendency to
go for high yield. In the early 1990s this pushed some of
them towards high coupon stocks standing above their
redemption prices. In effect they were quasi annuities. The
inevitable loss of capital resulting from such policies is not
widely appreciated.

Investors can, of course, choose suitable gilts themselves
as a complete or partial substitute for trusts investing in
bonds. This has the considerable advantage of saving
management costs. But for investors who do not need the

* Gilts are the most obvious bond investment for British investors, although the introduction of personal equity plan tax concessions for holdings of corporate bonds has skewed the argument.
(See Appendix C for PEPs.) Gilts have both capital and income
guaranteed by the government, but that does not mean they have
no risks. All long term bonds pose the risk that the investor will be
locked in at what with hindsight appears to be a very unfavourable
interest rate. Short term bonds pose the risk that the investor may
not be able to reinvest his capital on such favourable terms when
the bond matures. All bonds carry the risk that the interest cannot
be reinvested on such good terms.

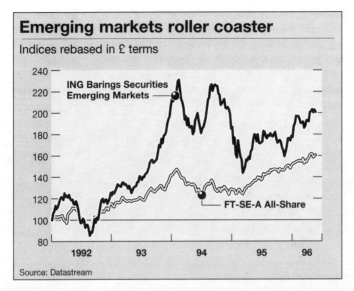

Emerging markets roller coaster

Indices rebased in £ terms

ING Barings Securities
Emerging Markets

FT-SE-A All-Share

1992   93   94   95   96

Source: Datastream

Fig 14.1 Any overseas investments should be counted as part of the high risk portion of your portfolio. But investments in some overseas markets, such as those of emerging economies, are especially risky

income, the snag is that it is not easy to reinvest the income cost-effectively. The introduction of gilt strips, which work like a zero coupon bond, should solve this problem, though the investor will need to keep an eye on the tax implications.* Zero coupon preference shares are another theoretical possibility, but most have a fairly short period left to maturity.

Financial planners and portfolio managers often suggest that sterling investors should have some exposure to overseas markets. Most reckon that around 60 to 80 per cent of the total should always stay in UK investments, rising to 100 per cent for older retired people. Any overseas investments should be counted as part of the high risk portion of the portfolio: specialist and growth trusts. The risks of

* Zeros pay no interest. The investor buys at a substantial discount to the eventual redemption value, with the gain to redemption compensating for the income foregone. It should be possible to buy a gilt strip whose redemption date precisely matches the investor's chosen maturity but returns will be liable to income tax.

investing overseas even in large markets such as Wall Street are high because of the additional currency risk.

- **Lump sum investment.** Investors who inherit a lump sum at any stage in their life should follow a slightly modified portfolio strategy, because they are faced with the problem of market timing. This makes it sensible to be rather more cautious than would otherwise be appropriate. For example, someone getting a substantial inheritance while still young and growth-oriented should probably aim for a 70:30 equity:bond split rather than 80:20.

It is also sensible to invest the money gradually over a period of at least a year. Start by parking the largest share (say 70 per cent) in a safe short term high interest cash fund and build up the portfolio over a period, in order to avoid the risk of putting the whole sum into the market just before a sharp set-back.

Some people get a lump sum to invest when still fairly young but have to rely on it for both their immediate and their future income. Examples include anyone who suffers a disabling accident, a young widow or widower with children who receives compensation for the death in service of the spouse, or a divorced person. Such investors should also adopt a modified strategy. They need both a safe and a growing income. Different elements in the portfolio can meet these different requirements.

Putting a relatively high proportion in long term and medium dated bonds with high yields should cope with the short-term need for a reliable income. That is the first leg of the race, but then another part of the portfolio takes over the baton. For this type of investor should also have a substantial proportion of the total portfolio in equity trusts aiming to produce capital and income growth. These will reduce the initial yield on the portfolio as a whole, but are necessary to ensure that the income does not start shrinking when the investor is still only middle-aged.

Here is model portfolio allocation for growth and income-oriented investors who have a lump sum to invest while still relatively young. But again, treat it as a yardstick, not a strait-jacket.

| | Lump Sum Investor | |
	Growth-oriented %	Income-oriented %
Equity trusts		
Growth	35	15
General	20	25
Equity income	0	20
Specialist funds	15	0
Total equity	*70*	*60*
Bond funds/gilts		
Long term	20	25
Medium term	10	10
Short term	0	5
Total bond	*30*	*40*
Total portfolio	**100**	**100**

The case for index funds

The argument for all investors having at least some of their
money in index funds is compelling. These unit trusts, also
known as tracker funds, construct portfolios designed to
mimic the performance of a particular stockmarket index,
through full replication, selective sampling or the use of
derivatives. Running a portfolio in this way is known as
passive management, in contrast to the active management
style of a trust whose managers use their stock selection
skills to try to beat the market.

Tracker funds routinely produce a better performance
than most actively managed funds aiming to beat the same
index. There are two reasons for this. First, it is not possible
for fund managers in aggregate to beat the market, since
together they own the market. Their aggregate return will be

the stockmarket performance minus their transaction costs. Second, since index funds always have lower transaction costs and usually impose lower management charges than actively managed funds, both their investment performance and their returns to the investor should outstrip those of the average actively managed fund.

What is more, even though individual managed funds do beat the market over short periods, over the long term comparable funds tend to drift back towards the average. So, for the long term investor, the case for investing through tracker funds appears irrefutable.

But that does not stop people trying to refute it. One argument against trackers is that their market risk is normally higher than that of comparable actively managed funds – such as general growth trusts. (See Chapter 13 page 303 for an explanation of betas as a measure of market risk.) In a bear market trackers do worse than general growth trusts, whose managers normally try to reduce risk to below the market average. Thus an investor who does not know whether he wants to be in the market or out of it will find that a general growth trust hedges some of his bets for him. Investors who take the tracker route should make sure that their overall portfolio allocation includes enough cash to cushion the market risk of their tracker.

● **Picking winners is hard.** Even supporters of active management do not dispute the arithmetic argument that, other things being equal, lower costs spell better returns. They concentrate on the fact that some fund managers do better than others. Pick the right managed funds and their superior investment performance will outweigh the additional costs, runs the argument. They have two different strategies to suggest: picking a series of outstanding funds, or picking consistent long term winners and sticking with them.

First, a strategy for traders: chasing performance. Since some funds always do significantly better than others over particular periods, an investor who succeeds in catching each fund while it is on the roll should be able to achieve an above average performance.

Second, a buy and hold strategy. A few outstanding fund managers, such as Warren Buffett or Peter Lynch, manage to beat the market over the long haul. So an investor who backs managers like them can himself beat the market.

● **Chasing performance.** The commonsense view, supported by most research, is that actively trading funds is akin to betting on horses, and often about as successful. For how do you pick tomorrow's winners? Relying on a short term above average performance is often fatal. Trusts which do exceptionally well in one year often do unusually badly thereafter. Even the organisations which measure fund performance admit they have no predictive power. And actively trading trusts will be very costly for the investor.

Some interesting recent American research both contradicts and confirms this thesis.* It suggests that past performance is a good predictor of future performance over fairly short periods of time. But this improved investment performance only brings a better return to the investor if the funds have no initial charge, so that switching does not cost him money. A minority of sophisticated investors does chase good performance. But bad funds survive because of the 'disadvantaged clientele': unsophisticated investors who pay attention to advertisements and brokers, investors tied to a particular fund management group which does badly, and people who do not want to switch for tax reasons.

● **Buy and hold.** The buy and hold strategy also poses practical difficulties. As Benjamin Graham might have said, a small number of unusually good managers do exist, but reliable means of identifying them do not.† Statisticians like a long term track record in order to state confidently that a particular fund has a consistently superior performance: some suggest as much as 25 years. But, since unit

---

* *Another puzzle: the growth in actively managed mutual funds* by Martin Gruber, 1996.
† What he actually said about managed funds was that there may be special risks in looking for superior performance by investment fund managers. Funds chasing performance aggressively usually take risks which means they are bound to come a cropper sooner or later. The best that can be hoped for from a large soundly managed fund is 'only slightly better than average results over the years'. The only obvious bargain in the investment fund business is buying a selection of shares in closed end funds (investment trusts) selling at a discount of say 10–15 per cent.

trusts' managers often change every few years, not many trusts have a record long enough to assess in this way. And by the time the statisticians are satisfied, the next Peter Lynch will probably have retired.

Since hope springs eternal, many investors will continue to test their skill by trying to pick winning managers. But even optimists cannot deny that the higher costs borne and imposed by actively managed funds puts them at a disadvantage. And joining the 'disadvantaged clientele', trapped or locked into the funds which pull the averages down, has no attractions for any intelligent investor.

● **Counting the costs.** Unit trust costs inevitably hamper performance. The question here for the investor wondering whether to use trusts or invest directly in shares is whether he would in practice be paying even more if he invested himself or paid an expert to invest for him. The answer depends mainly on how active he would be as a direct investor. The combined costs of buying and selling shares in a leading company add up to around 5 per cent, and perhaps treble that for a second line share. If you are a long term investor who seldom changes his holdings, trusts are probably more expensive. If you are fairly active, the balance of advantage could swing the other way.

Costs on managed funds are normally more than on trackers. Many actively managed equity unit trusts have both an initial charge of around 5 or 6 per cent and an annual charge of 1.0 to 1.5 per cent. Some trusts with no initial charge have an exit charge for short term investors. These charges are usually set at a level which allows the management group to pay financial advisers an initial fee of 3 per cent and in many cases an annual renewal commission of up to 0.5 per cent. And even if the investor buys directly from the fund manager, he will normally be unable to get a discount, though discount brokers do offer cheap deals.

Many trackers have no initial charge and annual charges as low as 0.5 per cent. This is partly because you do not need expensive fund managers to run a 'passive' fund, partly because increased competition in the tracker market has brought costs down.

A front end charge hampers performance in the early years of investment; an annual charge hampers it for ever. If two identical funds offered a choice between a 5 per cent initial charge and a one per cent annual charge, the investor who paid the initial charge would only catch up after six years.

But the longer the investment period, the more damage apparently modest annual charges can do. An annual charge of 1 per cent a year reduces the total return (capital and income) by around 18 per cent over a 20 year period, by around 26 per cent over 30 years, by around 33 per cent over 40 years, and by around 40 per cent over 50 years.

So the active fund manager has to perform substantially better than the passive fund even to keep level in terms of the return to the investor. But active fund management has another layer of hidden costs: those the fund itself pays when buying and selling shares. The level of portfolio turnover can vary from under 10 per cent to over 100 per cent a year. And these transaction costs can amount to a 0.5 to 2 per cent levy on the fund's assets each year. Again, an energetic manager has to produce a very superior performance to justify this costly activity.

• **Choice of trackers.** Until the mid 1990s tracker funds were one of the best kept secrets of the UK fund management industry. Most large pension funds and life insurance companies put a significant proportion of their own money into index funds. But index funds were seldom promoted to the general public. This was partly because of the way retail funds are sold.

Management groups put their biggest marketing push behind new unit trusts, which are often launched to catch popular enthusiasm for a particular stockmarket or sector which has been doing unusually well. Index funds were considered unglamorous and were not allocated large marketing budgets. Nor did they make much money for the fund management groups. One group, Gartmore, did run a tracker with no initial charge and a low annual charge. But it was an exception. However, when Richard Branson's Virgin chose a tracker fund as the vehicle for his entry to the personal equity plan market in early 1995, a marketing war broke out and charges on tracker funds came down to match.

There is now a wide variety of trackers following different UK stockmarket indices. Many people argue that tracking the broadest index, the FT-SE-A All-Share is the most neutral choice, but fans of large and small companies alike can find an index fund to match their desires. In the US investors can also choose between investing in a growth index fund and a value index fund. This is not yet possible in the UK. Nor are there as yet any UK index funds tracking the bond markets.

The itchy-fingered investor should resist the temptation actively to manage a tracker portfolio, since that will raise costs and remove the funds' intrinsic advantage.

● **How to use trackers.** The investor in the UK stockmarket can use a tracker either instead of direct holdings, or as the core of his portfolio. Putting 90 per cent of the total portfolio into a mainstream tracker and buying individual stocks with the remaining money would be a sensible option for anyone who enjoys choosing and owning shares but is reluctant to entrust his future prosperity to his stockpicking talents.

Anyone wanting to invest some money overseas should also consider the index fund route. As yet trackers exist only for the main overseas markets, such as the US, Japan, Germany and France, but the number looks set to grow. Their record overseas has been a bit patchy: sometimes they have failed to match the relevant market index.

Fans of index funds argue that they should prove a good way of investing even in less developed and hence ineffi-cient markets. For although such markets arguably give active fund managers greater scope for beating the average, identifying the winning managers in advance remains as hard as ever. And the costs and charges of funds investing overseas are often much higher than on domestic funds. But the case for using indexed funds in markets dominated by particular sectors, such as Spain, is a bit dubious. A lop-sided portfolio produces an equally lop-sided spread of risk.

How not to choose a managed fund

Avoiding losing money is one of the most important tasks of any serious investor. Here are some common traps in picking actively managed funds.

- **Random selection.** This is dangerous because of the wide divergence between funds which do well and those which do badly.
- **Following fashion.** Picking 'cult' funds or cult market sectors is usually a mistake, because such fashions seldom last. This applies particularly to new issues.

New unit trusts tend to be launched when the market or sector in which they specialise is near its peak. This is normally exactly the wrong time to buy even if the underlying idea is sound. For example, emerging markets were excessively popular at the start of 1994, and the basic concept is probably sound enough, but buying emerging market trusts in early 1994 was a quick way to lose money in the short term.

In 1995 the *Financial Times* checked out the performance of all new unit trusts launched over a two year period. The vast majority had performed less well than the All-Share index since their launch.*

- **Buying top performers.** Many specialist newspapers and magazines publish tables showing the best performing trusts in particular sectors over periods such as one, five and ten years. But according to analysis by Fund Research Limited, picking the best performing fund from such a table gives you only a one in five chance of doing unusually well over the next five years.

Most funds which make the number one slot do so by taking above average risks. This may work when the whole sector is doing well because the background is favourable. But this kind of investment strategy often means that the fund does unusually badly in adverse circumstances. A single really bad year can seriously hamper a trust's long term performance and pull down the overall return from a portfolio of unit trusts.

---

* The 74 new authorised unit trusts launched in 1993 produced an average return of 12 per cent up to September 1995, compared with an average 30 per cent on the All-Share index; only ten managed to outstrip the index. A control check using the 64 new trusts launched in 1994 showed that their average return was roughly a third that of the All-Share index. Many of the newcomers were overseas trusts, but on average they also did substantially worse than the FT/S&P World Index.

How to pick an equity fund.

John Bogle, who runs the $100bn Vanguard group of funds in the US, and was a pioneer of index funds, provides a check-list for fund investors.* His basic thesis is that most broadly-based funds revert to average performance sooner or later. The only consistent exceptions are funds at the bottom of the league tables, which do unusually badly because of above average costs. Equity funds investing overseas or concentrating on a specific type of share may do significantly better or worse than average over most time periods. But they also tend to carry above average risk.

Since most unit trust investors will not want an exceptionally risky portfolio, they should keep most of their equity portfolio in broadly-based funds. Anyone who needs a high immediate income to live on, should consider an equity income fund. But once you know what kind of fund you want, how do you pick a particular trust?

● **Compare like with like.** Make sure the trusts you are comparing have similar investment characteristics: the fact that they are included in the same category in league tables is no guarantee that they are actually similar. Points to look at are the extent to which the fund's performance simply follows that of the market index, its relative volatility and the gross yield before expenses.

The first point shows whether the fund manager is adding any value, the second measures risk, the third measures return. Together they should give the investor an idea of whether the fund manager is doing a good job. This can be defined as an above average return achieved partly because of the investment strategy but without taking on additional risk.

Any fund whose portfolio closely resembles that of the relevant stockmarket index, and whose performance roughly shadows it, may be a closet index fund, that is to say it works much like a tracker but charges more. Such funds are likely to produce worse returns to the investor and are bad value.

* See *Bogle on Mutual Funds*.

Most fund measurement services nowadays measure the absolute volatility of funds, the standard deviation.

The fund management group should, if asked, tell a potential investor what the portfolio yield is and whether the management charge is levied against capital or income or a bit of both*.

● **Age of fund.** A track record of at least five to ten years is preferable, unless the new fund is launched by a good management house, with experience in the chosen area. And even then, size could be against it at the beginning, for it will not yet have the critical mass to absorb its expenses.

● **Size.** A fund which is too small is likely to have high expenses. However, one which is very large will find it hard to produce an above average performance.

● **The tenure of the fund manager.** Star fund managers are often peripatetic. Buying a fund after its star has left can lead to disappointment. But the importance of the individual manager depends both on whether the fund management group has a dominant investment style, and on how much of the manager's success can be attributed to the research team, how much to his individual flair. But note that even star managers seldom shine equally in all markets.

● **Costs.** They can be a killer. Although they are not such a crucial determinant of total returns in an equity fund as they are in a bond fund, excessive costs can still turn a good investment performance into a bad fund performance. Remember: a large initial charge holds back performance in the early years; a high annual charge hampers it for ever.

● **Relative performance.** Look at relative returns for the last ten years, but look for consistency not sudden spurts.

● **Winners.** Avoid funds at the top of the performance tables with outstanding recent records.

● **Losers.** Avoid funds at the bottom of the performance tables. Failure is more resilient than success.

● **Specialists.** Keep specialised funds to a maximum of 20

---

* Until recently unit trusts charged expenses against income. Nowadays they are allowed to charge against capital, and many income funds do so wholly or in part. This makes accurate comparisons even harder. But work by Fund Research Ltd suggests that the charging policy makes little difference to performance.

per cent of the portfolio in aggregate. And do not try to beat the market by sector switching.

How to pick a bond fund

Bond funds are a relatively underdeveloped market in the UK, and investors do not yet have the choice available in other countries, such as the US. In particular, few funds state their objectives or portfolio strategy clearly.

Bogle points out the differences between investing in bonds and investing in bond funds. He argues that predicting the probable return on a bond is relatively easy: the primary determinant of returns on long bonds is the initial yield. The investor should pay attention to this rather than the long term record of bonds when working out what return he can expect from a bond. And if he holds to redemption, he eliminates all risk to principal, although the reinvestment rate – which affects the total return – cannot be known in advance.

Predicting the return on a bond fund is actually harder than predicting the return on a bond, because a bond fund does not have a pre-set maturity date. This is one reason why investors seeking certainty may prefer to invest directly in bonds. Direct investment is easy and usually sensible for anyone happy to buy gilts. Investing in corporate bonds is harder and riskier. But the government has now given investors an incentive to consider corporate bonds, including them in the list of investments which can qualify for personal equity plan tax-exemptions. Working out the tax implications adds an additional layer of complication to bond investment.*

One of the most important facts for the bond fund investor to grasp is that there are only two reliable ways for the fund manager to improve the returns on a bond fund. He can accept a higher risk by holding bonds of a longer average maturity or a lower investment quality. Or he can reduce his

* Gilts are free of capital gains tax. But anyone buying corporate bonds through a personal equity plan is exempt from both income and gains tax.

expense ratio. The investor needs first to decide what maturity and quality of bonds he is happy to invest in. Then he should choose one of the low cost funds which meet his criteria. Other points to consider are:–

- **Your probable holding period.** If the average maturity of the bonds in the fund is much longer or much shorter than your investment period, your capital and income respectively are at risk. If your holding period is shorter than the average life of the bonds in the portfolio, and interest rates rise sharply in the interim, you may make a capital loss when you sell. But buying a fund which concentrates on very short term bonds can endanger your income: it both reduces the initial yield and increases the risk of a reduction in your income later on, if interest rates fall.

The impact of interest rate changes on bond investors is more complex than some investors realise. A rise in interest rates during your holding period will have a negative short term impact on market prices of bonds: the longer the bond and the lower the nominal interest rate, the greater the impact. A bond's sensitivity to interest rate changes can be measured by its 'duration'*. But an interest rate rise has a positive long term impact on total returns from bonds if the income can be reinvested at higher rates on a sustained basis.

- **Risk.** Decide how much risk – both to principal and to income – you are willing to accept in terms of average maturity. Ask the managers about the average duration of the portfolio so that you can measure its sensitivity to interest rates.
- **Expenses.** Look hard at the fund's expense ratio. If two funds have the same maturity and quality, lower costs are likely to lead to higher returns.
- **Quality.** Look equally hard at the quality of the portfolio. First, find out the yield on the portfolio and compare it with those of similar funds. (The net yield after expenses does not necessarily reflect portfolio quality.) Then check what is in the portfolio, for some managers push up the

---

* This period is shorter than the bond's remaining life, except for zero coupon stocks.

portfolio yield by including some high yielding but risky bonds. Remember, money in a defaulted bond is gone for ever.

● **Value for money.** Never purchase a bond fund with a lower-quality portfolio and a relatively high expense ratio, when one with a higher quality portfolio and a relatively low expense ratio provides an equal or higher yield.

● **High yields.** Ignore advertisements highlighting above average yields if they do not also disclose quality, maturity, coupon structure and other relevant characteristics.

● **Compare like with like.** A comparison between funds with different quality portfolios and different average maturities is a futile exercise.

● **Currency risk.** Even funds investing primarily in domestic corporate bonds sometimes include some foreign bonds to spice up the yield. Foreign bonds always import currency risk. And very high yielding ones can import credit risk as well.

The investment trust route

The investment portfolios of unit and investment trusts are often very similar nowadays, for many management groups have started selling both. Virtually identical unit and investment trusts are sometimes run by the same investment manager. But there are still differences:

● **The fixed pool of assets.** Investment trusts operate with a relatively fixed pool of money. Other things being equal, this makes it easier for the fund manager to invest sensibly and for the long term. This is particularly important in illiquid markets, such as stockmarkets in newly developing economies, where both buying and selling large quantities of shares rapidly can be very difficult.

However, what is good for the fund manager may be bad for the investor, at least in the short term. For fluctuations in investors' enthusiasm for an investment trust affect the price of the investment trust's shares. And since investor enthusiasm tends to rise with a rising market and fall with a falling

one, investment trust shares often exaggerate the performance of the underlying market.

● **Discounts.** Most investment trust shares normally sell at
a discount to their asset value. This traditionally made it hard
to launch new trusts. And although management groups
have got round the problem by offering packages of shares
and warrants when launching new trusts, new issues of
investment trusts on average do worse than existing trusts.

Occasionally trust discounts narrow and shares in some
trusts rise to a premium. This is usually a dangerous time to
buy. However, existing trusts whose shares are selling at
substantial discounts can sometimes offer good value.
Hence Benjamin Graham's argument that buying a selection
of investment trust shares at substantial discounts to asset
value is one of the few obvious bargains in managed funds.

● **Gearing.** Unlike unit trusts, investment trusts can gear
up through borrowing. This improves their performance if
the value of their portfolios is rising, but can compound
losses on the downside. It can give investment trusts a
significant advantage over unit trusts in a low inflation, low
interest rate environment, such as that of the mid 1990s.
Most trusts do not gear up, but a few do. For example, in
1996 a new trust called Loot, created to buy second hand
endowment policies of life companies likely to be taken
over, said it would be gearing up the portfolio as part of its
overall strategy.

● **Expenses.** New investment trusts often charge as much
as unit trusts. But some of the large old established trusts
have expense ratios of around 0.5 per cent of assets – much
the same as a tracker fund.

● **Institutional involvement.** A large proportion of the
capital of many investment trusts is held by other institutions, notably life insurance companies. This has both good
and bad consequences for the private investor.

Several stockbrokers do thorough research on investment
trust companies. But the market is not particularly efficient,
since many of the institutions hardly ever change their
holdings. This means that it is often relatively easy to spot
anomalies, but that these anomalies tend to persist.

Many of the smaller specialist trusts being launched are in
response to specific requests from institutions wanting to

plug a hole in their portfolio. They are often then offered to the public. Many are not suitable for private investors.

● **Retail mark-up.** Investment trusts specifically aimed at the public can have specific disadvantages. Large new trusts, often targeting the personal equity plan market, usually sell through intermediaries, which means that their costs are likely to be similar to those of unit trusts.

● **Corporate engineering.** Unlike unit trusts, investment trusts' structure leaves scope for corporate engineering. Hence the 1980s fashion for split level trusts, which have different classes of share catering for income and growth oriented investors, and usually zero dividend preference shares which provide additional gearing. Some of these shares are intrinsically risky. And several of the trusts have found it impossible to reconcile the interests of different classes of investor.

● **Corporate activity.** As quoted companies, investment trusts can be the subject of bids against the wishes of the incumbent management. As in most businesses, it is usually the companies which have done badly that get bids. Terms can be exceedingly complicated, and are sometimes less advantageous to one class of shareholders than others.

Sizing up investment trusts

Most investment analysis consists of two interlocking parts. First you weigh up the company's business, management and prospects. Then you consider whether the share price looks good value given your assessment of those factors, particularly the prospects. Buying shares purely because they look cheap on some standard yardsticks such as yield or PE ratio is generally agreed to be a certain way to lose money.

Analysing investment trusts is a very different skill. There is no underlying business for the analyst to look at, just an investment portfolio and its manager – another investment professional like himself. Unsurprisingly, many trust analysts tend to rely more heavily on number crunching than those looking at other sectors. But their approach does depend greatly on what kind of trust they are looking at.

There are lots of ways of slicing up trusts. The simplest is to divide them into three. First, the broad international trusts, such as Foreign & Colonial, which aim to provide investors with a complete well balanced portfolio. Second the specialists: geographic specialists who target a particular continent or country, and UK trusts which concentrate on a particular investment objective or sector, such as high income or venture capital. Third, split level trusts which use financial engineering to try to achieve different investment objectives for different types of shareholder.

• **General trusts.** Many of the general international trusts are large, but many stockbrokers' analysts spend relatively little time scrutinising them. For their shares are increasingly held by private investors for the long term, and stockbrokers' analysts are, as always, targeting institutions.

Analysts can look at the overall portfolio split, the management's record and philosophy, the gearing and the discount. For example, if a particular manager has a known aversion to North America and liking for Japan, his fund will not do well if Wall Street is rising and Tokyo falling. If the fund has no borrowings, it will not do as well in rising markets as one which does. If the discount – the gap between the share price and the value of the underlying assets – is small, or if the share price is actually above the value of the underlying assets, its shares may well be expensive.

Such sweeping statements can be refined. Discounts tend to narrow when markets are rising and widen when they are falling or expected to fall. For demand tends to increase when markets are rising and decrease when they are falling – or expected to fall. So although trusts with narrow discounts or premiums may look expensive, they may stay expensive until something triggers a fall in the underlying markets.

The only obvious way of measuring customers' appetite for investment trust shares is the growth in investment trust saving schemes. One broker supplements these by also looking at net retail sales of unit trusts. Thus, if unit trust sales fall sharply, a similar lack of enthusiasm for investment trusts could produce a wider discount.

• **Specialist trusts.** Somewhat similar calculations are

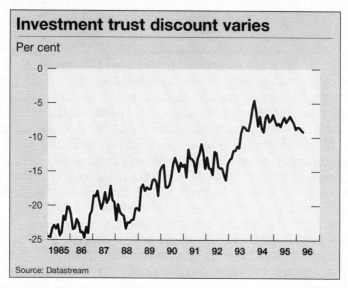

Investment trust discount varies

Per cent

Source: Datastream

Fig 14.2 Investment trust shares normally sell at a discount to their asset value, but the size of the discount varies. It often narrows when the market is rising, but don't count on it.

used with specialist trusts. But these trusts are primarily catering for professional investors. Fund managers use specialist trusts as a cost-effective way of getting exposure to countries or particular types of company which they do not have the expertise or ability to invest in themselves. Normally the first question they ask themselves is whether they want to increase or decrease their exposure to a particular area. The choice of trust is secondary, although managers with a good record do acquire a following.

Most professionals prefer to use trusts with a very clear specialisation, since this makes it easier for them accurately to implement their asset allocation decisions. For example, in 1995 one trust which had covered both Japan and other Asian markets split into two to please its institutional shareholders.

Private investors should probably be wary of investing in such highly specialised trusts unless they have a very large portfolio. And if they do, they need to be aware that such trusts are extremely vulnerable to fashion, even if hindsight proves that fashion misguided.

A discount which might be tempting in a general trust could carry on getting wider if professional fund managers simply don't like the market. For example, in early 1996 the average discount on trusts specialising in America topped 20 per cent. There were some specific reasons for the discount rising quite this high.* But the basic explanation for the above-average discount on American trusts was that UK fund managers remained disinclined to increase their Wall Street weightings.

Their attitude meant that private investors who read the market correctly did not get their just rewards. The US market may have done much better than expected, and asset values duly rose. But the widening discount meant that investors in American trusts did not get the benefit of the increase in asset values. Contrarians may prefer to stick with unit trusts.

● **Split capital trusts.** Split level trusts are where the number crunchers come into their own. But they are also a classic example of financial engineers getting too clever for investors' good. Many splits revealed fundamental construction faults in the 1990s, because the engineers who built them erroneously assumed that the heady equity growth rates of the 1980s would continue throughout the trusts' lives.

A typical split capital trust has three types of share. The income shares get the lion's share of the income on the investment portfolio, but have often only a nominal claim on the capital when the trust reaches its pre-set wind-up date. The zero dividend preference shares are issued at a substantial discount to their eventual redemption value, and the whole of the investor's return comes in the form of pre-

* One of the biggest American trusts, Fleming American, was faced with a sudden claim for pollution damages in a liability suit dating back to the last century when the company owned a creosote factory for treating railway sleepers in Louisiana. Its share price plunged so far that analysts decided that, with a discount of over 30 per cent, the shares were making excessive allowance for the probable settlement costs. So they recommended investors to switch out of the other big American trust into the Fleming American, despite the pending law suit. So shares in the other trust, American Trust, were also weak.

determined capital growth. The capital shares get the lion's share of the assets left in the portfolio at the wind-up date, but only after the zeros' claims have been met. The larger the zero element, the higher the gearing of the capital shares. For the capital value of the portfolio has to increase sufficiently to meet the zeros' claims in full before the capital shares acquire any value. But once assets top this barrier, the value of the capital shares rises faster than that of the underlying portfolio.

It is clear that the total return on the equity market is crucial to the sums. When this fell in the 1990s, the only way portfolio managers could satisfy the expectations of the income shareholders was to run a high-yielding portfolio. But soon it became clear that such portfolios were producing little or no capital growth. In most cases it seemed probable that there would be enough in the kitty to pay off the zeros in full, but prospects for the capital shares were dim. In several cases the managers elected to reduce the portfolio yield in order to increase the prospect of capital growth: this meant chopping dividends and upsetting the income shareholders, but improved prospects for holders of the capital shares.

Those who did unnaturally well in most cases were the owners of the zeros. Long term holders enjoyed 1980s-style returns right through the first half of the 1990s because those returns were bankrolled by owners of the other classes of share. The zero holders were innocent cuckoos in the nest.*

Attempting to analyse split capital trusts on an ongoing basis is a nightmare. As already explained, the vast majority

---

* One of the worst hit trusts, Exmoor Dual, had raised the stakes by investing only in the shares of other split level trusts. Alas, it was hit on two fronts. The yield on its portfolio dropped when managers of other trusts cut the payout on their income shares. And the value of its holdings of capital shares also suffered as it became clear that 1990s growth rates could not finance a bonanza. Just before Christmas in 1995, the managers announced both that they were cutting dividends, and that the portfolio strategy would be changed to allow the fund to invest in a wider range of investment trust shares. Shareholders could console themselves that they were martyrs to a financial engineer's idea of beauty.

of their assets are in the UK in relatively high yielding portfolios. And there is not really that much the managers can do except try to keep on course. But every change in the value of the underlying assets means a change in the vital statistics of each of the different classes of shares which make up the capital.

One way of looking at them is to treat all the securities like fixed interest stocks and calculate redemption yields (ie a theoretical annual yield based on the total return from both income and capital over the life of the trust). This works reasonably well for zeros, which have a set redemption price as well as a set redemption date. But calculating redemption yields for other types of share involves lots of assumptions about probable growth rates.

An alternative approach is to base your calculations on the current share price, and ask what kind of future portfolio growth/shrinkage is necessary for that price to be justified. A variant asks what needs to happen for a class of shares to be worthless.

Most private investors should not tangle with splits unless they have expert advice at hand – and perhaps not even then. Remember Benjamin Graham's advice that you should only be receptive to unconventional suggestions from a trusted adviser if you have learnt so much that you can pass independent judgement on the suggestions.

How the pros analyse trusts

Fund Research Limited, which sells detailed research to financial advisers, reckons that selecting funds from the newspaper league tables gives only a one in five chance of picking a future top performer. The firm itself uses a combination of quantitative analysis and qualitative appraisal to search for funds which produce consistently good performance.*

* The firm's research is not, alas, on sale to the public. If you use a financial adviser, you can check if the adviser uses the research. If you are buying direct, phone the unit trust management group and ask what their Fund Research rating is before you make your final

First it screens out those which are not worth looking at, either because they are consistently bad, or because they are too erratic. To do this it breaks each five year period down into five separate one year periods: this reveals which funds owe their apparent superiority to an isolated spurt in one year, and which are excessively volatile. The latest years are given slightly more importance in the assessment. Only 15 per cent of all the trusts it looks at pass its screening procedures. Funds which do pass have a one in three chance of performing well in future.

The firm then does detailed research on this minority, and concludes by giving all the funds it researches a rating: A, AA or AAA. Only 40 per cent of the total 'marks' on which these ratings are based relate to the statistical analysis. The other 60 per cent is produced by qualitative appraisal. Roughly 30 per cent relates to the fund manager, about 20 per cent to the management group and the final 10 per cent to the fund itself. (With fixed interest funds the manager understandably counts for less, the management group for more.)

The analysts both pore over each fund's reports and discuss the portfolio, performance and investment strategy with the fund manager. What they are trying to find out is whether the fund's good performance is likely to be repeated in future. Did it result from luck or judgement? Did the rewards justify the risks? Was it produced by a disciplined investment process or by someone flying by the seat of his pants?

There are a number of items that Fund Research routinely checks out. But what it is looking for is not so much 'right' answers as reasonable explanations. It accepts that a fund manager is governed by the stated objectives of his fund: you cannot expect the manager of a smaller companies fund to benefit from a boom in utility shares.

It also accepts that there are several different ways of running a fund successfully. Some funds work to very tight 'top down' processes, with a central committee deciding which markets and sectors are likely to prosper under

choice. Groups with good ratings may even send you a copy! If the fund is not rated, ask why.

certain economic conditions, and which types of companies should benefit. Others are run by stockpickers. What the analysts are checking is that there is a disciplined process of some kind behind the selections: the manager knows why he bought each share.

Fund Research recognises that different management styles excel at different times in a market cycle. Interestingly, it observes that bottom-up stockpickers tend to do better on the way up, top down strategists on the way down. The analysts reckon it is generally disastrous if a manager tries to change his style to suit market conditions. And their rating system allows him to have a relatively poor year without being ejected.

A Fund Research checklist

When analysing a particular unit trust portfolio Fund Research routinely considers a number of different points. They are all ones you can check out yourself:

• **The portfolio's broad composition.** What countries is it investing in (for example, US versus Europe), what types of company (for example small or large), what businesses (for example utilities versus consumer shares), what type of securities (bonds, shares or convertibles).

If, for example, an equity income fund has a high proportion of convertibles it can mean various things. Perhaps the manager is getting into growth areas of the market in the only way feasible for a fund which has to produce an above average income – which should mean that the fund will produce better capital growth than some of its rivals. Alternatively, he may be boosting the fund's overall income by buying the high yielding convertibles of companies with a dubious future – in which case he is probably importing unacceptable risk to the fund.

The analysts also compare the current portfolio with that shown in the last report to spot changes in strategy. Did the manager move from FT-SE 100 shares down to Mid-Cap and Small-Cap stocks, when the right time came? If the answer is 'No' it may be that he missed a trick – but not always. If it is a blue chip fund, its objectives probably rule out smaller companies.

- **The spread of risk.** How many different companies does it own and does it have roughly the same amount in each? How much of the total portfolio is in a small number of large holdings. If it has a large number of tiny holdings is that because the manager is gradually building up its stakes or are they the residue of earlier unsuccessful ventures? Many funds have less than 100 holdings, a few have less than 50 and very large funds or index funds may hold 300 to 400 different stocks. The number of holdings will be influenced by the size of the fund, but is not dependent on it.

A glance at the 20 largest holdings will also tell you some useful things about a fund's strategy. Most broad funds have perhaps 35 to 40 per cent of their money in the 20 largest holdings. So if you find one with 60 per cent it is worth asking why. Is this concentration integral to the investment strategy or the incidental result of a change in strategy or an unusual flow of money in or out?

Are the biggest holdings fairly predictable? To check the norms you can check the portfolio either against that of the relevant index fund – if there is one – or against competitors'. If the percentage holdings are very much out of line with the relevant index, you can probably infer that the fund's performance will depend on the manager's stock-picking abilities. So it is worth reading the manager's report very thoroughly to see if you agree with his approach.

- **Portfolio turnover.** Warren Buffett argues that high portfolio turnover equates to an unacceptable tax on an investment fund. And certain types of fund, notably index funds have, by their nature, low turnover. But practice varies considerably even among funds in the same sector. A check on UK general funds in 1994, for instance, showed that turnover ranged from just 5 per cent to almost 140 per cent, with most around 25 to 50 per cent.

Fund Research has done some work on the correlation between high turnover and poor performance, and says there does not appear to be one. It has found that unusually high turnover, of between 300 and 400 per cent, is often associated with bad performance. But there are – as always –

exceptions. If market conditions are changing, unusually high turnover can be appropriate for some funds.

It is also worth delving beneath the raw turnover figures. If, for example, half the portfolio is unchanged on the year, you may well find that turnover on the other half is double the published figure. That is sometimes a bad sign. So check whether the performance justifies the high turnover.

● **Volatility.** Fund Research measures both the relative volatility of a trust and its standard deviation. The former shows whether the fund is more erratic than its peers; the latter how volatile it is in absolute terms. Essentially a fund which is more volatile than average needs to justify that with an above average return. Some fund measurement services publish sector relative risk/return ratings.*

● **Size of fund.** Very small and very large funds both have problems because of their size. Very small funds tend to have very high expense ratios, which can undermine a good investment performance. Very large funds find it difficult to produce an outstanding investment performance, though their expense ratios are usually modest. Even Fidelity's Magellan fund, Peter Lynch's original vehicle, did less well when it had $30bn under management than when it had $200m.

If a very small fund does well, it is worth checking

---

* But sector relative ratings of any type can be misleading if the sector classifications include disparate funds. John Cuthbert, a freelance fund analyst, argues that the methods currently used to classify funds in the UK are misconceived. Autif, the trade body, groups them by their investment aim. Cuthbert argues that they should instead be classified according to two criteria, the manager's investment approach and the fund's risk characteristics. There are, for example, many different ways of obtaining a high yield and the probable returns from funds using different methods are so dissimilar that they should not be grouped together. Yield should not be a criterion for inclusion in a sector; it is simply a by-product.

This purist approach is, however, unlikely to commend itself to the marketing men who run the British unit trust industry. Their view tends to be that the customer is solely interested in objectives, not the means by which they are achieved. A view sadly reinforced by the popularity of many high income products which put investors' capital at risk.

whether there is any particular reason for this. For example, was it being piggybacked by larger funds in the same group? Were all the new issues being channelled its way? If so, it may be unable to keep this performance up in later years. Fund Research tends to knock a few points off a new fund's apparent score for the first couple of years – because it is worried about the new fund effect.

Large size can be a problem if the fund gets so big that the managers cannot buy the shares they want in the quantity they want without moving the price against themselves. This is more likely to occur with funds specialising in smaller companies or smaller markets. Normally a general fund can grow fairly large with impunity. But being large can also hamper a general fund in certain types of market.

Unit and Investment Trusts

IN A NUTSHELL

1. Investing through trusts is a good way for investors to get a spread of shares. They can be used either as the whole of a portfolio or as the majority of a portfolio, leaving the investor to invest directly in the area which interests him. Trusts can be bought and sold easily. The investor only needs to bear the costs relating to his own investment period. Investing through trusts leaves the investor more time to consider his overall asset allocation.

2. Different mixes of funds suit investors at different stages of their lives. Broadly, most investors should start with a relatively aggressive growth-oriented portfolio and reinvest the income. Later in life they should increase the proportion in bonds and other income producing trusts. Lump sum investors should be more cautious than those building up a portfolio gradually.

3. All unit trust investors should consider investing all or part of their portfolio in index (tracker) funds. They perform better than the average actively managed fund and cost less. Remember, though, that they carry greater market risk and do worse in bear markets.

4. Front-end charges on unit trusts hamper performance in the early years. But annual charges hamper it for ever. An annual charge of 1 per cent a year cuts around 18 per cent off the total return over a period of 20 years.

5. Ways not to choose a fund include: random selection, following fashion, and buying top performers.

6. Points to consider when picking an equity fund

include: age, size, the fund manager and costs. What you want is consistently good performance, due at least partly to the management strategy, which is achieved without taking on excessive risk. It is important to make sure that you are comparing similar funds when making your choice.

7. The most important determinant of bond fund returns is the initial yield on bonds when you invest. Points to consider when choosing a fund include: how long you expect to invest for, how much risk you are prepared to take, the quality and maturity of the portfolio, and costs. Be wary of trusts advertising very high yields – that may be part of your own capital they are selling you. Other things being equal, go for the low cost fund.

8. Investment trusts are different from unit trusts in some ways. Points to pay attention to include: discounts, costs, institutional involvement, gearing and other forms of corporate engineering.

9. Professional fund analysts use a mixture of quantitative and qualitative checks when trying to pick winning funds.

Appendix A
Sources of Information

City fund managers have an enormous array of information at their fingertips. The daily delivery of research reports from brokers is usually inches thick, while the telephone rings non-stop with salesmen wanting to share their latest ideas. Electronic screens provide up-to-the-minute news services and price information. Databanks, such as Datastream and the *Financial Times'* Analysis, supply instant history tailored to their specific requirements. Other screen services allow those with a technical bent to display prices as Candlesticks within the elastic confines of Bollinger bands, and add in the trading volume and Gann levels.

Private investors are more meagrely provided for. The services professionals use are prohibitively expensive. And even basic company information can be surprisingly hard to get hold of. But the supply, particularly of electronic information, is improving. Anyone who makes full use of all the sources listed below will be in danger of suffering from information overload. Remember that although many professionals experiment with a number of options, they usually end up by relying on a small number they are comfortable with.

Information from companies

Most companies will supply a copy of their latest annual report and interim statement free of charge. But finding out who to talk to, particularly if the head office is outside London, can be a hassle. Traditionally companies used to devolve this chore onto the company registrar, and many still do. Nowadays some have shareholder relations departments which have taken it on instead. But getting copies of reports relating to earlier years can be difficult or impossible: spare copies have often been pulped.

Investors interested mainly in the larger companies can save themselves trouble by using the **free annual reports service** offered by the *Financial Times* (FT). This supplies both annual and interim reports for many major UK-listed companies and some international ones. It has around 1,200 companies on its list: they are the ones whose names are annotated with a club on its London Share Service pages (inside the back page of the second section during the week and inside the back page of the first section on weekends). The reports are sent out by second class post the next working day, provided they are in stock.

The telephone number of the service is (0181) 770–0770 and it is open 24 hours a day including weekends. Reports can also be ordered by fax on (0181) 770–3822. (The telephone numbers and a daily code number are given in the bottom right hand corner of the right hand page of the share service.)

The staff manning the FT telephone service even have details of where to get reports for around 30 of the most popular companies not available through them. Tracking down the source of annual reports for others can be tedious. But a subscriber to any of the Hemmington Scott company publications (see below) will find the telephone numbers of both the company and its registrar listed.

Company information specialists

The two best commercial sources of retail information on companies are Hemmington Scott Publishing and Edinburgh Financial Publishing. But the number of suppliers and services is growing as companies with databanks look for ways of recycling information they already have.

Of the two established firms, Hemmington Scott has a slightly worthier feel with a very strong databank and solid publications offering good value for money. They will appeal to the value investor who likes hard work. Edinburgh, run by a couple of former stockbrokers notable for charm and entrepreneurial flair, is a little more user friendly: its *Inside Track* products may appeal to the growth investor who still has a sneaky hope that there is a fast track to stockmarket profits.

- **Hemmington Scott (HS).** The firm's original publication is the *Hambro Company Guide*, which provides brief financial details on some 2,000 companies quoted on the London stock exchange, both fully listed and those on the Unlisted Securities Market (USM) in its dying days and the newer fringe Alternative Investment Market.

The p&l record shows turnover, pre-tax profits, FRS3 and normalised earnings and dividends. The balance sheet precis lists sources of finance: ordinary capital and reserves, minorities, short and long term creditors. It shows how the money is deployed: intangibles, fixed assets and investments, stocks, debtors and cash and securities, and works out the gearing and return on capital. Information on which sector and index the company belongs to, directors, major shareholders and contact numbers are also standard. Larger companies also get consensus brokers' forecasts for the next couple of years, and a chart showing the absolute and relative share price.

For any investor who wants a birds-eye view of a company's recent record, this is an excellent handbook. The slight snag is that it is only normally available on a subscription basis which provides an updated version every quarter. A subscription for four quarters costs £115,* with a full refund if you cancel during the trial period. Investors who simply want one copy as a reference book can order it from a bookshop for £40.

The serious private investor will probably find *Company Refs – Really Essential Financial Statistics –* a better buy than a sub to the *Earnings Guide*. *Company Refs* comes in three bits. First, a guide book, *How to Use Company Refs*, written by Jim Slater, which both runs though the main ratios used by financial analysts and explains the layout of *Company Refs*.

Second, a *Companies* volume which includes a large number of financial and investment ratios: summaries of

---

* All prices are those obtaining in early 1996.

performance figures, gearing, earnings and dividend estimates plus investment ratios such as PEs and PEGs, with
pictograms showing how the company measures up against
both its sector and the market as a whole.

Third, the *Tables* volume, which approaches stockpicking
from the opposite angle. It runs a series of screens over the
companies it monitors and produces tables ranking companies by criteria such as relative strength, growth rates, PEs
and PEGs, return on capital, price-cash flow multiples and
so on. It is a treasure house for the value investor who
enjoys experimenting with stockpicking methods based on
mathematical screens. It also carries sector tables giving
standard statistics such as growth rates and PEGs. What is
unusual and useful about these statistics is that earnings
figures used (derived from another HS publication) are
based on a brokers' consensus forecast for the coming twelve
months.

Company Refs is available on either a monthly or a
quarterly update basis. The monthly service costs £675 for a
year and the quarterly one £250. The introductory guide
comes free to subscribers or can be bought independently in
bookshops for £29.95 (with the money refunded if you
subsequently take out a subscription).

The third publication, the *Earnings Guide*, puts together
the company profit forecasts from 30 leading stockbrokers. It
is available quarterly for £75 or monthly for £210. But
anyone who gets *Company Refs* would probably find the
Earnings Guide superfluous.

For all these publications contact Hemmington Scott
Publishing Ltd, City Innovation Centre, 26–31 Whiskin
Street, London EC1R OBP. Telephone: (0171) 278–7769.
Fax: (0171) 278–9808.

● **Edinburgh Financial Publishing.** The firm sells its
expensive services to institutions, its cheaper ones to
private individuals. It produces one set of information based
on directors' share dealings, another based on brokers'
estimates.

The *Estimates Directory* is similar to the *Earnings Guide*
but has a wider broker panel – 56 compared with 30 – and
costs substantially more. The *UK Directory*, covering 1,300
companies, costs £495 for one year's subscription to a

monthly service, and £170 for a quarterly service (less if you pay by credit card or direct debit). Single copies can be bought for £45. It is also available on floppy disc at a minimum cost of £3,000 for the professional market.

The *Estimates Directory* may by now provide a slightly swankier product than the *Earnings Guide*, but the best value for money is still *Company Refs*: it includes so much in addition to brokers' estimates. *Estimates Directories* are also available for overseas markets: continental Europe, the Pacific basin, Japan, Emerging Markets and very soon the US.

Edinburgh, originally known as Directus, started life monitoring all directors' share deals announced through the UK Stock Exchange, and has built up a useful databank. All information on directors' dealings is now supplied under the catchy name *The Inside Track*, which produces publications of varying frequency. First, the monthly newsletter, which provides focused comment on four different companies with buy/sell recommendations and a review of earlier recommendations. It is essentially a newsletter rather than an information source. Cost £49 for the first year's subscription and £89 thereafter.

The weekly *Inside Track* service consists of a pack of information sheets about important deals during the previous week with some comment and relevant background information on the company concerned. The service aims to cover all the significant deals and screen out those which the staff consider irrelevant. So the number of companies covered each week varies. The cost is £325 a year if they are delivered by post in a batch once a week. If you want them faxed it costs £450. For the addict there is also a daily fax service winging out within four hours of an announcement at a cost of £1,750 a year. A daily list giving comprehensive details of dealings is also available.

The daily services are intended for professionals. Best choice for a serious private investor who likes making his own mind up is probably the weekly postal service.

The *Inside Track* also supplies information for various national newspapers. The *Weekend Money* section of the *Financial Times* on Saturday lists all directors' deals worth more than £10,000, without attempting to winnow out the unimportant ones, plus a chart of one of the significant deals, with sells usually outnumbering buys by about 3:1. There is also a small amount of supporting text. The *Sunday Times* carries one chart with comment each week and the *Sunday Telegraph* carries a monthly sector comment.

Other firms periodically try to rival Edinburgh Financial Publishing's directors' dealing publications. Some can supply similar data, but they often fail when it comes to interpreting them. As yet the *Inside Track* remains the market leader.

For details of the *Estimates Directory* and *Inside Track* services write to Edinburgh Financial Publishing at 16 Randolph Crescent, Edinburgh EH3 7TT. Telephone: (0131) 538–7070. Fax: (0131) 538–8030.

● **Sharefinder.** This offshoot of execution-only broker Sharelink supplies a near identical Company Focus information pack to customers of Sharelink, the *Investors Chronicle* and the *Financial Times*.

The basic information package for each company includes a five year summary of the p&l and balance sheet, and a few ratios such as gearing; analysts forecasts for profits, dividends and earnings stretching ahead for the next two years and company announcements for the past 18 months. The plain version sells for £4.95 per company, the IC version including cuttings from the IC sells for £5.95, and the FT version garnished with FT cuttings sells for £6.45.

Telephone number for the FT service is (0121) 200–4678; for the IC service it is (0121) 200–4660.

The Financial Times

Most daily newspapers are carrying an ever increasing amount of financial information. But the *Financial Times* (FT) still contains more than the others. And, as addicts will realise, the FT's statistics are still evolving, albeit at a seemingly glacial pace. Very serious investors may find it necessary to get the paper every day; others could content themselves with a once a week fix on Saturdays.

First **the weekday paper.** The front page of the main paper gives a daily snapshot of stockmarket and other financial highlights, such as the closing prices of major stockmarket indices, money market and currency rates. But many enthusiastic investors start with the second section.

Even habitués sometimes lose their way in this information jungle. Frustrated foragers should note that the front page of the second section contains a page index, called market statistics, showing where to find, for example, gilts prices or the London share service. There is also an index of companies mentioned in the issue. Early recourse to these guides can considerably reduce reader stress levels.

The weekday paper's best known feature is its *London Share Service*, the two pages of share prices and basic investment statistics inside the back page of the second section Monday to Friday. Shares are grouped in categories according to the classification system used for compiling the FT-SE-A All-Share index. Coverage is very extensive but not totally comprehensive: companies have to pay for the coverage, and most do as regards the ordinary share price; they are more reticent when loan stocks and preference shares are concerned. Companies listed on the less regulated Alternative Investment Market (AIM), designed for small companies, are in a separate section. So are overseas companies with a London listing.

On Tuesday to Saturday, statistics for each ordinary share listed include the closing mid-price (the middle of the dealing spread), change on the day, rolling 52 week high and low, market cap, yield and PE ratio. For investment trusts the market cap and PE ratio are replaced by the net asset value and discount.* In Monday's paper the information relates to the previous week and gives dividend payment details: Friday's closing price is flanked by the

---

* Split capital trusts are segregated, but no satisfactory way of showing the relevant statistics for the different types of share has yet been found. The current compromise is to publish the same figures as for other trust shares. This can be confusing for novices who find a seemingly attractive double figure yield without realising it belongs to an income share with little hope of a significant capital repayment on wind-up. The FT continues to work on the problem. The best answer perhaps would be for some *deus ex machina* to remove this troublesome hybrid sector from the face of the earth.

change over the week, the net dividend, cover, payment months, the last ex dividend date and the relevant code for the premium rate Cityline real time telephone share price service.

The share price service is also available on the Internet at http://www.FT.com.

The back page itself, which includes the equity market reports (except on Mondays), also contains the sector indices, against which investors can compare statistics for individual shares, and the day's trading volume for major shares. Other useful tables are those listing which sectors showed relative strength, which individual shares hit new highs and lows, and how the main equity indices moved on an hour by hour basis. Other information relating to the UK equity market requires forays even deeper into the second section, where you will find details of rights issues, recent new issues, and the most actively traded equity options.

Just before the London share service comes the FT managed funds service, which gives details of the initial charge, buying and selling prices, change and yield for most onshore unit trusts and many offshore ones. It even states whether expenses are charged to capital or income. The snag is that the funds are grouped by unit trust management group, not by sector. So hunting all the relevant ones down can take time.

The Weekend FT. Published on Saturdays, this newspaper is organised in a different way from its weekday parent, and contains additional information for the personal investor. The basic principle is that virtually all the information which would normally appear in the second section during the week appears towards the back of the first section on Saturdays, plus a few additional bits. The second section, *Weekend Money*, aimed at personal investors and savers, contains additional material which is not carried during the week.

For example, the first section of the *Weekend FT* contains the London share service, the report on Friday's trading, volume figures, the sector indices, new highs and lows, recent issues and rights issues. It also includes a comprehensive list of how the different sectors have moved since the start of the calendar year, and a page of London Stock

Exchange dealings in securities not included in the main share service. This is a particularly useful service for private investors. The snag is that securities only feature if there have been dealings in them.

The dealings page used to be invaluable to investors holding shares dealt under the fringe Rule 4.2 dealing facility, killed by the Stock Exchange. Now it is a cross between a senior common room and a freak show. It is the investor's best hope for tracking down a price for most corporate bonds and preference shares, permanent interest-bearing shares issued by building societies, and a handful of ordinary shares – often better known 20 years ago than they are today. Investment trust esoterica also feature.

Rule 4.2 shares which have taken refuge on AIM are listed each day in the main London share service. But a neat little advertisement near the Saturday dealings page, called Ofex Facility, notes any trades in several other former Rule 4.2 companies, including one or two substantial groups such as National Parking and Weetabix. Ofex is an unregulated dealing facility run by a small company market maker John P Jenkins.

Weekend Money has a back page which summarises the week in the stockmarket. Tables show which shares performed best and worst in the Footsie, Mid-250 and Small-Cap indices, and among the market sectors. It shows weekly changes in the major foreign markets and popular shares, and lists investment yardsticks such as the gilt/equity yield ratio, interest rates and inflation.

The front page index to *Weekend Money* explains where to find additional statistics, such as directors' dealings, lists of company results for the previous and forthcoming weeks, current bids and issues, the best gilts for investors with different tax rates, building society permanent interest-bearings shares (PIBS), annuity rates and capital gains tax indexation allowances. Editorial news reports and comment always cover the UK and US stockmarkets and some of the major company news of the week.

A unit and investment trust page, listing the funds which have produced the best and worst performances over three years by sector, gives the existing unit trust investor some yardsticks against which to judge his holdings. It includes yield, volatility and performance for some other periods in addition to the one on which the funds are ranked, and also tables giving details of current launches, if any. It is not intended to offer buying suggestions, since pundits are unanimous that funds which come top of a performance table are most unlikely to continue to excel. The managed funds advertisement pages follow in a pack.

The FT's daily cost of 70p means an annual bill of just over £36 for the investor who buys it once a week, and around £200 for a daily purchase.

The Investors Chronicle

The *Investors Chronicle* (IC) remains the only specialist stockmarket weekly. Its traditional strength is its company coverage, but it aims to set company developments into their business and stockmarket context. Again, use the main index at the front and the Companies index near the back to find your way round.

Both the Market View at the front of the magazine and the Investment Snapshot further inside explain how the IC interprets the current economic and political scene. These views are explained in greater detail on a week by week basis on Market Strategy pages. Each week these pages discuss the outlook for both the UK gilt and equity markets and the main overseas markets. A supplementary page of analysts' views precis a selection of recent circulars.

A couple of regular columns, A Week in the Markets and Fund Manager's Diary add a more personal view. The Bearbull page gives a practical demonstration of building portfolios for specific purposes. And the traded options page serves a dual purpose. It is an exercise in short term speculation on the traded options market, buying puts and calls. But it is unusual in that the investment decisions are based on technical analysis: the share price charts usually contain three different moving averages.

The *Investors Chronicle* is best known for its detailed reporting of company news. The second half of the magazine analyses both the annual and the interim results of roughly 1,000 of the largest companies on the UK stockmarket, with a five year table of key statistics for each company. It also reports the more interesting of the results from smaller companies, and includes them all in a table with key figures and a line of comment. The smaller companies section has regular comment on AIM and Ofex shares. Major international companies are covered as well.

Additional statistical tables give details of current rights issues and open offers, takeover bids, scrip issues and new issues. And again each entry has a line of text, setting out the key facts and, where appropriate, offering advice.

Both the main companies section and the smaller companies section make a certain number of investment recommendations each week. The company tips are often the pick of the results which have been analysed that week; smaller company tips tend to be individually researched. And in both cases the recommendations are reviewed at regular intervals or when necessary.

The statistics section at the end gives a selection of statistics on UK and overseas markets, UK sectors and economic information, and there is a page showing directors' dealings for three companies each week. The personal finance section always has some unit and investment trust coverage.

Anyone getting a daily newspaper with a good City section may find the background comment in the IC superfluous. The magazine's two great advantages are first the sheer scope of its company comment, second its format. Despite the monstrous regiments of computer screens, many people still like to do their investment research sitting comfortably in a chair with a weekly dose of company news to browse through. Other publications may offer alternatives; it is hard to see any attempting to compete head on with the IC in its traditional niche. With a cover price of £2.20 a weekly purchase costs around £112 a year, with various subscription discounts. That is good value compared with the products sold by company information specialists.

The IC's nearest rival is a much glossier monthly magazine called the *Analyst* which specialises in lengthy articles on investment systems and company profiles, plus detailed analysis of selected smaller companies. Many of the free-lance writers who write for the *Analyst* have worked as professional analysts in the City. The *Analyst* is available on subscription for £90 a year. Telephone: (0171) 247–4557.

Information on technical analysis

The best known supplier of charts for UK private investors is **Investment Research of Cambridge** (IR) (01223) 356251, which sells a number of different services. Its monthly UK Equity Chart book, with charts on over 650 companies costs £520 a year (£49.50 for a single issue). It can be supplemented by a daily market fax, a fortnightly service covering the traded option stocks, a monthly market leaders update of the firm's views on the 200 leading shares in the UK market. Most charts are based on daily high/low figures for over three years, plus moving averages, market relatives and a longer term chart as background. IR also runs intensive two day courses costing around £400.

Investors who prefer point and figure charts should try **Chart Analysis** (0171) 439–4961.

Most of the leading investment software houses (see following appendix for details) include technical analysis packages. Some, such as MetaStock, support a wide variety of different types of chart format; others are tailored to a particular technique such as Gann or Candlesticks.

Information on unit and investment trusts

Full unit trust performance tables classified by sector are carried by *Money Management,* a sister publication to the *Investors Chronicle. Money Management* itself is a distinctly heavyweight publication aimed at financial advisers. The magazine can be bought in many large newsagents. One issue costs £4.50, an annual subscription £59.

Most performance statistics come from one of two per-formance measurement services. HSW tel: (01625) 511311, the older, and Micropal (tel: (0181) 741–4100, the more entrepreneurial. They do not, however, deal directly with the public.

Books

There are lots, and investors who can spare the time should go to a specialist bookshop to see what is available. One good specialist bookshop is Parks, which now operates under the Blackwells name, and has branches in London and some other cities. The telephone number of its central London branch is (0171) 831–9501. It also operates a postal service. The *Analyst* also runs a book club, whose particular niche is getting hold of American classics. Some general bookshops have surprisingly good investment sections and even those that do not will get books to order. Much depends on the local demand.

Here are some suggestions for further reading.

• **The Investors Chronicle Beginners' Guide to Investment** by Bernard Gray. This is the companion volume to the book you are reading now. And you need to understand what's in the first book to get the most out of the sequel. *Beginners' Guide* is a clear, comprehensive and practical introduction to financial markets, financial planning and companies, and is the under-the-desk cribsheet favoured by many financial journalists. It is published by Random Century. Cost: £12.99 paperback.

• **Charters on Charting** by David Charters. An accessible introduction to technical analysis by the managing director of Investment Research of Cambridge. Published by Rushmere Wynne. Cost £12.99 hardback.

• **The Investors' Guide to Technical Analysis** by Elli Gifford. A more advanced but still extremely lucid exposition of the subject by one of David Charters colleagues at Investment Research. Published by Pitman Publishing. Cost £50 hardback.

• **Interpreting Company Reports and Accounts** by Geoffrey Holmes and Alan Sugden. An excellent and thorough guide through company accounting. Its use of practical examples is particularly helpful. Published by Prentice

Hall/ Woodhead Faulkner in both hardback and paperback. Cost: £21.95 for the paperback.
- **Accounting for Growth** by Terry Smith. A racy guide to creative accounting by an investment analyst. Useful as a supplement to Holmes and Sugden but in no way a substitute. Published by Century. Cost £14.99 paperback.
- **New Creative Accounting** by Ian Griffiths. Lacks the pizzazz of Terry Smith's book but is helpful on some of the trickier bits of smoke and mirrors. Published by Macmillan. Cost £15.99 hardback.
- **The Intelligent Investor** by Benjamin Graham. Described by Warren Buffett as the best investment book ever written. Very easy to read and as compelling today as when it was written. Published by Harper & Row in the US.
- **Warren Buffet's letters to shareholders** in the Berkshire Hathaway annual reports. The perfect antithesis to investment theory by a man who has proved his methods work. Available in two volumes free for a modest postal charge. Contact Berkshire Hathaway, 3555 Farnham Street, Suite 1440, Omaha, Nebraska.
- **One Up on Wall Street** by Peter Lynch with John Rothchild. The better of two investment books by the former maestro of Magellan fund. Fun but perhaps a touch too journalistic for some. Published by Simon & Schuster and Penguin Books in the US.
- **The Money Masters** by John Train. Still the best of his many books on investment practitioners. Others include the *New Money Masters* and *The Midas Touch* (a book on Buffett). Train's analysis of how great investors do it is both clear and accessible. Published by Harper & Row in the US.
- **The Warren Buffett Way** by Robert Hagstrom. Much less enjoyable to read than John Train, let alone Buffett himself, but illuminating on the investment sums. Published by John Wiley & Sons. Cost £11.95 paperback.
- **An Introduction to the Risk and Return from Common stocks** by Richard Brealey. Those who feel reassured by understanding the theory of modern investment management will enjoy this pleasingly unpompous book. Published by the MIT Press in Cambridge Massachusetts but available from Basil Blackwell in the UK. Cost: £17.99 paperback.
- **Bogle on Mutual Funds** by John C Bogle. This introduction to investment in unit trusts is endorsed both by Warren

Buffett and by Economics Nobel Laureate Paul Samuelson, who puts it in the same league as Benjamin Graham's *The Intelligent Investor*. Samuelson is one of the many Americans who invest with Bogle's $100bn Vanguard mutual fund group. The book is extremely clear though not a holiday read. Published by Irwin Professional Publishing, 1333 Burr Ridge Parkway, Burr Ridge, Illinois 60521.

All prices are those obtaining in early 1996.

Appendix B
Computer Software

Professional investors use information technology in three main areas, portfolio management, share selection and share trading.

Traders and fund managers at the large investing institutions use it to keep track of what they have bought, what profit they have made and to measure their own performance against various yardsticks.

Traders, fund managers and analysts also use information technology as an aide to making investment decisions. There is a vast amount of information available about companies, industries and stockmarkets. And it is a daunting job for any individual to try to keep track of the basic information available in any area, let alone assess its implications. Computers both provide a means of storing this information in an easily accessible form, and help investors to spot investment opportunities before everybody else does.

In addition, professionals use computers to help them trade. Indeed, in some markets, such as foreign exchange, dealing-room systems provided by firms such as Reuters have become the mechanism by which members trade with each other, sometimes without any human intervention. In the UK stockmarket price display and order execution systems provide the forum where market makers display their constantly changing prices to both customers and rivals. And screen-based news services keep them abreast of the latest developments in whichever markets they specialise in.

No modern investment firm would attempt to operate without some of the appropriate information technology. The systems they use are generally far too expensive for private investors. And most of those involved in the actual process of share trading are also inappropriate. But there is a growing number of much cheaper systems for portfolio management and share selection designed specifically for private investors.

Computer software programs aimed at the retail market offer some of the same features as those catering for professionals. The majority of packages are suitable for use on most modern personal computers. But they vary considerably in what they are trying to do. And individual investors need to select programs which suit the size of their portfolio, their investment style and share selection techniques, their understanding of computers – and their pockets. Spending a couple of thousand pounds on a real time information system or top of the range technical analysis packages is pointless if you have a small portfolio of shares which you expect to hold for a long time.

Basic functions

Several products are designed to reduce the chore of managing your own portfolio. They start with basic book-keeping: recording how many shares in particular companies you have bought or sold, and noting when the transaction took place and at what price. Provided you update the share prices you can monitor your profits or losses both on individual shares and on a portfolio of shares, both in actual money and in percentage terms.

You can also keep a record of the brokers you deal with, their commissions, which bank accounts payments for shares are drawn from and your dividends are paid into. If you enter your personal tax rate and allowances you can calculate your tax liabilities. You can also adjust your records when shares you hold have scrip or rights issues.

Measuring the performance of individual shares or your overall portfolio against yardsticks – such as the relevant stockmarket index, inflation or a professionally managed fund – can be done in figures or by plotting the information on a chart. If you run a couple of different portfolios you can measure them against each other, and you can of course run as many dummy portfolios as you want.

This is just basic housekeeping which any investor needs to do. The computer does nothing you could not do manually; it just makes it quicker and easier to get the chores done. If you are an expert on computer spreadsheets, you could probably use one to devise a program which would carry out all these tasks, and build in any specific requirements of your own. The advantage of commercial packages designed purely to do investment chores is that you are guided through a series of simple questions, and the main calculations needed to produce your reports are built in. So again you save time. And if your time is limited you can probably spend it to better effect making sure your share selections are right in the first place.

Fundamental analysis

Computers have two functions in share selection. These correspond broadly with fundamental share analysis (picking shares on the basis of their business and financial ratios, and how they compare with other shares') and technical analysis (determining whether a share price is going to rise or fall purely on the basis of its past performance).

Most professional investors probably use information technology mainly for fundamental analysis. Databanks, such as Datastream, contain more historical data of various types than any normal business library. And it can be manipulated in a number of different ways. For example, when the *Investors Chronicle* produced a portfolio of 'Bargain shares' on the Ben Graham model, it did so by feeding criteria into Datastream and asking its computer to comb through all 2,000 odd shares on the London stockmarket to find the small number that qualified.

The IC High Yield portfolios also rely on Datastream to find the shares which meet its criteria. There is also a wealth of relevant information in a broader area: economic statistics for overseas countries if you are thinking of buying an overseas unit trust, dozens of foreign stockmarket statistics with which to assess the relative cheapness of UK shares, industry statistics to provide a business snapshot when trying to predict the outlook for specific companies. And even more specialised databanks, such as the FT's Analysis, contain summaries of several years' annual accounts for quoted companies. Such databanks are continually being updated, and can be used in conjunction with current share prices.

Cautious professionals tend to check the data before they act on it. Sometimes computers can eliminate genuinely interesting opportunities. There is a pleasant story of George Soros's erstwhile partner Jim Rogers discovering that the reason nobody was interested in the Austrian stockmarket was that the Morgan Stanley index was showing an unrealistically high PE ratio of nearly 70. He made a lot of money there. But as a way of sifting through a lot of facts fast computers are unbeatable and most professionals use them.

As yet this is an area where private investors remain at a disadvantage. Tapping into a professional databank is simply too expensive. Many of the companies which produce software also supply data, both when you first buy the package and through regular updates thereafter. But this is necessarily much more limited than that in a professional databank.

Although some software packages allow you to search for shares and rank them according to their financial performance, as reported in their annual accounts, the information available is often not much more sophisticated than dividends, pre-tax profit, earnings per share and turnover. But even that can be useful as an initial sorting mechanism, particularly when used in conjunction with current share prices. You can always send for a copy of the full accounts of any company which interests you.

Technical analysis

Many of the more advanced software packages for private investors concentrate on technical analysis. Reasonably enough, since they can offer many of the basic tools used by professional investors. And since technical analysis is concerned with comparing individual share prices with stereotypes – typical patterns – these tools can work as well for private investors as for professionals. Even the basic technical analysis packages are visually attractive.

The simplest packages allow you to display conventional

line charts, showing how a share price has moved over certain periods of time. Those showing each day's high, low and closing price can reveal information not obvious to anyone relying purely on closing prices. And index relative charts show whether a share has risen on its own merits or because the whole market or sector has risen. This kind of information is relevant to all investors, not just technical analysts.

Share prices tend to follow strong trends. And charting aims to spot when a share price has moved away from a trend and is likely to move back, or when the trend is about to change. Its real power derives from a range of indicators developed to give early warning that a share is on the move. (See Chapter 2 on Charts for a more detailed explanation of what technical analysts are looking for and some of the tools they use.)

More advanced software packages allow you to analyse moving averages, oscillators and other overbought/oversold indicators. Chartists get excited both by the relationship of the actual share price to the averages and by the relationship of the averages to each other. Oscillators present share price information in a way which magnifies movements. This can highlight when a share has risen or fallen worryingly fast. Volume indicators are used in conjunction with price movements to show whether the movements are supported by heavy buying or selling of the shares.

Different indicators are generally agreed to work better in different circumstances. Professional analysts both check out several different indicators before taking a decision and fine tune aspects of individual indicators, such as the time period. Some more advanced software packages help you with the tuning; more basic ones leave you to work by trial and error or refer to a textbook. The more advanced packages also offer more esoteric tools, such as the Gann theory, Fibonacci analysis, based on formal mathematical relationships, and Japanese Candlesticks.

Knowing where to look is as useful in share selection as any other hunt. And some products allow you to search your database for shares showing a buy or sell signal. Again you will probably want to check it out in more detail. But it is another useful timesaver, particularly if you have built up a large database.

Data collection

Building up your database is one of the more difficult parts of using investment software. Even the basic portfolio management programs can absorb a lot of time if you need to type in all the up-to-date share prices every time you want to review your portfolio. Several of the more advanced products allow you to update your portfolio automatically from the Teletext pages of your TV. And downloading from Internet looks set to be the fashion in the future. This aspect of the investment software market is changing very fast.

Efficient data collection is particularly important with charting programs. Typing in four values a day for every share you are interested in is a back-breaking task. But most suppliers have ways of shortcutting the process nowadays. Putting in the initial record of historic share prices is a one-off operation. Updates are sometimes supplied on discs, sometimes down a telephone line. Real time data is generally expensive and probably unnecessary for most personal investors.

What kind of software is worth considering depends not just on your investment needs but also on your computer's capacity, and on how comfortable you are with your computer. Most software runs on DOS, but some is now tailored for Windows. Do consider both the mechanics and the cost of data collection when making your choice. Most of the more expensive programs will supply a demonstration disc before you commit yourself. It is probably a good idea to choose a package from a company with a range of products, so that you can upgrade later. Most suppliers let you upgrade by paying the difference between the product you want and the one you previously bought from them.

Lists of software programs have a rather limited shelf-life. But many of the suppliers have been around for some time and are steadily expanding their ranges. First, decide what you want your software to do for you, how much you are prepared to pay, and what data collection method would suit you. Then phone your way down the list below to find out what bits of the market each firm serves, what their price range is, what programs they have available, and what data collection methods they offer. Many are specialists and many are rivals. So get your information first hand.

Some UK investment software suppliers

Company	Telephone No.
• Alibro Software:	(0181) 208–1067
• Comcare CPAS:	(0161) 902–0330
• Dividend Associates:	(01264) 737642
• Dolphin Software:	(01702) 545984
• Fairshares:*	(01372) 741969
• Financial Software:	(0121) 236–3180
• Genie:	(01273) 771865
• Indexia:*	(01442) 878015
• Meridian:	(0181) 309–5960
• MESA (UK):	(0181) 303–7407
• Portfolio Control:	(0171) 378–0657
• Pricetrack:	(01275) 472306
• Qudos:	(0161) 439–3926
• Share Genius:	(0117) 957948
• Synergy:*	(01582) 424282
• Trading Edge:	(0181) 810–0607
• Trendline:	(01707) 644874
• TTL:	(01277) 353126
• Updata:*	(0181) 874–4747
• Winfolio:	(01204) 385159.

* Market leaders offering a range of products at different price levels.

Appendix C
Tax Efficient Investment

Saving tax should never be an investor's main objective: that leads to bad investment decisions. But it makes sense for any investor to make full use of all the tax shelters available to him, provided they fit in with his investment objectives and that the cost of the shelter does not exceed the tax saving. The higher an individual's tax rate, the more beneficial tax shelters should be.

Examples of tax-efficient investments that saved tax but lost the investor his investment are legion. Both the Business Expansion Scheme (BES) and its predecessor, the Business Start-up Scheme (BSS) produced a large number of schemes which lost investors some or all of their capital. This is hardly surprising. Generally speaking government creates tax breaks in order to persuade people to do something they would not otherwise do, or persuade investors to put money into something they would not otherwise choose to invest in.

The UK government encouraged individuals to save for their old age because it did not want the burden of looking after them. It gave companies generous allowances on capital investment to compensate for the fact that the early years of a new project are seldom profitable. It created Regional Development Grants and Enterprise Zones to encourage business into parts of the country they would not otherwise have chosen. It invented the BSS and BES to create a source of finance for very small businesses which even the existing venture capital firms could not be bothered with. The Personal Equity Plan (PEP) was dreamed up partly for a similar reason – to create a new source of equity finance for companies.

Many of the more publicised tax-efficient investments are a three-way fight:
- The government is trying to encourage money into a politically favoured but risky area, and is not particularly

interested in whether investors make a worthwhile return from it.

● Investors are hoping that they will get a better return from their money than the net return available from a comparable taxable investment. They are seconded by the better financial intermediaries, who are trying to interpret the rules in ways which allow them to cherry pick the relatively safe investments, and offer their clients relatively high returns with disproportionately little risk.

● Less honourable or less skilled salesmen and intermediaries merely emphasise the tax breaks to all and sundry without bothering about risks or suitability, whilst ensuring themselves a large commission or management fee.

Some tax-saving investments are suitable for most people, some only for people with lots of money, some are just bad investments. One useful way of classifying them is into non-taxable investments, tax-free investments and tax shelters. As a crude rule of thumb, most people should consider non-taxable investments, most serious investors should consider tax-free investments, but only relatively rich investors with a high risk tolerance should even contemplate tax shelters.

Every investor should work his way up the risk scale. Make sure that you have taken full advantage of all the available non-taxable and tax-free investments before considering tax shelters.

Non-taxable investments

The government offers income tax allowances and capital gains tax allowances to all UK residents. These are intended to help low earners and encourage small investors. But they are only of use to people with some income or capital gains to relieve from tax. Basic tax planning aims to ensure that all qualifying members of the family take advantage of the available income and gains tax reliefs, even if their own earnings or assets would normally be too small to allow them to do so.

This way of saving tax is useful to more people than any other. It is not advertised, because no one makes money out of selling it. But any competent tax adviser or planner should mention it. It is most useful to firmly married couples.

Unlike many tax efficient investments, non-taxable investments involve no additional risk, unless the family subsequently splits up. To ensure that every family member uses all the available allowances, it is usually necessary for assets to be irrevocably spread around the family. Hence the caveat that this type of financial planning is suitable only for closely knit families which expect to stay that way.

The benefits are greatest when different members of the family would otherwise pay different rates of tax. Many of the tax allowances and tax rates are subject to Budget changes. Rates used here are for the 1996/97 tax year.

- **The individual personal allowance:** £3,765. Every adult is entitled to a personal allowance: the money you can earn from any source without paying income tax. If either husband or wife pays tax at the top rate of 40 per cent and the other has no taxable income, an annual income tax saving of £1,506 can be achieved by transferring assets producing an income of £3,765.

Assume, for example, the husband is the high earner, and has a substantial portfolio with a 6 per cent gross yield. He could transfer assets worth £62,750 to his (non-earning) wife, and cut the family tax bill by £1,506. (The comparable savings are £753 for a 20 per cent tax payer and £903 for a 24 per cent tax payer, though of course this saving can only be achieved if the assets exist in the first place.) If the family's assets lie in a family business rather than the stockmarket, a similar result can be achieved if the husband pays the wife a salary of around £3,000.

Caveat. The Inland Revenue does not like fictitious transfers or fictitious jobs.

- **Children's personal allowance.** Children get the same personal allowance as their parents. But if the assets are given to them by their parents, and the income on those assets is more than £100 a year, their parents are taxed on the whole of the child's income from those funds while it is under 18. There are three ways to make the most of this concession.

First, parents can limit the amount given to the child to around £1,666 (again assuming a 6 per cent yield. Second, parents can put the assets into a bare trust, under which they hold the assets as nominees for the child, and no tax is payable provided the income is rolled up until the child reaches 18. Third, interested adults, such as grandparents, can make an absolute gift of capital to the child and the income will in this case count as the child's.

Cash gifts of up to £3,000 a year can be made by anybody (both husband and wife in a married couple) without building up an inheritance tax (IHT) liability. And anyone who failed to use the previous year's exemption can give away up to £6,000 in a year. Other gifts are only outside the IHT net if the donor survives for seven years, unless they can be shown to be just part of the donor's normal expenditure.

We are not dealing with estate planning here. But people blessed with a superfluity of assets should consider carefully which assets to hand over. For example, if adventurous grandparents want to give their grandchildren both a non-taxable income and assets with growth potential, they might decide to make regular transfers of shares in emerging markets trusts, which normally have extremely low yields.

● **Capital gains tax exemption: £6,300.** This allows any UK resident over 18 to make up to £6,300 of gains each year without having to pay gains tax. For a 40 per cent taxpayer the tax saving is £2,520 a year. The detailed rules are extremely complicated and expert advice is necessary.

Most financial advisers recommend that investors with substantial portfolios who do not already have £6,300 of taxable gains should bed and breakfast their shares each year in order to make use of the £6,300 capital gains tax exemption. This means selling shares producing a £6,300 capital gain one day and buying them back the next. The price at which they were bought back then forms the new base price for gains tax calculations. Again, it makes sense for all family members to use their £6,300 exemption each year. So a husband or wife with large unrealised capital gains should consider handing some of the relevant assets over to a less fortunate partner, so that both can bed and breakfast the assets.

Caveat. Once more, remember that the Revenue is not amused by transparent fictions.

Tax-free investments

Most tax-free investments offer reasonably attractive but not stupendous returns. They would often not be appealing in the absence of the tax breaks. And some are inflexible and restrictive. This means that anyone who cannot meet the conditions they impose may end up with an investment which produces a lower return than one which had never held out the tax-free carrot.

Many have a minimum normal holding period. This has three possible consequences for investors who cannot stick to the prescribed time scale. First, those who want their money back earlier may lose the tax exemption which gave the investment its original appeal. Second, they may fare comparatively badly, because of surrender penalties imposed by the rules of the investment scheme. Third, early encashment may expose them to market or liquidity risk which was not a feature of the investment if held for the full term.

The type and degree of risk varies. Safest are government-backed National Savings certificates, which guarantee a pre-determined total return. Then come Tax Exempt Special Savings Accounts (Tessas) and Gilts. Tessas offer return of capital, subject to normal commercial risks but the income is often variable. Gilts can offer a pre-determined total return, but only to people who buy and hold to maturity. Personal equity plans (PEPs), which invest in equities and nowadays in corporate bonds carry a variable amount of market risk as well. All these investments are suitable for many ordinary investors. The final tax-free investment, timber, is much riskier: it is an illiquid long term holding, only to be considered by those who already have everything else.

Financial firms who package these products up have started selling some of them with guarantees attached. These reduce the risk, provided the guarantee comes from a credible firm. But in many cases the cost of the guarantee substantially reduces the return from the investment.

The range of tax free investments on offer is now wide and confusing. Investors who feel the need to pay for advice from an intermediary on picking a suitable investment will find their return still further reduced. As with all tax-saving investments, the higher your tax rate, the more you stand to benefit from the tax breaks.

• **National Savings Certificates**. These provide a government-guaranteed tax-free total return on up to £10,000 of capital per person per issue. The prescribed investment period is five years and there are penalties for early surrender. No interest is paid during the holding period. Conventional issues offer a fixed rate of interest set in advance. Index-linked issues offer a comparatively low rate of interest in addition to inflation-proofing. The maximum holding of £10,000 per issue can be doubled if the certificates are held in trust.

Advantages. Very low-risk. Total security of capital and a known total return for the conventional certificates, while the index-linked are one of the two main ways of protecting your capital against inflation.

Disadvantages. The early surrender penalties make them an inflexible investment, though not as bad as Tessas. The rates of interest offered are often not competitive compared with alternatives. Children's certificates (Bonus Bonds) offer better rates of interest offset by stiffer penalties for early redemption.

• **Tessas**. These allow you to invest up to £9,000 over five years in a bank or building society deposit account with no tax on the income, which you can leave to roll up in the Tessa. The rules vary slightly depending on whether you took out a Tessa when they first became available and are reinvesting it into a second generation one, or are a new saver. If you are reinvesting an existing Tessa, you can re-invest up to £9,000 of your original capital in a new one. If you are a new saver, the investment has to be done in stages.

All guarantee return of capital. Most have a variable rate of income, sometimes with loyalty bonuses at the end of the five years. A few offer an alternative of an equity linked return.

Advantages. Low risk. Capital is as safe as it would be in a normal bank or building society deposit, and you probably get a better return.

Disadvantages. Tessas are extremely inflexible. If you need to withdraw any of your money (other than the interest) before the end of the prescribed five years, you lose the tax concessions for the lot over the whole period. The rates are often variable. So even if the interest rates on offer look attractive at the beginning of the investment period, they may look less appealing at the end. Better returns with greater flexibility are probably available from riskier alternatives such as personal equity plans.

● **Gilts.** These fixed interest securities offer a government guarantee of return of capital on maturity (save for undated issues) and no tax is payable on capital gains. They can be bought in any quantity, have no prescribed holding period, and are easy to buy and sell. But they need to be handled with care.

First, the government's capital guarantee applies only when the security reaches its pre-set maturity or redemption date. Gilts expose the holder to substantial market risk in the run-up to redemption. Second, the exemption from capital gains tax is only useful if there are gains to tax. Gilts sometimes sell for more than their redemption value. If you purchase a gilt above par (its redemption value) you may make a capital loss and are certain to do so if you hold it to maturity. Capital losses on most securities can be offset against gains on others to reduce your capital gains tax bill. But capital losses on gilts cannot be offset against profits elsewhere.

Since income from gilts is subject to income tax, high taxpayers need to minimise the amount of their total return, which comes from income rather than capital gain. Working out which gilt offers you the best net return can be a tricky calculation, even if you intend to hold the gilt to maturity.

Advantages. Very low risk provided you hold to maturity. Redemption value is guaranteed by the government and interest rate is fixed. Index-linked gilts are an alternative way for investors to protect their capital against inflation, provided they hold the indexed gilt to maturity.

Disadvantages. Exposure to market risk if you do not hold

the gilt to maturity. The longer the gilt and the lower the nominal rate of interest, the greater its volatility. If interest rates fall during your holding period you may get a lower rate of interest on your reinvested income. If interest rates have been falling for a long time before you buy, it may be hard to find many gilts likely to produce capital gains.

● **Personal Equity Plans (PEPs).** These allow adult UK taxpayers to invest up to £6,000 a year in suitable equities, trusts or corporate bonds free of both income and gains tax. Another £3,000 a year can be invested in a single company PEP. PEPs have to be run by an approved plan manager, and the costs may outweigh the income tax benefits for a low taxpayer. There is no minimum holding period.

Most serious investors will benefit from using PEPs to shelter some of their investments from tax. The most heavily advertised PEPs are wrappers for unit and investment trusts. But several stockbrokers offer self-select PEPs, which allow the investor unrestricted choice over the investments put into the PEP. They do, however, often charge for each transaction, so pick a PEP manager to suit your own activity level.

Many advisers suggest putting securities with relatively high yields into the PEP, while keeping those with more immediate capital growth prospects outside – with the intention of bed and breakfasting them each year. Some financial advisers offer packaged investment systems with a PEP wrapper, such as shares selected according to the O'Higgins system. But it is probably cheaper to do it yourself.

Advantages. The risk depends on the underlying securities. All serious investors, who would already be investing in the underlying securities, should have them. Investments held in a PEP are extremely liquid. If you pick the right PEP, you can buy and sell the underlying securities readily without losing the tax exemptions.

Disadvantages. They may not be suitable for investors with less money, or those who are very risk averse. Low taxpayers may find that the charges outweigh the savings in income tax. The capital risk may deter others. Investors who buy a PEP used as a wrapper for a particular trust or share may need to change plan manager if they want to change the underlying investment.

● **Timber.** Forestry profits are free of income and capital gains tax and the investments have advantages for inheritance tax planning.* But that does not necessarily make them an attractive investment. Buying immature timber is a very long term very illiquid investment, and usually involves very high minimum investments. Nowadays several pooled schemes buying relatively mature plantations offer shorter term investments for smaller amounts of money, sometimes a regular income through serial felling, and sometimes a guaranteed minimum return. Although their structure makes it appropriate to classify them as a tax-free investment, their illiquidity and potential riskiness make them more akin to the tax shelters described below.

Advantages. The tax attractions are considerable, provided the profits are there to shield.

Disadvantages. Timber exposes investors to a variety of risks. It should be possible to insure against physical disasters, such as fire or storm damage. But some investors have in the past been sold unsuitable timber – in places where it would not grow well or would be prohibitively expensive to extract. Average long term returns have not been good, even taking account of the tax advantages. And although there have been some good years, the long investment period makes it more than normally difficult to predict returns. Guarantees are comforting but only as good as the guarantor.

Tax shelters

These should be considered only by people with a high taxable income or gains on other investments that they want to shield from tax. The risks are in all cases considerable, and the probable risk/return trade-off is only designed to appeal to people who can benefit from the tax breaks.

* CGT is payable on any gain in the land element; it is the sale of the crops which is tax-exempt. To get the tax exemption the woodland has to be run on a commercial basis.

Investors who are not in that position should avoid them. And many who are in that position may prefer to find other homes for their money.

With the exception of Venture Capital Trusts most of them are unquoted. There are no meaningful track records and no formal monitoring processes for this type of investment. This makes them in some ways akin to the old Business Expansion Scheme, where there was plenty of anecdotal evidence of investors losing money, but no reliable source of statistics.

Tax shelters should only be considered by investors with special knowledge of the business concerned, reasons for confidence in the management and the ability to keep abreast of events. Investors who have good reason to believe that their financial adviser is himself in that position, and equally good reason to place implicit trust in their adviser, may be willing to delegate responsibility to him. But always remember how many formerly affluent people became Names at Lloyd's without understanding the mechanics – just because their trusted adviser told them it would save tax.

● **Venture capital trusts (VCTs).** These are classified as investment trusts but have particular investment and tax characteristics. The investment portfolio consists of stakes in small unquoted investments, and if the investment manager fails to stick to the rules, the investor could lose his tax reliefs.

Provided he invests for five years, the investor can get income tax relief at 20 per cent on the cost (up to £100,000) of new shares in a VCT. He can also defer capital gains tax (CGT) on up to £100,000 of gains realised in the previous 12 months. Thus the initial relief can be up to 60 per cent. Any dividends paid are free of income tax and gains made on selling the VCT are also exempt from CGT, although the reinvested gain which provided the initial capital is not.

Advantages. The tax reliefs could turn a modest return into a good one.

Disadvantages. These are speculative investments and one or all of the underlying investments could go bust. Management fees tend to be high. The investor loses his income tax relief if he sells before the five years are up, and the shares will be difficult to buy and sell anyway. Any calculations of the probable return need to recognise that the original gain will be taxable when the shares are sold.

- **Enterprise Investment Schemes (EISs).** These involve a high-risk investment in a single unquoted company. Again, they allow an investor who re-invests up to £100,000 of gains to defer CGT and also enjoy 20 per cent income tax relief on the initial investment. The minimum investment period is five years, and may in practice be longer. Any gains when the investor eventually sells the EIS are free of CGT, but the reinvested gain which provided the initial investment becomes chargeable. One or two EISs have come with a guaranteed exit. The normal caveat about guarantees applies.

Advantages. Similar to those of VCTs, but the investment is more concentrated and thus riskier. Hands-on investors may enjoy the fact that with the right EIS you can sit on the board and get paid: a nice if potentially expensive retirement hobby.

Disadvantages. As for VCTs but more so. Very high risk. Inflexible investment period. Normally no pre-determined exit.

- **Enterprise Zone Trusts (EZTs).** These are medium to long term pooled investments in single properties in enterprise zones. The better ones are pre-let to a good tenant, though even this does not guarantee the tenant will still be there at the end of the seven year minimum investment period. Although they may sound similar to property companies, they count as unregulated collective investments, and several investors have lost money on them. The lure is full income tax relief on the investment in the building, though not the land. Interest on money borrowed to fund the investment can also be offset against the rents from the tenants, provided the building remains fully let to credit-worthy tenants.

Advantages. A self financing tax shelter for high earners if all goes according to plan.

Disadvantages. Risky and illiquid. You may lose all your money. The reason the government classifies certain areas as enterprise zones is that they are ones most firms would not chose to work in. So it is often hard to get and keep tenants,

even at low rents. And although many EZTs arrange for
investors to borrow money to invest, the investor remains
liable to repay this money even if the scheme goes bust. The
schemes may run for 25 years, and there is seldom a ready
exit if you want to get out early.

● **Oil and gas partnerships.** Another long term investment
for high income tax payers. The investor belongs to a limited
partnership which drills for oil and produces a tax-deducti-
ble trading loss. The basic idea is that you get tax relief on
development expenditure in your high earning years and
the oil well produces an income stream in later years when
your tax rate may be lower. The wells tend to be in the
southern United States.

Advantages. Again the sums normally look fine on paper.

Disadvantages. Very risky and illiquid. You can lose all
your money if the well is dry. Revenues may be less than
you expect if the oil price moves against you during the
investment period. And the revenues depend heavily on
obtaining all the expected tax allowances. Ownership can
be a contentious issue in some places. Many partnerships
last for 15 years, and that is a long time to have your money
tied up in a desert half way round the world.

Bibliography

The Beardstown Ladies Investment Club with Whitaker L., (1994), The Beardstown Ladies Common-Sense Investment Guide, Hyperion, New York.

Bogle, J.C., (1994) Bogle on Mutual Funds, Irwin, Illinois.

Bodie, Z., Kane, A., and Marcus, A.J., (1983 and 1993) Investments, Irwin, Illinois.

Brealey, R.A., (1983) An Introduction to Risk and Return from Common Stocks, MIT Press, Massachusetts.

Buffett, W., (1977–1993) Berkshire Hathaway Inc. Letters to Shareholders 1977–1986 and 1987–1993, Berkshire Hathaway, Nebraska.

Calverley, C., (1995) Pocket Guide to Economics for the Global Investor, Probus Publishing, Cambridge.

Charters, D., (1995) Charters on Charting, Rushmere Wynne, England.

Gifford, E., (1995) Investor's Guide to Technical Analysis, Pitman Publishing, London.

Graham, B., (1973) The Intelligent Investor (Fourth Revised Edition), Harper & Row, New York.

Gray, B., (1991, 1993) Investors Chronicle Beginners' Guide to Investment, Century Business, London.

Griffiths, I., (1995) New Creative Accounting, MacMillan, London.

Hagstrom, R.G., (1995) The Warren Buffett Way, John Wiley & Sons, Inc. New York, Chichester.

Holmes, G., and Sugden, A., (1994) Interpreting Company Reports and Accounts (Fifth Edition), Prentice Hall/Woodhead-Faulkner, Hertfordshire.

Kindleberger, C.P, (1978, 1989) Manias, Panics, and Crashes, Basic Books, Inc, New York, MacMillan Press Ltd, Basingstoke, Hampshire.

Lynch, P. with Rothchild, J., (1989) One Up on Wall Street, Simon & Schuster, New York, and Penguin Books USA Inc. (1990).

Lynch, P. with Rothchild J., (1993) Beating the Street, Simon & Schuster, New York.

Luft J., (1963, 1970, 1984) Group Processes, Mayfield Publishing, California.

Mackay, C., Extraordinary Popular Delusions and the Madness of Crowds, originally published in the 19th century, published 1995 in Ware Hertfordshire by Wordsworth Editions Ltd.

Morton, J., Editor (1995) The Financial Times Global Guide to Investing, Pitman Publishing, London.

O'Higgins. M., with Downes. J., (1991) Beating the Dow, Harper-Collins, New York.

Pepper, G., (1994) Money, Credit and Asset Prices, MacMillan, London.

Schwager, J.D., (1989) Market Wizards, Simon & Schuster, New York.

Schwartz, D., (1996) The Schwartz Stock Market Handbook, Burleigh Publishing, Gloucestershire.

Slater, J., (1992) The Zulu Principle, Orion, London.

Smith, T., (1992) Accounting for Growth, Century Business, London.

'Smith, A.', (1968) The Money Game, Michael Joseph, London.

Soros, G., (1987,1994) The Alchemy of Finance, John Wiley & Sons Inc. New York, Chichester, Brisbane, Toronto, Singapore.

Train, J., (1980) The Money Masters, Harper & Row, New York.

Train, J., (1987) The Midas Touch, Harper & Row, New York.

Train, J., (1989) The New Money Masters, Harper & Row, New York.

Index